A-4

NEXT STOP, NEVADA

Nevada's legendary railroads accomplished a lot in their time. They created mining boomtowns seemingly overnight, helped build the Hoover Dam and after playing a role in taming the Wild West, went on to become Hollywood icons, starring in hundreds of movies and television shows. Their unforgettable stories live on in Nevada's three fascinating railroad museums, which are perfect stops for the entire family.

NEVADA STATE RAILROAD MUSEUM, CARSON CITY · 2180 S. CARSON STREET · 775.687.6953
View a superstar cast of trains and the largest collection of Nevada railroad artifacts.

NEVADA STATE RAILROAD MUSEUM, BOULDER CITY · 601 YUCCA STREET · 702.486.5933
Ride the scenic and historic Union Pacific Railroad Boulder Branch, the line that helped build the Hoover Dam.

EAST ELY RAILROAD DEPOT MUSEUM, ELY · 1100 AVENUE A · 775.289.1663
Learn the history of the Nevada Northern Railway and the copper mining industry that kept it running for nearly a century.

**Download your FREE Nevada Railroad Brochure
at TravelNevada.com/rr**

DIVISION OF MUSEUMS AND HISTORY – NEVADA DEPARTMENT OF CULTURAL AFFAIRS   **nevăda**

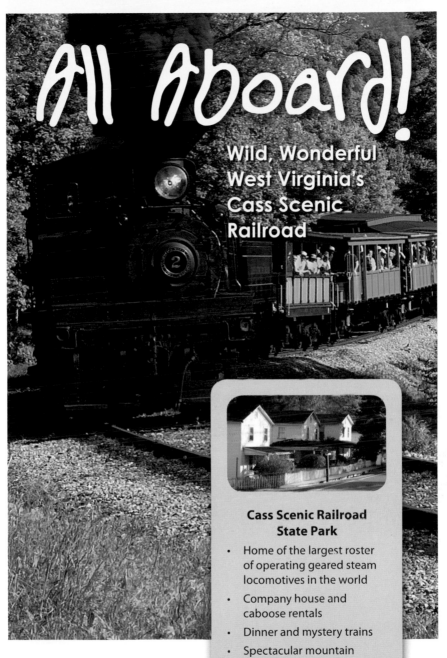

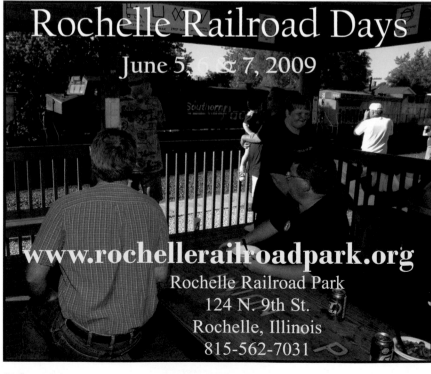

EXPERIENCE THE STRASBURG RAIL ROAD!

Experience it all...
Connect with the past through fun, interactive opportunities:

- Ride Trains
- Shop
- Eat
- Relax
- Watch the Trains & the Model T's
- Experience, Enjoy, Have Fun

... All day long!

Your 45-minute train ride is only the beginning ...

Unique railroad activities for the whole family:
- Mechanical shop tour • Interaction with real railroad workers

Amazing gift shops:
- Train Toys & Treasures • Model Railroading • Railroad Gifts

Casual dining spots:
- Dining Car on the train
- Trackside Café at the station
- Sweets & Treats for a quick snack

Seasonal adventures & opportunities:
- Cagney steam train ride
- Pump car ride
- Cranky car ride
- Themed dinner trains

Mailing Address: Route 741 East, Strasburg, PA 17579
GPS Address: 301 Gap Road, Ronks, PA 17572
General Information: 717-687-7522
Dining Car Reservations: 717-687-6486
Gift Shops: 877-475-8990
StrasburgRailRoad.com

STRASBURG
SINCE 1832
RAIL·ROAD

THOMAS & FRIENDS™

CHUGGING INTO A STATION NEAR YOU!

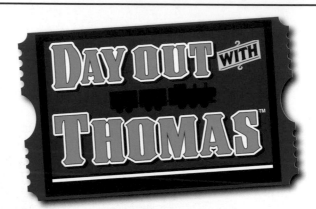

DAY OUT WITH THOMAS™

ALL ABOARD FOR FUN:

Take a 25-Minute Ride with Thomas

. . . .

Meet Sir Topham Hatt!

. . . .

Enjoy Storytelling,
Live Music & Much More

For tickets and information, visit
www.ticketweb.com/dowt or call 866.468.7630

Advance purchase is recommended. Ticket sales are final. Events are rain or shine.

www.thomasandfriends.com/dowt

HiT entertainment™

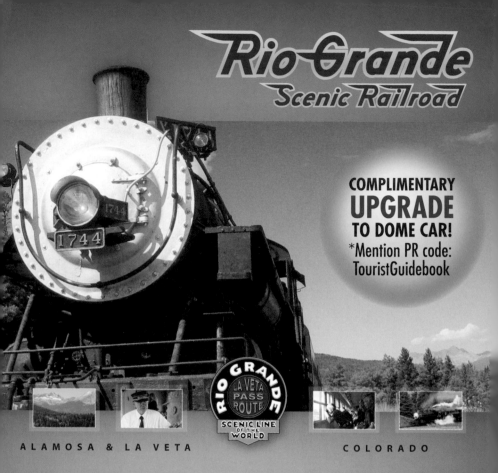

Rio Grande Scenic Railroad

COMPLIMENTARY UPGRADE TO DOME CAR!
*Mention PR code: TouristGuidebook

ALAMOSA & LA VETA

COLORADO

Soaring 14,000 - foot peaks.

Dramatic mountain passes.

Abundant wildlife.

Service to the Great Sand Dunes National Park.

Steep cliffs and colorful canyons.

Miles of historic mountain rails.

Charming mountain towns.

Standard gauge comfort.

Scenic dome cars.

Seven days of steam power.

Your next great adventure.

www.riograndescenicrailroad.com • 1-877-726-rail

Colorado RAILROAD Museum

Featuring over 100 engines, cabooses and coaches.
Also renowned library, roundhouse restoration
facility and working turntable.

Train ride opportunities throughout the year.

GOOD TIME TICKET

– Good for –

$2 OFF ADULT ADMISSION

Must present your Railroad Discount Card for discount.
Coupon Expires December 31,2010
NOT VALID FOR DAY OUT WITH THOMAS

Lose track of time.

ColoradoRAILROADMuseum.org   303-279-4591 or 800-365-6263
17155 W. 44th Avenue, Golden Colorado 80403

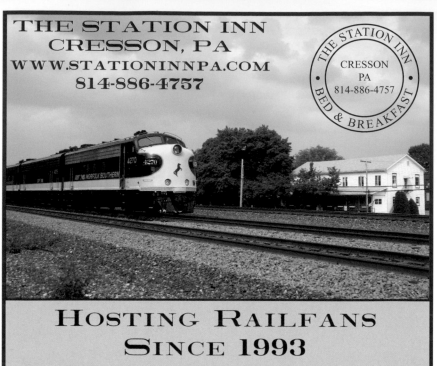

LEADERSHIP IN CREATIVE RAILROADING

Tourist Railway Association INC

TRAIN, Inc., the Tourist Railway Association, Inc. was formed in 1972 to foster the advancement of the tourist railway and museum industry. Full or Associate membership is open to all interested persons.

Members receive the organization's bi-monthly publication **TrainLine**, which includes comprehensive information and news from the industry.

Our 2009 Spring Meeting will be hosted by Texas State Railroad in Palestine, TX; 2010 Spring Meeting will be hosted by Strasburg Rail Road in Strasburg, PA and will be joint with ARM and RPCA. Spring 2011 will be in French Lick, IN hosted by Indiana Railway Museum.

TRAIN Annual Convention 2009 will be hosted by Grand Canyon Railway at the South Rim. TRAIN Annual Convention 2010 will be hosted by San Luis Rio Grande/Rio Grande Scenic Railroad in Alamosa, CO. TRAIN Annual Convention 2011 will be a joint convention of TRAIN/ARM and will be hosted by TVRM in Chattanooga, TN. For more details check out our updated Website at www.traininc.org.

TRAIN, Inc. is a leader and serves as a voice on all issues which affect the operation and display of vintage and historic railway equipment and the industry.

GET ON TRACK NOW if you are not currently a member call for membership information or if you are a member **STAY ON TRACK** by renewing your membership, contributing to **TrainLine** and attending Spring and Annual meetings.

For More Information Contact:
TOURIST RAILWAY ASSOCIATION, INC.

P.O. Box 1245
Chama, NM 87520-1245
1-800-67TRAIN (1-800-678-7246)
(575) 756-1240 • FAX (575) 756-1238
Email address: train@valornet.com
Visit our website at *http://www.traininc.org*

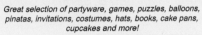

TRAINPARTY.com

Train Themed Party Supplies, Toys, and Gifts!

Great selection of partyware, games, puzzles, balloons, pinatas, invitations, costumes, hats, books, cake pans, cupcakes and more!

Themes include Thomas & Friends, Amtrak, Little Chug, Whistle Stop, and many others!

1-800-761-4294
www.trainparty.com

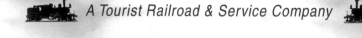

WESTERN MASS. EXCURSION TRIPS

20 mile round trips along the Housatonic River over former New York New Haven & Hartford track in the beautiful Berkshire Hills between restored stations in Lenox and Stockbridge, Massachusetts. Diesel hauled trips in former DL&W 1920s coaches. Alco and EMD power. 90 and 45 minute trips Saturdays, Sundays and holidays only, June through October. HO train layout, train, trolley and Gilded Age exhibit. For schedules, pricing and special 2009 25th anniversary events visit go to www.berkshirescenicrailroad.com Just 5 miles from MassPike Exit 2 follow US Rte. 20 west, go right on Housatonic St. and continue 1.5 miles. (413) 637-2210 10 Willow Creek Road, Lenox, MA 01240

Berkshire Scenic Railway MUSEUM

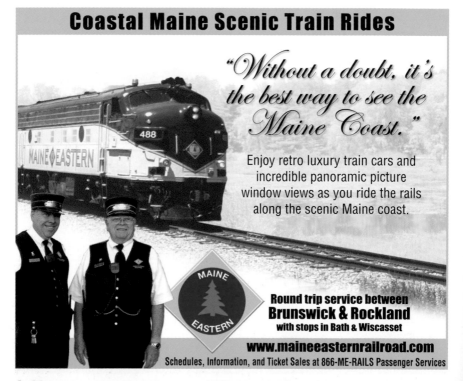

Railroad Discount Card Participants

Alder Gulch Shortline

Big South Fork Scenic Railway

Boone & Scenic Valley Railroad

Camp Five Museum

Cass Scenic Railroad State Park

Chehalis-Centralia Railroad & Museum

Colorado Railroad Museum

Conway Scenic Railroad

Cooperstown & Charlotte Valley Railroad

Danbury Railway Museum

Durand Union Station

Durango & Silverton Narrow Gauge Railroad

Durbin & Greenbrier Valley Railroad

Gold Coast Railroad Museum

Golden Spike Tower

Great Smoky Mountains Railroad

Green Mountain Railroad

Heber Valley Railroad

Illinois Railway Museum

Indiana Railway Museum

Jackson Street Roundhouse

Kentucky Railway Museum

Lake Shore Railway Museum

Leadville, Colorado & Southern Railroad

Medina Railroad Museum

Mid-Continent Railway Museum

Middletown & Hummelstown Railroad

Midland Railway

Monticello Railway Museum

National New York Central Railroad Museum

Nevada Northern Railway

Osceola & St. Croix Valley Railway

Potomac Eagle Scenic Railroad

Railroad Museum of Pennsylvania

Sacramento RiverTrain

Sierra Railroad

Skunk Train

Strasburg Rail Road

Tanana Valley Railroad

Texas State Railroad

Upper Hudson River Railroad

Waterloo Central Railway

Wilmington & Western Railroad

Check the listings for details of each participant's discount offer.

ADV-PRO-BK09050RH

CLIP & SAVE!

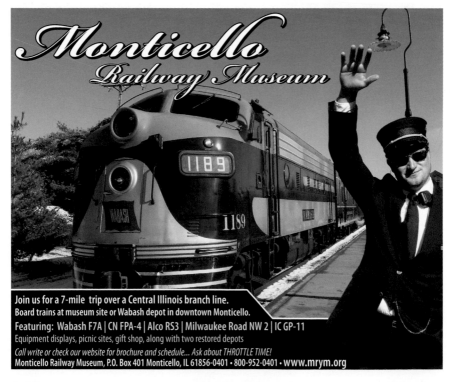

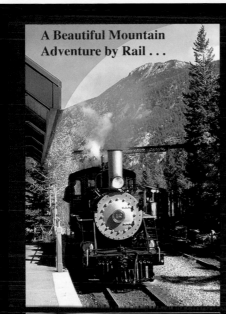

The Train Where Eagles Fly

In 2005 through 2008 eagles were seen on every Train Ride

Historic
Locomotives & Trains
in Romney, West Virginia

Regular 3.5 hour excursions & selected all-day trips available
First class & coach seating available on all trains

**Excursions operate Saturdays & some Sundays May – September
Daily departures in October, check out our website for schedule**

POTOMAC EAGLE

Information and Reservations:
www.potomaceagle.info
304-424-0736

West Virginia
Wild and Wonderful

Potomac Eagle Wappocomo Station, Route 28 North, P.O. Box 657 Romney, WV 26757

Andy Fletcher's CUSTOM*Trains*

Over 1,500 railroad magnets from your favorite tourist railroads, museums, and class one railroads of today and yesterday. There are steam, electric, traction, diesels, cars, and cabooses so you can build your favorite trains. All magnets are $3 each. Magnets are approximately 1.5" by 3"-7". Actual size samples below:

to see the full catalogue, go to:
customtrains.org
andyfletcherartist@gmail.com
(530) 574-3365

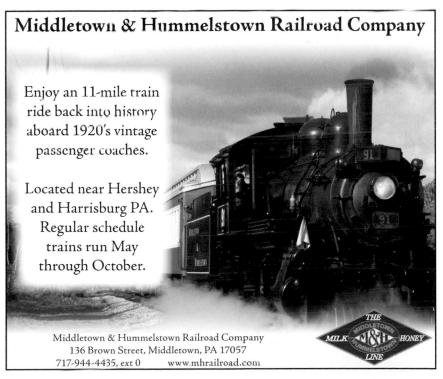

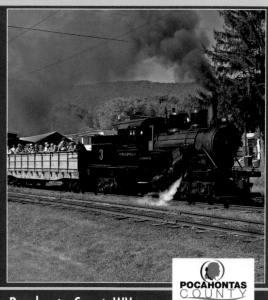

HISTORIC MACHINERY SERVICES CORPORATION

34 Years Experience • Museum Quality Restoration and Conservation

- Repairs to Operating Equipment
- Extensive Rebuilding or Minor Repairs
- Steam Locomotives and Steam Engines
- Industrial Machinery - metal and woodworking
- Portable Crank Pin Turning
- King & Paxton-Mitchell Rod & Valve Stem Packing

- Boiler Work:
  - Form 4 inspections and calculations
  - Repairs and Alterations
  - ASME certified welders
- Part Replication:
  - From your drawing or old part
  - Injector Nozzles
  - Lever Operated Alemite Crank Pin Grease Gun
  - Washout Plugs, Bronze
  - SB-61 Pressure Part Bronze Castings

P.O. Box 856 • Springville, Alabama • SHOP PHONE AND FAX (256) 538-6938

www.HistoricMachineryServices.com

ILLINOIS RAILWAY MUSEUM

ILLINOIS RAILWAY MUSEUM
7000 Olson Rd. (Mailing Info: P.O. Box 427)
Union, IL 60180

SPECIAL EVENTS
THROUGHOUT THE SEASON

RR DC

Operating days:
Saturdays – *May through October*
Sundays – *April through October*
Weekdays – *Memorial Day through Labor Day*

GROUNDS OPEN – NO CHARGE –
ON WEEKDAYS IN MAY BEFORE MEMORIAL DAY, ALSO IN SEPTEMBER AFTER LABOR DAY.

For recorded information: **1-800-BIG-RAIL** or **1-815-923-4000**
or see Web site: **www.irm.org**

Advertiser Index

TOURIST TRAINS GUIDEBOOK
✛ SECOND EDITION ✛

KB
KALMBACH BOOKS

Kalmbach Books
21027 Crossroads Circle
Waukesha, Wisconsin 53186
www.Kalmbach.com/Books

Published in 2009
13 12 11 10 09   1 2 3 4 5

Manufactured in China

ISBN: 978-0-87116-273-1

Front cover photo: Wilmington & Western Railroad by Jim Wrinn
Back cover photo: Baltimore & Ohio Railroad Museum by Alexander Mitchell IV

Publisher's Cataloging-In-Publication Data

Tourist trains guidebook. -- 2nd ed.

    p. : col. ill., maps ; cm.

    ISBN: 978-0-87116-273-1

1. Railroad museums--United States--Guidebooks. 2. Railroad museums--United States--Directories. 3. Railroad museums--Canada--Guidebooks. 4. Railroad museums--Canada--Directories. I. Kalmbach Publishing Company.

TF6.N75 T68 2009

625.1/0074/013

Contributors

The following people provided reviews of the tourist train sites: Matt Austin, Bryan Bechtold, Erik Bergstrom, Marvin Clemons, Joe Cooper, Dave Crosby, Steve Glischinski, John Godfrey, Peter Hansen, Mike Harbour, Scott Hartley, David Hoge, J. David Ingles, Bob Johnston, Joel King, Tom Kline, Kathi Kube, G. Wayne Laepple, Robert LaMay, J. Parker Lamb, Elrond Lawrence, Erik Ledbetter, David Lustig, Rob McGonigal, Jackson McQuigg, Hal Miller, Alexander Mitchell IV, Don Nickel, Steve Patterson, Mark Perri, Bob Withers, Jim Wrinn, Karl Zimmermann

Contact us

To improve future editions of the guidebook, we would like to hear from you. Let us know about the sites you visited, your experiences, and if our descriptions were accurate. Please send your comments to Tourist Trains editor, Kalmbach Books, 21027 Crossroads Circle, PO Box 1612, Waukesha, WI 53187-1612. You can also enter your comments at www.Kalmbach.com/Books.

Contents

Canada

Introduction

In search of history? Looking for that scenic view that you can't get from the highway or from an airplane? If so, you've found it. Scores of railroad museums and scenic railroads are ready to transport you back in time or into the rugged wilderness. And they're all found within the pages of this guide.

The *Tourist Trains Guidebook* is a passport into the exciting world of heritage railroading. If you want to view spectacular sights, enjoy a meal while passing through incredible vistas, or marvel at some of the magnificent machines that made America and Canada great, we'll put you on the right track.

You'll learn where to find real operating steam locomotives. You'll discover trains that run within sight of, or right through, some of our land's greatest national parks. You'll find trains that take you to see wildlife up close, relive history, or provide rafting or biking adventures.

We'll also put you in touch with the places that preserve railroading's most treasured artifacts, as well as its most common items, to keep the heritage alive. You'll find out where you can step inside a genuine roundhouse, learn about narrow gauge trains that once climbed the Rockies, and discover places that tell the story of man and machine vs. the mountains. Some museums even have programs that allow you to run a locomotive.

Here's a bit of advice about how to use this guidebook. Do not sit back and relax with it. Pick out a destination, flip through the pages, and see what awaits. I encourage you to do as I do: let it steer you to the nearest set of railroad tracks, where adventure and excitement are just around the next bend.

Jim Wrinn, Editor
Trains

Using the guidebook

Tourist Trains Guidebook describes 453 excursion trains, trolley rides, rail museums, and historical depots across the United States and Canada. Of those, 179 of the top attractions were reviewed by *Trains* magazine staff and contributors. In this second edition, 25 additional sites have been reviewed. New sites have also been added as directory listings.

The reviews provide an in-depth look at each attraction. They give you an idea of when to go for the best experience and what each site offers. They point out activities that are worth doing and what you shouldn't miss to make your visit enjoyable.

We have used the most up-to-date details possible for every attraction. However, due to the nature of the tourist train industry, we recommend that you contact any site before planning your visit. Steam engines may not be running, hours and prices may change, and museums may be under renovation.

At the front of the book, there is a Railroad Discount Card. You can use this card to receive a discount offer at 43 different attractions found in the book. Each site's specific offer is found in its listing.

Maps

The second edition of the guidebook has also been made easier to use. The continental United States has been divided into seven regions, and states are color coded according to their region. (Canada is one region and one color.)

Under each state, the directory entries are listed first and then followed by the full-page reviews. Each group is in alphabetical order. After each attraction's name, there is a number in a circle or a square. Squares represent train and trolley rides, and circles represent museums, depots, and other sites. (Some train sites have museums, and some museums offer train rides, so the symbols are keyed to the site's name.) You can turn to the regional maps, beginning on page 290, and find a site's location using its number.

ALABAMA

Foley Railway Museum ❶

The Foley Railway Museum houses Louisville & Nashville Railroad artifacts, as well as artifacts representing the history of Foley and Baldwin County. It displays an L&N diesel switch engine, several boxcars, and a caboose. The museum is open Monday through Friday.

SITE LOCATION: 125 E. Laurel Avenue, Foley
PHONE: 251-943-1818
WEB SITE: www.cityoffoley.org/html/depot_museum.php
E-MAIL: foleymuseum@gulftel.com

Fort Payne Depot Museum ❷

Located in northeast Alabama, the museum is a former train depot from the late 1800s and displays railroad artifacts, memorabilia, and a caboose. It also includes historical items from every war since the Civil War and 95 dioramas. The depot is open Monday, Wednesday, Friday, Saturday, and Sunday.

SITE LOCATION: 105 Fifth Street NE, Fort Payne
PHONE: 256-845-5714
WEB SITE: www.fortpaynedepotmuseum.org
E-MAIL: depotmuseum@bellsouth.net

Huntsville Depot & Museum ❸

Built in 1860, the depot is one of the nation's oldest remaining railroad structures and is listed on the National Register of Historic Places. You can read graffiti left by Civil War soldiers and climb aboard several steam locomotives for an up-close look. The museum is open Wednesday through Saturday March through December.

SITE LOCATION: 320 Church Street NW, Huntsville
PHONE: 256-564-8100
WEB SITE: www.earlyworks.com
E-MAIL: info@earlyworks.com

North Alabama Railroad Museum ❹

The museum runs a diesel-powered, 10-mile excursion on select days April through December. The museum offers guided tours on these train days. Otherwise, you can view 30 pieces of rolling stock, the restored Chase Depot, and other rail exhibits on a self-guided walking tour seven days a week.

SITE LOCATION: 694 Chase Road, Huntsville
PHONE: 256-851-6276
WEB SITE: www.northalabamarailroadmuseum.com
E-MAIL: narm-mail@comcast.net

Heart of Dixie Railroad Museum ⑤

SITE LOCATION: 1919 Ninth Street, Calera
PHONE: 800-943-4490 or 205-668-3435
WEB SITE: www.hodrrm.org
E-MAIL: bmorrow@hodrrm.org

Alabama

Marvin Clemons

The museum features exhibits housed in a restored depot from Wilton, Ala. It operates two trains and displays a variety of locomotives and rolling stock. The Heart of Dixie has been designated as the official railroad museum for the state of Alabama.

CHOICES: The museum's Calera & Shelby Railroad operates over 5.5 miles of the Louisville & Nashville's former Alabama mineral railroad through the forested countryside. Two one-hour, diesel-powered excursions run every Saturday. On the first and third Saturdays of each month, the two-foot narrow gauge Shelby & Southern also operates 15-minute trips. The museum is open Tuesday through Saturday from mid-March through mid-December. Admission to the depot museum and outdoor exhibits is free (donations are welcome). A shaded picnic grove is available for lunches.

WHEN TO GO: With comfortable temperatures and lower humidity, spring and autumn are ideal seasons for a visit, as well as the best time to enjoy the colorful foliage along the heavily wooded Calera & Shelby right-of-way. For family outings, the museum regularly operates a number of theme-related excursions including the Cottontail Express, Day Out with Thomas, Mother's Day (and Father's Day) Limited, Pumpkin Patch Express, Santa Express, and the ever-popular Polar Express.

GOOD TO KNOW: In addition to its regular excursion train, the museum offers monthly dinner trains aboard the *William Penn*, a beautifully refurbished Pennsylvania lightweight parlor car built in 1952 for the *Congressional*. It features an onboard gourmet meal and wine tasting at nearby Ozan Vineyards.

WORTH DOING: Located only a 15-minute drive from the museum, the American Village provides a delightful setting for a Revolutionary-era village, complete with replicas of early American sites, such as Mount Vernon, with a cast of early American heroes including George Washington and Thomas Paine.

DON'T MISS: Housed in an early 20th century L&N freight house, the museum's W. A. Boone Memorial Library contains an extensive archive of books, periodicals, maps, and other local railroadiana. It is open on Thursdays and Saturdays.

GETTING THERE: The museum is located 30 miles south of Birmingham, just one mile off I-65 at Exit 228. Drive towards Calera and turn left onto Ninth Street to the museum.

9

ALASKA

Museum of Alaska Transportation & Industry ❶

The museum is home to the trains and other machines that helped develop the state. It features a train yard with locomotives and cars, a renovated section house, and a short train ride. The museum is open Tuesday through Sunday during the summer months.

SITE LOCATION: 3800 W. Neuser Drive, Wasilla
PHONE: 907-376-1211
WEB SITE: www.museumofalaska.org
E-MAIL: form on Web site

Tanana Valley Railroad ❷

The railroad operates a restored 1899 Porter 0-4-0 steam locomotive on a narrow gauge railroad around the perimeter of Pioneer Park in Fairbanks. The locomotive was used to bring residents and supplies to Fairbanks. A historical museum is open daily Memorial Day through Labor Day, and steam trains run on select weekends during summer and fall.

SITE LOCATION: 2300 Airport Way, Fairbanks
PHONE: 907-459-7421
WEB SITE: www.ftvrr.org
E-MAIL: ftvrr.inc@gmail.com
DISCOUNT: One free train ride, up to two adults.

Alaska Railroad 3

SITE LOCATION: 411 W. First Avenue, Anchorage
PHONE: 800-544-0552 or 907-265-2494
WEB SITE: www.akrr.com
E-MAIL: reservation@akrr.com

Bob Johnston

Completed in 1923, the Alaska Railroad was built to link the Pacific seaport of Seward with Anchorage, Fairbanks, and the natural resource-rich interior long before there were highways. Passenger service offers breathtaking excursions into rugged back-country terrain that is often inaccessible by car.

CHOICES: The *Denali Star* operates daily between Anchorage and Fairbanks with stops at Talkeetna and Denali National Park. The train features a fascinating combination of refurbished "lower 48" heritage domes, Korean-built coaches, new Gold Star dome cars sporting open-air viewing decks, and cruise line double-decker domes. Other offerings include the *Coastal Classic* south to Seward and the *Glacier Discovery* to remote Spencer Glacier and Whittier. The *Hurricane Turn* operates with 1950s-era Budd railcars on a four-day round-trip out of Talkeetna.

WHEN TO GO: Trains operate mid-May to mid-September when the weather is warm and the days are long. Early in the season is best when there is still snow on the mountains and little rain. The *Hurricane Turn* operates the first Thursday of every month but starts the winter trip in Anchorage. Colorful September or snowy March offer more light than the short days of December and January, yet winter's Northern Lights deliver a bonus.

GOOD TO KNOW: There are all-inclusive hotel packages to Denali, Seward, and Talkeetna from Anchorage featuring winter excursions that include Anchorage-Fairbanks airfare. With its variety of equipment and room to roam, the *Denali Star* is a better bet than the more deluxe but confined-to-one-car atmosphere of the cruise line domes.

WORTH DOING: The *Hurricane Turn* provides a welcome escape from sightseeing and tourism overload and a chance to visit with friendly Alaskans on their way to remote cabins. The town of Talkeetna is off the main road, has plenty of accommodations, and is reminiscent of the television series *Northern Exposure*.

DON'T MISS: Try either the *Coastal Classic* or *Glacier Discovery* trains. The scenery south of Anchorage is more varied and breathtaking than most of the Denali route, and the *Glacier Discovery* can be arranged to include a rafting tour along Spencer Glacier.

GETTING THERE: Alaska Airlines has the most flights to and from Anchorage, but Anchorage is also served by other carriers. Cruise ships from Vancouver and Seattle that dock at Seward or Whittier are another option.

White Pass & Yukon Route ◢

SITE LOCATION: 231 Second Avenue, Skagway
PHONE: 800-343-7373 or 907-983-9827
WEB SITE: www.wpyr.com
E-MAIL: info@whitepass.net

Karl Zimmermann

With the reopening of the line from Bennett to Carcross, the White Pass & Yukon's 67.5 route miles make it once again the longest operating narrow gauge railroad in North America. More importantly, virtually every one of those miles is knock-out beautiful – a potpourri of lakes, rivers, and snow-capped mountains. Completed in 1900, the railroad was built to link the Yukon and other booming gold-mining districts with tidewater at Skagway.

CHOICES: There are many options for riding. The most popular is the half-day, 40-mile round trip to White Pass Summit. Other possibilities include going seven miles farther to Fraser. Even better are the six-hour trips along the full length of the line, Skagway to Carcross, that are available in either direction with motor-coach return.

WHEN TO GO: The White Pass & Yukon operates from early May to late September, and any time in that window is fine for a visit – though it is likely to be bracingly chilly early and late. As compensation, the snow-capped mountains will be more scenic.

GOOD TO KNOW: The few hotels and handful of B&Bs in Skagway are best booked in advance. As you might expect of a tourist town, there's an ample variety of restaurants.

WORTH DOING: One of the railroad's two steam locomotives, either Mikado no. 73 or Consolidation no. 69, operates on summer Sundays. Unique and colorful diesels – shovel-nose General Electric units dating from 1954 to 1966 and newer chop-nose road switchers built by Alco and then MLW – handle all the other trains.

DON'T MISS: Though the entire line is spectacular, pay particular attention to the first 20 miles to White Pass Summit. Here the railroad uses grades of up to 3.9 percent to climb 2,885 feet. For the best views, grab seats on the left side of the train.

GETTING THERE: Most passengers arrive at Skagway by cruise ship, but the railroad successfully caters to independent travelers as well. You can get to Skagway from Bellingham, Wash., or Prince Rupert aboard the comfortable ferries of the Alaska Marine Highway. For motorists, Skagway is 110 miles south of the Alaska Highway, via the South Klondike Highway. A commuter airline serves Skagway directly from Juneau.

ARIZONA

Arizona Railway Museum ❶

The museum focuses on restoring and displaying railroad equipment and artifacts of the Southwest and has more than 30 pieces of equipment including locomotives, freight cars, and passenger cars. It is open weekends September through May, with work sessions taking place on many Saturday mornings.

SITE LOCATION: 330 E. Ryan Road, Chandler
PHONE: 480-821-1108
WEB SITE: www.azrymuseum.org
E-MAIL: azrymuseum@cox.net

Sierra Madre Express ❷

For a different vacation, try a weeklong rail adventure to Mexico's Copper Canyon aboard classic sleepers and railcars. During the trip, the train travels through 80 tunnels, crosses nearly 40 bridges, and climbs rugged landscapes through almost every climate zone.

SITE LOCATION: 4415 S. Contractors Way, Tucson
PHONE: 800-666-0346 or 520-747-0346
WEB SITE: www.sierramadreexpress.com
E-MAIL: adventure@sierramadreexpress.com

Southern Arizona Transportation Museum ❸

The centerpiece of the museum is locomotive no. 1673, which was built in 1900, converted to an oil burner in 1906, and is listed on the National Register of Historic Places. You can learn more about no. 1673 on Locomotive Saturdays and tour the former Southern Pacific Railroad Depot Tuesday through Sunday. Guided tours are available by appointment.

SITE LOCATION: 414 N. Toole Avenue, Tucson
PHONE: 520-623-2223
WEB SITE: www.tucsonhistoricdepot.org
E-MAIL: contactus@tucsonhistoricdepot.org

13

Arizona

Grand Canyon Railway 4

SITE LOCATION: 233 N. Grand Canyon Boulevard, Williams
PHONE: 800-843-8724 or 928-773-1976
WEB SITE: www.thetrain.com
E-MAIL: info@thetrain.com

Steve Glischinski

This train doesn't take passengers into the canyon, or even along the rim, except for a short distance, but what it does do is provide a unique way to reach one of the great scenic wonders of North America in style. Steam- and diesel-powered trains take riders from Williams on a 65-mile journey to the Grand Canyon's South Rim through high desert and pine forests. An exceptional ride, the trip is also a great value in that it saves you time in trying to find a parking space at the ever-popular South Rim.

CHOICES: Grand Canyon offers five levels of service: coach, club, first-class, dome, and parlor. Service and attention are hallmarks of this railroad. Coach passengers won't be disappointed with the strolling musicians and complimentary soft drinks, while those in cars with higher levels of service will be pampered with extra room, private bars, and exceptional views.

WHEN TO GO: Traveling this area any time of the year is fascinating. The only two days the railroad doesn't run are December 24 and 25. The summer's heat is foiled by air-conditioned cars.

GOOD TO KNOW: You can ride from Williams, spend the night at South Rim, and return on the next day's train. Packages are available from the railroad. Also, the railroad has its own hotel, restaurant, RV park, and pet-sitting services available at Williams. Williams itself is a charming western town with plenty of shops and restaurants worth checking out. The Williams depot, built in 1908, was originally home to a Harvey Hotel and is listed on the National Register of Historic Places.

WORTH DOING: At South Rim, the train arrives at the old Santa Fe Railway depot. Walk up the hill to El Tovar, the historic railroad hotel, and you'll stand in awe of nature at its finest.

DON'T MISS: Ride the parlor car for the ultimate experience: the chance to stand on the back platform of your private car for the day.

GETTING THERE: Williams is about 50 miles west of Flagstaff. Take I-40 to Exit 163 and follow Grand Canyon Boulevard to the depot.

14

Verde Canyon Railroad 5

SITE LOCATION: 300 N. Broadway, Clarkdale
PHONE: 800-320-0718
WEB SITE: www.verdecanyonrr.com
E-MAIL: info@verdecanyonrr.com

Jim Wrinn

On the Verde Canyon Railroad, you'll ride a former copper mining spur down a lush green valley where eagles often soar. Ride across bridges, around rock formations, and through a 680-foot tunnel.

CHOICES: The four-hour, historic route from Clarkdale to the deserted Perkinsville Ranch travels between two national forests and into Verde Canyon, which is accessible only by rail. Narration describes the history, archaeology, geology, and wildlife of the area. Open cars offer canopies to protect riders from the intense sun, and air-conditioned cars are also an option to beat the heat. Special events on the Verde Canyon are too numerous to mention. Among our favorites are the Grape Train Escape, a wine tasting train, and Throw Mama on the Train, a Mother's Day special.

WHEN TO GO: Trains run year-round, but summer can be exceptionally hot. In winter, you can view nesting bald eagles in their natural habitat.

GOOD TO KNOW: The railroad's pair of streamlined diesel locomotives from the 1950s features a special eagle paint scheme. Located in Clarkdale, the Verde Canyon Railroad depot opened in 1997 on the same site of two previous depots.

WORTH DOING: Visit the Tuzigoot National Monument, where an ancient Sinagua pueblo was built. The 42-acre site includes guided tours of the pueblo ruins and hiking trails.

DON'T MISS: Watch for the railroad trestle over 175-foot-deep gorge and the Perkinsville covered bridge.

GETTING THERE: The railroad is about 40 minutes from Sedona and two hours from Phoenix. From Sedona, go southwest toward Cottonwood on Highway 89A to Mingus Avenue. Turn right on Mingus Avenue and go two miles to Main Street. Turn right on Main Street and travel through Old Town Cottonwood. Look for the sign and turn right on Broadway. From Phoenix, take I-17 north to Exit 287. Go west on Highway 260 and then turn left at Main Street through Old Town Cottonwood. Look for the sign and turn on Broadway.

ARKANSAS

Arkansas Railroad Museum ❶

This museum, located in the former Cotton Belt locomotive shops, contains the last two Cotton Belt steam engines, several Alco diesel locomotives, and various railcars. On display are SSW 4-8-4 no. 819 and 2-6-0 no. 36. The museum is open Monday through Saturday.

SITE LOCATION: 1700 Port Road, Pine Bluff
PHONE: 870-535-8819
WEB SITE: www.geocities.com/thetropics/8199/cb819

Eureka Springs & North Arkansas Railway ❷

This railway takes you on a 4.5-mile round trip through the Ozarks, complete with narration. You can chat with the conductor and crew as the train is switched. Dinner trains offer the chance for a relaxed meal. Around the depot, you can inspect a turntable, rolling stock, and other equipment. The railway is open Tuesday through Saturday April through October.

SITE LOCATION: 299 N. Main Street, Eureka Springs
PHONE: 479-253-9623
WEB SITE: www.esnarailway.com
E-MAIL: form on Web site

Fort Smith Trolley Museum ❸

Visit this working museum and you can see restoration work in progress as well as railroad and streetcar exhibits. You can ride on no. 224, a restored Fort Smith streetcar. The museum is open weekends, and trolleys run daily May through October and on weekends the rest of the year.

SITE LOCATION: 100 S. Fourth Street, Fort Smith
PHONE: 479-783-0205
WEB SITE: www.fstm.org
E-MAIL: info@fstm.org

Frisco Depot Museum ❹

This restored Victorian depot was built in 1886 and operated by the Frisco Railroad. Take a self-guided tour and hear the stories of 14 figures representing passengers, station workers, and train crew. You can also take a guided tour, view several short films, and examine a caboose. Located in Mammoth Spring State Park, the depot is closed on Mondays.

SITE LOCATION: Highway 9 and Highway 63, Mammoth Spring
PHONE: 870-625-7364
WEB SITE: www.arkansasstateparks.com/mammothspring
E-MAIL: mammothspring@arkansas.com

Arkansas & Missouri Railroad 5

SITE LOCATION: 306 E. Emma Street, Springdale
PHONE: 800-687-8600 or 479-725-4017
WEB SITE: www.arkansasmissouri-rr.com
E-MAIL: brendab@arkansasmissouri-rr.com

David Hoge

From the highest point to down in the hollers, the Arkansas & Missouri operates excursion trains powered by its all-Alco roster of diesels from April to December. Rebuilt air-conditioned coaches transport riders over 100-foot trestles and through a 1,702-foot tunnel through some of the most rugged terrain between the Appalachians and the Rockies. The A&M operates 139 miles of former St. Louis San Francisco trackage from Monett, Mo., to Fort Smith, Ark., through the Boston Mountains of northwest Arkansas.

CHOICES: The longest ride is a 134-mile round trip from Springdale to Van Buren with a stop in Van Buren, where passengers can shop or dine near the 1901 Frisco depot. Another ride is a 70-mile round trip from Van Buren to Winslow with a ride through the Winslow tunnel. As an occasional special run, the Slots of Fun train takes casino goers from Springdale to Fort Smith, where they meet buses bound for the casinos in Pocola, Okla., for a few hours of gambling.

WHEN TO GO: Fall offers the best scenery, and fall trips sell out quickly, but spring is also popular because everything is blooming.

GOOD TO KNOW: Fares increase for all trips during the fall foliage season, and members in the A&M fan club receive a 10 percent discount. Three classes – first-class, upgraded coach, and coach – are offered on all trips, with lunch or snacks offered for first-class and upgraded coach but not coach. The A&M's oldest car starred in the film *Biloxi Blues* and was built in the late 1910s and used by the Delaware, Lackawanna & Western.

WORTH DOING: The A&M excursion fits in nicely with a trip to Branson or to the William J. Clinton Presidential Library in Little Rock. Eureka Springs offers shopping, and the nearby Buffalo and Mulberry Rivers provide camping, canoeing, and hiking opportunities. Two Civil War battlefields are nearby.

DON'T MISS: Groups can arrange a shop tour of the railroad's all-Alco fleet.

GETTING THERE: Various airlines offer flights into Northwest Arkansas Regional Airport. Travel over I-540 and I-40 gives the area quick access, making the A&M easily accessible for a day of fun.

CALIFORNIA

Colma Depot ❶

This former Southern Pacific depot was built in 1865 and is part of the Colma Historical Association's museum, which also includes a blacksmith shop and freight shed. The second stop between San Francisco and San Jose, the depot was built to shelter passengers at Colma, where farmers and teamsters stopped on the way to San Francisco.

SITE LOCATION: 1500 Hillside Boulevard, Colma
PHONE: 650-757-1676
WEB SITE: www.colmahistory.org
E-MAIL: colmahist@sbcglobal.net

Fort Humboldt State Historic Park ❷

The park includes a logging museum that displays historic, steam-powered redwood-logging equipment, including two 0-4-0 locomotives and a steam donkey. On select days, the Timber Heritage Association steams up the equipment, and short train rides are provided. The park also includes a historical museum on the site where Ulysses S. Grant briefly served.

SITE LOCATION: 3431 Fort Avenue, Eureka
PHONE: 707-445-6567
WEB SITE: www.parks.ca.gov/default.asp?page_id=665
E-MAIL: info@parks.ca.gov

Lomita Railroad Museum ❸

This museum is a replica of the Boston & Maine station at Wakefield, Mass. You can climb into the cab of Southern Pacific no. 1765, a 2-6-0 Baldwin built in 1902, and walk inside a 1910 UP caboose. Several freight cars and a wooden water tower are also displayed. The museum exhibits lanterns, china, and other artifacts. It is open Thursday through Sunday.

SITE LOCATION: 2137 W. 250th Street, Lomita
PHONE: 310-326-6255
WEB SITE: www.lomita-rr.org
E-MAIL: m.martinez@lomita.com

Millbrae Train Museum ❹

The Millbrae Historical Society operates a museum containing photos, artifacts, and documents related to the railroad history of the Millbrae area. Housed in the former Southern Pacific train station, the museum displays a 1941 Pullman sleeper, with its original configuration and paint scheme, from the *City of San Francisco* streamliner. The museum is open on Saturdays.

SITE LOCATION: 23 E. Millbrae Avenue, Millbrae
PHONE: 650-333-1136
WEB SITE: www.millbraehs.org

National City Depot ❺

Still in its original location, the National City Depot, built in 1882, is the oldest railroad-related structure in San Diego County. Operated by the San Diego Electric Railway Association, it exhibits railroad and local historical items. The depot is open Thursday through Sunday but closed on Thanksgiving and Christmas.

SITE LOCATION: 922 W. 23rd Street, National City
PHONE: 619-474-4400
WEB SITE: www.sdera.org/index.html?Info.shtml
E-MAIL: webmaster@sdera.org

Nevada County Narrow Gauge Railroad and Transportation Museum ❻

The museum's collection features NCNGRR engine no. 5. The 1875 Baldwin hauled timber, passengers, and freight. Other narrow gauge locomotives and wooden railcars are on display as are a 1901 steam-powered carriage and other historic transportation pieces. Docent-led tours of the museum are available. It is open Friday through Tuesday during summer and on weekends in winter.

SITE LOCATION: 5 Kidder Court, Nevada City
PHONE: 530-470-0902
WEB SITE: www.ncngrrmuseum.org
E-MAIL: contact@ncngrrmuseum.org

Nevada County Traction Company ❼

Discover a 90-minute, three-mile historic excursion in Gold Country. You ride in open-top cars over part of a narrow gauge line that was originally built in the 1870s, now on the grounds of the Northern Queen Inn. Along the way, you can see vintage rolling stock and a mine. A stop at History Hill allows you to visit a Chinese cemetery.

SITE LOCATION: 402 Railroad Avenue, Nevada City
PHONE: 800-226-3090 or 530-265-0896
WEB SITE: www.northernqueeninn.com
E-MAIL: depotpeople@nccn.net

Poway-Midland Railroad 8

You can ride a variety of railroad equipment on this railroad. It operates a 1907 Baldwin 0-4-0 steam locomotive, a trolley car, and a speeder. You'll also see restored historic buildings and rolling stock, a gallows turntable, and an expanded train barn.

SITE LOCATION: 14134 Midland Road, Poway
PHONE: 858-486-4063
WEB SITE: www.powaymidlandrr.org
E-MAIL: pmrr-info@cox.net

Rail Journeys West 9

Take a luxurious rail vacation aboard the *Silver Solarium*, an original dome sleeper from the *California Zephyr*. Riding in a private railcar over Amtrak or VIA Rail routes, you can take a day trip from the San Francisco area or take longer trips to other destinations in the United States and Canada.

SITE LOCATION: 3770 Flora Vista Avenue, Santa Clara
PHONE: 408-241-7807
WEB SITE: www.railjourneyswest.com
E-MAIL: info@railjourneyswest.com

Railway & Locomotive Historical Society, Southern California Chapter 10

Featuring classic gingerbread architecture, a former AT&SF depot was moved to the Los Angeles Fairplex. The museum includes indoor exhibits and outdoor displays of rolling stock and locomotives, including a Union Pacific Big Boy. You can visit the museum during the county fair in September or during open house weekends each month.

SITE LOCATION: Fairplex Drive, Pomona
PHONE: 909-623-0190
WEB SITE: www.trainweb.org/rlhs
E-MAIL: rlhs-pomona@rrmail.com

Sacramento RiverTrain 11

Leaving from Woodland, the train offers dining and entertainment options on a three-hour round trip. Operated by the Sierra Railroad, the RiverTrain follows the Sacramento River, crosses the long Fremont trestle, and travels through a wildlife refuge. Open-air cars offer an enjoyable experience for lunch, brunch, or dinner.

SITE LOCATION: E Street and Main Street, Woodland
PHONE: 800-866-1690 or 209-848-2100
WEB SITE: www.sacramentorivertrain.com
E-MAIL: info@sierrarailroad.com
DISCOUNT: 10% off tickets and gift shop purchase.

San Francisco Municipal Railway [12]

The San Francisco Municipal Railway operates city transit services, historic streetcars and cable cars. Cable cars run on three lines: Powell and Hyde, Powell and Mason, and California. Streetcars run regularly on the F-Market and Wharves line that connects the downtown area with Fisherman's Wharf.

SITE LOCATION: 1145 Market Street, San Francisco
PHONE: 415-701-2311 or 311
WEB SITE: sfmta.com/transit

Santa Clara Depot [13]

This restored former Southern Pacific depot houses a collection of artifacts and memorabilia that highlights western railroads, with a focus on signaling, and local railroaders. Along with the depot, which dates to 1863, the site features a restored 1926 tower, a section tool house, and a speeder shed. The museum is operated by the South Bay Historical Railroad Society.

SITE LOCATION: 1005 Railroad Avenue, Santa Clara
PHONE: 408-243-3969
WEB SITE: www.sbhrs.org
E-MAIL: information@sbhrs.org

Society for the Preservation of Carter Railroad Resources [14]

Visit this museum on a work day and you'll see restoration efforts of wooden cars completed using hand tools and 19th century techniques. Most cars the society preserves were built by Carter Brothers in Newark. For a one-of-a-kind experience, April through November, you can ride a train car pulled by Belgian draft horses. Narrow gauge steam trains operate once a year.

SITE LOCATION: 34600 Ardenwood Boulevard, Fremont
PHONE: 866-417-7277
WEB SITE: www.spcrr.org
E-MAIL: curator@spcrr.org

South Coast Railroad Museum [15]

The museum's centerpiece is the historic Goleta depot, a Victorian-styled Southern Pacific country station. The museum features hands-on exhibits and a SP caboose. Special events are scheduled throughout the year, and handcar rides are offered. In the Gandy Dancer Theater, you can view films on a variety of railroad topics. It is open Wednesday through Sunday.

SITE LOCATION: 300 N. Los Carneros Road, Goleta
PHONE: 805-964-3540
WEB SITE: www.goletadepot.org
E-MAIL: form on Web site

Trolley Barn 🄯

The replica trolley barn recaptures the form of early California barns. Located in History Park, the structure houses the trolley restoration projects of the California Trolley and Railroad Corporation. The barn contains trolleys and other historic vehicles including a horse-drawn streetcar. Trolley rides take place on park grounds on weekends and during special events.

SITE LOCATION: 1650 Senter Road, San Jose
PHONE: 408-287-2290
WEB SITE: www.ctrc.org or www.historysanjose.org

Waterfront Red Car Line 🄰

The Red Car line runs along the Port of Los Angeles waterfront as it did in the 1900s. It operates a restored car, no. 1058, as well as several replicas. You can board at World Cruise Center, Downtown, Ports O' Call, and Marina Stations. Cars run Friday through Monday and on select weekdays when cruise ships are in port.

SITE LOCATION: Sixth Street at Harbor Boulevard, San Pedro
PHONE: 310-732-3473
WEB SITE: www.portoflosangeles.org/recreation/waterfront_rcl.asp

Western America Railroad Museum 🄱

Housed in the restored Casa Del Desierto, a 1911 Harvey House, the museum features railroad art, artifacts, and memorabilia. Its outdoor displays include locomotives, rolling stock, and other equipment, highlighted by a Santa Fe 95 in classic warbonnet scheme and a Santa Fe horse car. It is open Fridays, Saturdays, and Sundays.

SITE LOCATION: 685 N. First Street, Barstow
PHONE: 760-256-9276
WEB SITE: www.barstowrailmuseum.org
E-MAIL: warm95@verizon.net

Cable Car Museum ⑲

SITE LOCATION: 1201 Mason Street, San Francisco
PHONE: 415-474-1887
WEB SITE: www.cablecarmuseum.org

Jim Wrinn

Of all the transportation systems in the United States, one – the cable car – is forever linked to the City by the Bay, San Francisco. Here's a museum that tells the history of the cable car in the city, from its start in 1873. The museum houses several historic cable cars. Also on display are photos, tools, and models.

CHOICES: As part of the Washington-Mason line powerhouse and carbarn, the museum isn't static. You'll see cable cars come and go all day. Make sure to descend the steps from the museum deck into the winding room to see the cables that pull the cars along the city streets. You can also view three antique cable cars from the 1870s: the no. 46 grip car and the no. 54 trailer from the Sutter Street Railway and the Clay Street Hill Railroad no. 8 grip car.

WHEN TO GO: The museum is open every day (except New Year's Day, Easter, Thanksgiving, and Christmas), and there is never a bad time to visit San Francisco. But be sure to take a jacket no matter what time of year it is!

GOOD TO KNOW: Admission to the museum is free. During the 1980s, the cable car system was completely overhauled. Track and cables were replaced on 69 city blocks. The powerhouse was rebuilt, and the cable cars were repaired and updated.

WORTH DOING: There is always plenty to see and do in San Francisco. You can walk through the Presidio, tour Alcatraz, visit Chinatown, or just hang out at Fisherman's Wharf.

DON'T MISS: During summer, usually in July, you can take in the cable car bell-ringing contest in Union Square, which has been an annual tradition for more than 45 years.

GETTING THERE: No question about it – ride a cable car there! Both the Powell-Hyde and Powell-Mason lines stop right at the museum. From the California line, get off at Mason Street and walk three blocks north to the museum. Tickets can be purchased as you board the cable car.

California State Railroad Museum ⑳

SITE LOCATION: 111 I Street, Sacramento
PHONE: 916-445-6645 or 916-323-9280
WEB SITE: www.csrmf.org
E-MAIL: form on Web site

California State Railroad Museum

This is among the best interpretive museums about railroading. The museum mixes a magnificent large-artifact collection with plenty of details and a sense of drama that bring them to life. Displays, hands-on exhibits, and human interaction all combine to produce an excellent experience for everyone, from those with a passing interest in railroads to those with a deep appreciation for railroading. And if you want the real thing, the museum operates its Sacramento Southern Railroad, a short train ride, in season.

CHOICES: Made up of several buildings, the museum offers guided tours. The Railroad History Museum, at 100,000 square feet, is the largest exhibit space and contains 21 restored cars and locomotives. Be sure to climb the stairs that take you into the cab of one of the largest preserved steam locomotives, a rare Cab Forward with its crew compartment in front of the boiler.

WHEN TO GO: Weekends, April through September, is when the museum offers its Sacramento Southern Railroad train rides behind Granite Rock no. 10, a rebuilt 1943 tank engine. The 40-minute, six-mile round trip travels over the levees of the Sacramento River. The museum also runs special events and trains throughout the year.

GOOD TO KNOW: The museum is situated in the Old Sacramento district of the state capital near where the first transcontinental railroad was launched eastward in the 1800s. The district is a 28-acre National Historic Landmark District and state historic park.

WORTH DOING: The Old Sacramento State Historic Park contains a variety of museums, landmarks, and historical buildings. They include a military museum, a Central Pacific passenger station, and a Central Pacific freight depot.

DON'T MISS: Walk through the *St. Hyacinthe*, a 1929 heavyweight sleeper car. But this is no walk through a lifeless artifact. Inside the beautifully restored Canadian National Pullman car, sound, light, and motion combine to provide the sense that you are speeding through the night on this hotel on wheels.

GETTING THERE: When driving to Sacramento, take I-80 from San Francisco or I-5 from Reno. If you want the full rail experience, take an Amtrak train. The station is adjacent to Old Sacramento. The museum is at the corner of Second and I Streets.

Fillmore & Western Railway 21

SITE LOCATION: 351 Santa Clara Street, Fillmore
PHONE: 800-773-8724 or 805-524-2546
WEB SITE: www.fwry.com
E-MAIL: info@fwry.com

Dale Bolms

Operating over a segment of a former Southern Pacific branch line, the Fillmore & Western Railway is a well-run combination of weekend scenic excursion trains, murder mystery dinner trains, and special trains. It is also one of the premier movie location sets. Billing itself as the "Home of the Movie Trains," from wrecks to shootouts, Hollywood has used this scenic little Southern California line to represent Washington D.C., Florida, the Pacific Northwest, and just about every place in between.

CHOICES: On weekend excursion trains, you can ride in an open-air railcar or in restored vintage passenger coaches. For a full afternoon tour, the Museum or Murals Train offers a luncheon tour to Santa Paula with a choice of a walking tour of the city's murals or of the California Oil Museum. Mystery dinner trains offer a wide range of themes and can be combined with lodging options for weekend getaway packages.

WHEN TO GO: Any time is a good time in southern California, with summers obviously being hotter then other seasons. The rainy season, which is spotty at best, is from about November to March. The trains consist of vintage and antique pieces of rolling stock, which are not climate controlled, so wear weather-appropriate clothing.

GOOD TO KNOW: Fillmore is a suburb in a sea of suburbs north of Los Angeles. Lodging and dining can be found in Fillmore and nearby Santa Paula, Piru, Oxnard, and Ventura.

WORTH DOING: Just down the road from the F&W is a state-run fish hatchery at Piru, where you can view the ponds on self-guided tours. Farther north up the California coast is Santa Barbara, San Luis Obispo, and the Hearst Castle, the ultimate in opulence and home of the man who ran the Hearst newspaper and radio empire.

DON'T MISS: Explore the healthy roster of passenger and freight equipment in various states of repair found on the property.

GETTING THERE: Fillmore is about 60 miles northwest of downtown Los Angeles and about 25 miles east of Ventura. The nearest large-scale commercial airport is the Bob Hope Airport in Burbank. Flights also originate in Santa Barbara.

Knott's Berry Farm 🔢

SITE LOCATION: 8039 Beach Boulevard, Buena Park
PHONE: 714-220-5200
WEB SITE: www.knotts.com
E-MAIL: info@knotts.com

© Knott's

Knott's Berry Farm is a Southern California theme park that has morphed from its 1952 western-style operation to a world-class attraction with rides and events designed for every age. Part of the theme park is the original three-foot-gauge Ghost Town & Calico Railroad.

CHOICES: The railroad is just one part of this large theme park operation that rivals any other attraction in the United States. Most trains are powered by one of two Denver & Rio Grande Western 2-8-0s, either no. 41 (former Rio Grande Southern no. 41 and originally Denver & Rio Grande Western no. 409), or no. 340 (also a former D&RGW of the same number). There is also a Rio Grande Southern Galloping Goose and a number of authentic narrow gauge coaches, a parlor car, and a caboose.

WHEN TO GO: Southern California is enjoyable almost any time of the year. Summers can get very hot, so a hat comes in handy.

GOOD TO KNOW: If you're bringing the family, plan to stay all day. Like other theme parks in the area – Universal Studios and Disneyland – this is a kid-friendly destination with everything you need in one giant arena to tucker out even the hardiest person by the end of the day.

WORTH DOING: Southern California abounds in attractions, restaurants, and activities for everyone. Spend a week or a weekend.

DON'T MISS: In the park, be prepared to be overwhelmed by the amount of rides and sheer number of people. Good news for the railroad fan is that, by carefully selecting your photographic spots, you can come away with images that make it look like you snapped them in Colorado 60 years ago.

GETTING THERE: Buena Park is part of the greater Los Angeles area in Orange County and is near a number of local commercial airports. A vehicle is a must. Freeway exits are clearly marked.

Laws Railroad Museum ㉓

SITE LOCATION: Silver Canyon Road, Bishop
PHONE: 760-873-5950
WEB SITE: www.lawsmuseum.org
E-MAIL: lawsmuseum@aol.com

Laws Railroad Museum

The 11-acre Laws Railroad Museum is home to the largest collection of equipment that operated on the Southern Pacific's narrow gauge empire. At one time, the line's narrow gauge rails stretched almost 300 miles from Nevada, near Carson City, to Keeler, Calif., in the Lone Pine area of the Owens Valley.

CHOICES: Museum displays include SP 4-6-0 no. 9, one of the last three steam engines to operate on the line, various freight cars, a caboose, a turntable, and the original station. By the time the railroad was abandoned, Laws, four miles east of Bishop, existed pretty much in name only with the station being the only major building still standing. The museum has built a number of structures to show what Laws looked like in its heyday. A former Death Valley Railroad gas-electric doodlebug has been restored to operating status.

WHEN TO GO: The museum is open all year with a few exceptions. It is closed on several major holidays such as New Year's Day, Thanksgiving, and Christmas. It also closes occasionally due to severe weather conditions, and some buildings close during winter.

GOOD TO KNOW: The nearest city with restaurants and accommodations is Bishop. If you drive up from the south on Highway 395, there are numerous towns with hotels and eateries, starting with Lone Pine, Independence, and Big Pine. During the ski season, Highway 395 is the main route to and from the various resorts north of Bishop, so you might consider making reservations well in advance.

WORTH DOING: Owens Valley is known for the many motion pictures, mostly westerns, that have been filmed there over the years. A number of small nonrail museums dot the area. The remains of the Manzanar Relocation Center, one of the places where Japanese-Americans were interned during World War II is now part of the National Park Service and open to the public.

DON'T MISS: The area from Keeler to Laws is littered with narrow gauge artifacts, ranging from the remains of trestles and buildings to 4-6-0 no. 18 in Independence. The former SP standard gauge Lone Pine depot is intact as a private residence.

GETTING THERE: Laws is truly in the middle of nowhere, and the trip to the museum is half the fun. Locate Highway 395 on a California map and look about halfway between Reno, Nev., and Barstow, Calif. The highway is well traveled but consider bringing a cooler of refreshments for the long dry-spots between towns.

Napa Valley Wine Train 24

SITE LOCATION: 1275 McKinstry Street, Napa
PHONE: 800-427-4124 or 707-253-2111
WEB SITE: www.winetrain.com
E-MAIL: reservations@winetrain.com

Jim Wrinn

When you think of Napa Valley, you think of wine. And if you want a unique wine experience, take this ride through one of the world's most famous grape-growing valleys. You'll ride in elegant style onboard a fashionable train on a three-hour, 36-mile round trip while enjoying gourmet food and a glass of wine while watching the traffic along busy Highway 29.

CHOICES: Ride in a heavyweight passenger car, open car, or a vista dome, each with a different dining experience. The open-air *Silverado* features casual dining. Dining in the dome offers great views and a four-course meal. Aboard the restored Pullman cars, the menu includes a large selection of gourmet selections. As part of luncheon excursions, you can sample wines at the depot before boarding. A family fun train allows parents some quiet time together. While they dine, the children eat, play, and watch movies in a separate car. Winery tour trains are also available.

WHEN TO GO: Any time of the year is good, but the September grape-harvesting season is among the most popular. Special trains run around select holidays.

GOOD TO KNOW: Attire is generally casual at lunchtime, depending on the time of year or type of special event. Dinner is more dressy, and cocktail-party attire is acceptable. Jackets are suggested, but not required. One bit of advice: no blue jeans.

WORTH DOING: Enjoy the wine. The Wine Train offers a selection of more than 100 wines. Napa Valley is filled with hundreds of wineries to visit as well as having numerous special events.

DON'T MISS: Take a peek inside the kitchen to see the tiny space where all the meals are prepared and watch the chefs in action.

GETTING THERE: From San Francisco, take I-80 east to Exit 19. Follow Highway 29 north and exit at Napa/Lake Berryessa. Take Highway 221, which becomes Soscol Avenue, into Napa. Turn right on First Street and then turn left on McKinstry Street.

Niles Canyon Railway 25

SITE LOCATION: 6 Kilkare Road, Sunol
PHONE: 925-862-9063
WEB SITE: www.ncry.org
E-MAIL: pla_ncry@ncry.org

Jim Wrinn

This museum railroad, a project of the Pacific Locomotive Society, provides a magnificent ride through a dramatic canyon at the edge of the San Francisco Bay area. An outstanding collection of equipment and beautiful scenery make this an excellent day trip in central California.

CHOICES: The railway runs 70-minute round trips through scenic Niles Canyon between Sunol and Niles. Departures are scheduled at both stations. The railroad operates most Sundays during the year except in December, when holiday trains are the rule. On all trains, you can select from open cars, covered cars, or enclosed coaches. Trains are powered by either a diesel or a steam locomotive, when available, from the railway's impressive collection that also includes a variety of passenger cars, freight cars, and cabooses.

WHEN TO GO: Spring and fall can be most pleasant. During April and May, the trains run more often for wild-flower excursions. After Thanksgiving, there is a holiday schedule for the nighttime Train of Lights.

GOOD TO KNOW: Unlike other trips, the last daily train out of Niles is a one-way ride to Sunol, so make sure you have a ride back to Niles if needed. The line through Niles Canyon was the last completed link of the transcontinental railroad.

WORTH DOING: Visit the shops at Brightside, which is open on Saturdays, for a behind-the-scenes look at the railroad when the trains aren't running.

DON'T MISS: The restored Sunol depot was originally built in the 1880s, and the Niles depot, which features colonnade-style architecture and houses railroad exhibits, was built in 1901.

GETTING THERE: The Niles Canyon Railway is situated between Oakland and San Jose. From San Jose, you can take I-880 to Fremont and exit on Highway 84 east. Turn left onto Mission Boulevard and continue three blocks west to Sullivan Street, and the Niles station is on the left. To reach the Sunol depot from San Jose, just take I-680 to Highway 84. Travel west on Highway 84 one mile and turn right onto Main Street to Kilkare Road. From Oakland, take I-880 to Highway 84 east to get to either location.

Orange Empire Railway Museum ㉖

SITE LOCATION: 2201 S. A Street, Perris
PHONE: 951-943-3020
WEB SITE: www.oerm.org
E-MAIL: info@oerm.org

Orange Empire Railway Museum

The Orange Empire Railway Museum was organized in 1956 by trolley and electric railway enthusiasts to preserve a fast disappearing way of transportation. Visitors can ride on classic trolleys, passenger trains, and other railroad equipment from Southern California's past.

CHOICES: Two trolleys run on a half-mile loop line, and one is usually an early Los Angeles streetcar. Another train, pulling freight or passenger cars, operates on the 1.5-mile standard gauge main line. On the freight train, you can ride in either a caboose or open gondola. The cars and locomotives are rotated from the museum's collection, which contains more than 180 vintage pieces. There is also the opportunity to run a locomotive.

WHEN TO GO: The museum is located in Southern California's Inland Empire. The weather is usually bearable during most of the year; however, summertime temperatures can reach triple digits. Winter weather can be mild, but there is an occasional cold snap.

GOOD TO KNOW: The museum, situated on 100 acres of land, is about 20 miles south of Riverside. It has preserved, and is restoring, an eclectic mix of more than 225 pieces of railroad equipment, which includes electric, steam, and diesel power as well as a variety of freight and passenger rolling stock.

WORTH DOING: The museum can be part of a family vacation to Southern California that might also include such world-renowned attractions as Disneyland, Universal Studios, and Sea World.

DON'T MISS: The surrounding area, from Riverside to Temecula, is well developed with all the amenities a traveler would expect. For military aircraft fans, the March Field Air Museum has an extensive collection of aircraft adjacent to March Air Reserve Base in Riverside.

GETTING THERE: Dozens of airlines serve Southern California. Besides Los Angeles International Airport, Ontario International Airport is 35 miles from the museum, and Palm Springs International Airport is 50 miles away. Perris is about an hour's drive from either San Diego or Los Angeles. In Perris, exit at Route 74. Follow Route 74 (Fourth Street) west for one mile and turn left onto A Street.

Pacific Southwest Railway Museum ㉗

SITE LOCATION: Highway 94 at Forest Gate Road, Campo
PHONE: 619-478-9937 or 619-465-7776
WEB SITE: www.psrm.org
E-MAIL: support@sdrm.org

Randy Houk

The Pacific Southwest Railway Museum operates in two locations near San Diego. The main collection is at Campo, just north of the U.S.-Mexican border. At Campo, visitors can enjoy a number of train-riding options, including one to Tecate, Mexico. The other location is at La Mesa, about 10 miles east of downtown San Diego.

CHOICES: The museum has numerous pieces of equipment at Campo including a dozen diesel locomotives – among them, two rather rare EMD MRS-1 military road switchers – steam locomotives, freight cars, passenger cars, and cabooses. Train rides feature round-trip weekend excursions to Miller Creek or Division, and locomotive cab rides are available on either trip.

WHEN TO GO: The Campo facility is open on weekends and specific major holidays. The museum offers a variety of special events throughout the year, including some tailored to kids, such as Halloween and Christmas trains.

GOOD TO KNOW: San Diego is a great tourist destination. Sea World is just north of the city, and the coastline is tourist friendly. Amtrak's *Pacific Surfliner* makes it easy to get up and down the coast to Los Angeles, and the city's efficient light-rail system can take you almost anywhere you wish to go.

WORTH DOING: The greater San Diego area is brimming with places to visit, including Old Town. If you have always wanted to tour a U.S. Navy aircraft carrier, the decommissioned USS *Midway* is open to the public, with many types of aircraft positioned on its flight deck.

DON'T MISS: The only surviving San Diego and Cuyamaca Railway station, the restored La Mesa depot includes a telegrapher's station and exhibit area. A steam engine and freight cars are also on display.

GETTING THERE: The Campo site is 50 miles east of San Diego. San Diego is served by many major airlines and Amtrak. Traveling to the Campo museum requires an automobile. The La Mesa depot is located at 4695 Nebo Drive in La Mesa.

Railtown 1897 State Historic Park ㉘

California State Railroad Museum

SITE LOCATION: Fifth Avenue at Reservoir Road, Jamestown
PHONE: 209-984-3953
WEB SITE: www.csrmf.org/railtown
E-MAIL: form on Web site

Railtown 1897 State Historic Park is considered by many as the premier place for seeing California railroad history. It was originally part of the Sierra Railroad, arguably one of the best-known railroads in the world due to its extensive use in movies, television shows, and commercials. You can enjoy a ride over these historic rails behind a steam locomotive.

CHOICES: The historic shops and roundhouse have been operating as a steam locomotive maintenance facility for more than 100 years. One of the highlights of any visit is taking the roundhouse tour and experiencing for yourself what a working facility looks, feels, and smells like. On the six-mile, 40-minute round trip through California's Gold country, you can ride in open-air observation cars that were previously used in the Canadian Rockies.

WHEN TO GO: The park is open year-round. Tours of the roundhouse take place daily during the summer but have a more limited schedule during the rest of the year. Excursions run every weekend April through October. During the height of the tourist season, make reservations in the surrounding area well in advance.

GOOD TO KNOW: The state of California purchased the station, shops, and roundhouse facilities in 1982 to create Railtown 1897. Railtown is operated by the California State Railroad Museum and is part of the California State Parks System. With more than 200 credits, it is one of the most-filmed railroad locations. The first known filming was in 1919 for a silent movie, and scenes for *High Noon*, *Back to the Future Part III*, and *Unforgiven* were filmed here.

WORTH DOING: The Sierra Railroad operates through some of the most gorgeous countryside in the state. This area, up through Sutter's Mill, is where people settled during the gold strikes, so history abounds. If you like the outdoors and learning western history, this is a great place to explore.

DON'T MISS: On the guided tour of the roundhouse, be sure to examine the props that were used in the movies filmed on the railroad.

GETTING THERE: From any direction, you have to drive to get to the Jamestown area, but California's Gold Country is almost universally seductive, so you'll enjoy the trip. It is about a 90-minute drive from Stockton.

California

33

Roaring Camp Railroads 29

SITE LOCATION: Graham Hill Road, Felton

PHONE: 831-335-4484

WEB SITE: www.roaringcamp.com

E-MAIL: depot@roaringcamp.com

Elrond Lawrence

Located in forested coastal mountains, Roaring Camp Railroads features two distinct trains that offer the best of California scenery and vintage railroading. Roaring Camp & Big Trees runs small but powerful steam locomotives over a narrow gauge line through redwood forests, while the Santa Cruz, Big Trees & Pacific travels down a scenic river gorge to the ocean.

CHOICES: Roaring Camp & Big Trees operates Shay, Heisler, and Climax locomotives on a winding route up Bear Mountain. The 75-minute ride features open-air coaches, perfect for viewing the redwoods, and at the summit, you can explore the big trees. The adventurous can ride the steam train up the mountain and cycle or hike back. Santa Cruz trains employ passenger coaches pulled by an ex-Santa Fe CF-7 diesel. The three-hour round trip runs through Henry Cowell Redwoods State Park, down the San Lorenzo River Gorge, and through an 1875 tunnel before arriving at the seaside boardwalk.

WHEN TO GO: While crowds may be thick, summer is still the best time to go. The higher altitude and proximity to the ocean bring moderate temperatures, but the marine climate also brings chilly, foggy days. Less fog occurs during spring and fall. Special trains include moonlight dinner trains and a summer starlight train. October ghost trains travel through a haunted forest. In November and December, a holiday tree festival greets evening steam trains, and a beautiful holiday lights train rolls through Santa Cruz.

GOOD TO KNOW: Only six miles away, Santa Cruz is a typical resort town with plenty of lodging and a downtown filled with great dining and unique shops. The century-old boardwalk is a historic gem and features a 1924 wooden roller coaster.

WORTH DOING: Roaring Camp is a recreation of an 1880s logging town that includes a steam-powered saw mill, period buildings, antique cabooses, and picnic grounds. Access to the grounds is free, and picnicking is encouraged, but there is a charge for parking.

DON'T MISS: While riding the narrow gauge line up Bear Mountain, watch for a large trestle that was once part of the loop that carried trains to the summit. It was destroyed by fire in 1974, so today's trains navigate an old switchback.

GETTING THERE: Roaring Camp is located six miles north of Santa Cruz off Route 17 at Mount Hermon Road, which ends at Graham Hill Road. Turn left on Graham Hill Road and drive a half mile to Roaring Camp. It's less than an hour from the San Jose airport.

Shasta Sunset Dinner Train 30

SITE LOCATION: 328 Main Street, McCloud
PHONE: 530-964-2142
WEB SITE: www.shastasunset.com
E-MAIL: info@shastasunset.com

Shasta Sunset Dinner Train

The Shasta Sunset Dinner Train operates over part of the historic McCloud Railway that was built along the slopes of Mount Shasta in northern California. Ivory linens, fine china, and polished silver accent the four-course dining experience aboard refurbished passenger cars.

CHOICES: As you dine aboard the Shasta Sunset Dinner Train, you'll travel over steep grades, sharp curves, and the Signal Butte switchback that were constructed for the original route. The trip includes an elegant, four-course dinner that changes menu offerings throughout the year. Regular open-air excursions also take place on weekends during the summer, and a number of special events, including holiday and pumpkin trains, are scheduled every year.

WHEN TO GO: Operating every month of the year, the dinner train features a warm and festive atmosphere, especially in winter when it gets chilly in the northern California mountains. Thursday nights during the summer are special theme nights.

GOOD TO KNOW: The dinner train operates both steam and diesel locomotives that pull rebuilt heavyweight cars that were originally built for the Illinois Central Railroad in 1916.

WORTH DOING: There is always something doing in the McCloud area, including the Main Street Flea Market, Heritage Day, a lumberjack fiesta, and Christmas celebrations. In the greater McCloud area, there are a number of accommodations and restaurants. Depending on the time of year, the area is fertile ground for skiers.

DON'T MISS: The McCloud area in northern California is ideal for rail enthusiasts. The Union Pacific's north-south Los Angeles-Portland main line is nearby as are other short lines. The Yreka Western Railroad is north of McCloud on I-5.

GETTING THERE: McCloud is between Redding and Yreka, just off of I-5 on Highway 89. The best way to get there is by automobile. Commercial airports are located in Sacramento to the south and Medford, Ore., to the north.

Sierra Railroad Dinner Train ㉛

SITE LOCATION: 330 S. Sierra Avenue, Oakdale
PHONE: 800-866-1690 or 209-848-2100
WEB SITE: www.sierrarailroad.com/dinnertrain
E-MAIL: info@sierrarailroad.com

Sierra Railroad

The Sierra Railroad was formed in 1897 to connect the San Joaquin Valley to the Gold County. Today, the Sierra carries passengers, hauls freight, and makes movies. The Sierra Railroad Dinner Train, launched in 1999, provides visitors an opportunity to travel on the historic Sierra Railroad while dining and enjoying the passing countryside.

CHOICES: There are more than 20 different types of trips to choose from, including those featuring romantic dinners, murder mysteries, lunches, Sunday brunches, and Wild West shows. Along the route, you'll pass through distinct western scenery and the scenes of various Hollywood westerns including *High Noon* and *The Long Riders*.

WHEN TO GO: Any time is a good time to take a train ride through California's historic and fascinating Gold Country.

GOOD TO KNOW: The Sierra also offers spa and getaway packages and a rail-and-raft trip that lets you float along the Stanislaus River.

WORTH DOING: Being way out west, you can visit the Cowboy Museum in Oakdale. The museum is housed in a historic Southern Pacific depot.

DON'T MISS: The Sierra Railroad is also a functioning freight operation, so railfans can view more then just passenger cars. Also, take in Railtown 1897 Historic Park in nearby Jamestown to see an historic steam locomotive maintenance facility.

GETTING THERE: The Sierra Railroad is located at the junction of Highway 108 and Highway 120 in the city of Oakdale, which is 90 minutes from Sacramento. The train station, which is made of railcars, is on Sierra Avenue.

DISCOUNT: 10% off tickets and gift shop purchase.

Skunk Train 32

SITE LOCATION: 100 W. Laurel Street, Fort Bragg
PHONE: 800-866-1690 or 707-964-6371
WEB SITE: www.skunktrain.com
E-MAIL: info@sierrarailroad.com

Skunk Train

One of the most amazing attributes of the Skunk Train is its ability to make you feel small. Ride the train from the coastal town of Fort Bragg and you'll quickly find out why. The route travels through a scenic wilderness filled with giant redwoods. As the train takes you through the mountain scenery, the giant trees will make your neck sore unless you move to an open car, where you can stand in wonder.

CHOICES: You can ride from either end of the 40 mile line, boarding at Willits or Fort Bragg. The line features 30 trestles, two tunnels, and a route that snakes its way up the redwood-covered mountainside. At Northspur, the mid-point on the railroad, you can enjoy a picnic lunch and watch the locomotive turn on a wye for the return trip. A shorter 90-minute trip also operates out of Willits to Wolf Tree. A barbecue dinner train is another option.

WHEN TO GO: Trains operate all year, but most excursions to Northspur run April through December. Specials, limited runs, and a motor car also operate during the year.

GOOD TO KNOW: The railroad got its nickname from the yellow-painted, self-propelled gas-powered cars of the California Western Railway that provided transportation starting in 1925 and prompted local people to say, "You can smell 'em before you can see 'em."

WORTH DOING: Along the coast between December and April, you have a good chance to see a California gray whale as they migrate south from Alaska and then return. Whale-watching boats can be chartered out of Fort Bragg for an up-close experience.

DON'T MISS: Ride the train on days when steam locomotive no. 45 is running. A 2-8-2 Mikado type built by Philadelphia's famous Baldwin Locomotive Works in 1924, the locomotive is among the largest in regular service today. If you're really into the experience, this railroad offers a ride in the cab of the steam locomotive. Join the engineer and fireman for the chance to see how it all works.

GETTING THERE: Just over three hours north of San Francisco, the scenic drive to Fort Bragg starts on Highway 101. At Cloverdale, exit onto Highway 128 west, which turns into Highway 1, and continue north to Fort Bragg. The depot is at the foot of Laurel Street.

DISCOUNT: 10% off tickets and gift shop purchase.

Travel Town Museum ㉝

SITE LOCATION: 5200 Zoo Drive, Los Angeles
PHONE: 323-662-5874
WEB SITE: www.laparks.org/grifmet/tt
E-MAIL: traveltown@rap.lacity.org

David Lustig

Travel Town is a good place to enjoy a couple of hours looking at equipment that has been preserved nowhere else. The museum, part of the Griffith Park complex in Los Angeles County, has a collection of small- to medium-sized steam, diesel, and electric locomotives and rolling stock with a surprisingly diverse roster of equipment.

CHOICES: Operated by the Department of Recreation and Parks, the museum is free and kid-friendly, which sometimes takes its toll on the equipment. Nevertheless, the diversity of the saved equipment makes Travel Town worth stopping at if you're in the area. Steam equipment includes tank locomotives, 0-6-0s, 2-8-0s, a 2-6-2, a 2-8-2, a Shay, and a Heisler. Other equipment worth taking in includes an operating EMD Model 40 diesel, a Baldwin RS-12, a Santa Fe gas-electric, a Pacific Electric freight motor, plus various pieces of rolling stock.

WHEN TO GO: Summertime can get very hot in Southern California so bring a hat or other head covering.

GOOD TO KNOW: A food concession is inside, but eating and picnic areas are nearby in other parts of Griffith Park. If you would like to have lunch at a historic eatery, you can grab a chili dog at Pink's, which is 15 minutes away on La Brea Boulevard and has been operating since 1939.

WORTH DOING: Explore Griffith Park, a quiet oasis in busy LA, and especially take the time and visit the park's other sites including the famous observatory and world-class Los Angeles Zoo, which is right next to Travel Town.

DON'T MISS: If you want to take a break from walking, a rideable scale train encircles the collection.

GETTING THERE: Travel Town is near the confluence of I-5 and the 134 freeways. Freeway exits are clearly marked.

Western Pacific Railroad Museum ㉞

SITE LOCATION: 700 Western Pacific Way, Portola
PHONE: 530-832-4131
WEB SITE: www.wplives.org
E-MAIL: info@wplives.org

Western Pacific Railroad Museum

Here at one of the Western Pacific's last diesel locomotive shops is a great collection of rolling stock. The focus is on one of the West's most beloved railroads, which traveled through beautiful mountain scenery and hosted the legendary *California Zephyr*. The setting couldn't be more appropriate.

CHOICES: This 37-acre site displays more than 100 pieces of equipment. Three former Western Pacific streamlined diesels call the museum home, as do locomotives from the Union Pacific and Southern Pacific. Western Pacific 0-6-0 no. 165, a steam switcher, now under restoration, is the only steam locomotive in the collection. Rolling stock includes passenger cars, boxcars, cabooses, and maintenance-of-way equipment. The museum is hands-on, so you can climb into cabs and hop onto cars.

WHEN TO GO: The museum is open every day beginning in April until November. On summer weekends, caboose rides through a pine forest on a one-mile loop of track make for a fun train ride. In December, Santa trains run.

GOOD TO KNOW: Check in August for the annual Portola Railroad Days festival, which includes train rides, food, music, and a parade.

WORTH DOING: Close by is Lassen Volcanic National Park, where you can see hydrothermal features such as boiling mud pots, steaming ground, and roaring fumaroles.

DON'T MISS: Run a locomotive through the museum's program that puts you in the engineer's seat.

GETTING THERE: Portola is located in the Feather River Canyon between Sacramento and Reno. From the west, take I-80 to Highway 89 and go north to Highway 70, which runs into Portola. From the east, take I-80 to Highway 395 to Highway 70.

Western Railway Museum ㉟

SITE LOCATION: 5848 Highway 12, Suisun City
PHONE: 707-374-2978
WEB SITE: www.wrm.org
E-MAIL: form on Web site

Western Railway Museum

The Western Railway Museum gives visitors the opportunity to ride historic streetcars and interurban electric trains that once served California and other western states. There are more than 50 cars on display.

CHOICES: A trip to the Western Railway Museum begins in the mission-revival inspired visitor center. After purchasing admission tickets, explore Cameron Hall, a large display and exhibit hall designed in the grand railroad station style. The building contains many exhibits of historic interest including a permanent exhibit on the transportation history of Solano County. The museum offers 15-minute, one-mile-long streetcar rides around the grounds and a 50-minute interurban ride over the re-electrified portion of the former Sacramento Northern Railway main line to Gum Grove.

WHEN TO GO: The Western Railway Museum is open Saturdays and Sundays from September to May. From Memorial Day through Labor Day, the museum expands its schedule and is open Wednesday through Sunday.

GOOD TO KNOW: The admission ticket to the museum is good all day, and you can ride as often as you wish. The Depot Café offers hot dogs, ice cream, beverages, and snacks on weekends, and the museum features a 1.5-acre shaded picnic area that is well suited for family or group outings.

WORTH DOING: During October, special Pumpkin Patch Trains take visitors on a scenic five-mile journey to a pumpkin patch, complete with a hay-bale fort, hay rides, live music, animals, and, of course, pumpkins.

DON'T MISS: Visitors can stroll through the museum's large car house or take a guided tour of the building on weekends.

GETTING THERE: The museum is about 45 miles northeast of San Francisco, 12 miles east of I-80 on Highway 12. Restaurants and lodging are available in nearby Suisun City, Fairfield, and Rio Vista.

Yosemite Mountain Sugar Pine Railroad 36

SITE LOCATION: 56001 Highway 41, Fish Camp
PHONE: 559-683-7273
WEB SITE: www.ymsprr.com

Jim Wrinn

The Yosemite Mountain Sugar Pine Railroad is a four-mile railroad excursion at Yosemite National Park's south gate. The ride allows you to see what it was like when steam locomotives hauled massive log trains through the Sierra Nevadas. It is a restored segment of the old narrow gauge Madera Sugar Pine Lumber Company Railroad, with a portion of the original right-of-way reconstructed using the same techniques as 100 years ago.

CHOICES: Two geared Shay steam locomotives, formerly used on the Westside Lumber Company, power the excursion trains. An unique experience is riding a Jenny railcar powered by Model A Ford automobile engines. The *Moonlight Special*, which operates Saturday nights in the spring and fall and Saturday and Wednesday nights during the summer, begins with a steak dinner and includes masked bandits, moonlight, and campfire sing-a-longs.

WHEN TO GO: The Yosemite Mountain Sugar Pine Railroad operates daily from mid-March through mid-October and on select days during the winter months. At close to 5,000 feet elevation, it can get chilly at Fish Camp, even in the summertime. The height of tourist season in Yosemite is extremely crowded.

GOOD TO KNOW: Refurbished railcars, once used to transport logging crews, now carry excursion passengers.

WORTH DOING: Other activities in the Fish Camp area include fishing, backpacking, hiking, camping, and mountain biking.

DON'T MISS: Enjoy the beauty that is Yosemite and take in the entire experience, enhanced by the inclusion of an active narrow-gauge steam railroad. You can easily spend an entire day or longer in the area.

GETTING THERE: Fish Camp is 40 miles north of Fresno and 60 miles east of Modesto on Highway 41. The nearest big-time commercial airline service is at Fresno and Sacramento.

Yreka Western Railroad 37

SITE LOCATION: 300 E. Miner Street, Yreka
PHONE: 800-973-5277 or 530-842-4146
WEB SITE: www.yrekawesternrr.com
E-MAIL: yrekawesternrr@aol.com

Jim Wrinn

The *Blue Goose* excursion train takes you on a 15-mile, three-hour round trip over a railway that was first established in 1889. Providing scenic views of Mount Shasta, the train goes through Shasta Valley, crosses the Shasta River, and travels to the old cattle town of Montague. The depot includes some rail exhibits.

CHOICES: The railroad offers coach, caboose, special open-air car, and locomotive cab rides. Ride the train to Montague and along the way enjoy the sights of the ride – Mount Shasta in the distance, an operating lumber mill, and herds of cattle meandering trackside. When in Montague, enjoy a nice lunch at one of several cafés in this small town off the beaten path.

WHEN TO GO: The train runs most days during the summer and on weekends in the fall. This railroad holds several special events each year, including murder mystery trains, pumpkin trains, and Wild West events, but the most unique must be the Great Wild Goose Chase, in which participants on foot or bicycle try to race the train to Montague. (The race's name comes from the train's nickname, the *Blue Goose.*

GOOD TO KNOW: The Yreka Western is a classic lumber short line of the Pacific Northwest. It plays a role in the prosperity of its namesake community, connects businesses with the outside world, and hauls tourists on regular runs.

WORTH DOING: Explore the streets of Yreka. They contain more than 70 buildings that were built in the 1800s and early 1900s. Recreational activities, including rafting, hiking, and fishing, abound. Mount Shasta is located nearby in the Shasta-Trinity National Forest.

DON'T MISS: Walk down to the shop before the train runs to see the crew preparing 2-8-2 no. 19, a movie star having been in the 1973 movie *Emperor of the North Pole*, with Ernest Borgnine, Lee Marvin, and Keith Carradine. You'll see an inscription on the water tower that's a reference to the movie. The engine also appeared in *Stand by Me*, which starred Wil Wheaton and River Phoenix, in 1986.

GETTING THERE: Yreka is located in northern California, about 20 miles from the Oregon border. Take Exit 775 off I-5, head east, and turn right on Foothill Drive until you reach the depot, which is on the left.

COLORADO

Cripple Creek & Victor Narrow Gauge Railroad ❶

The four-mile, 45-minute trip takes you through gold country over a portion of the old Midland Terminal Railroad. Running south from Cripple Creek, the steam train crosses a reconstructed trestle and passes historic mines near the deserted mining town of Anaconda. Trains operate mid-May to mid-October, and they depart adjacent to the Cripple Creek District Museum, which is housed in the original MT depot.

SITE LOCATION: Fifth Avenue and Bennett Avenue, Cripple Creek
PHONE: 719-689-2640
WEB SITE: www.cripplecreekrailroad.com

Forney Museum of Transportation ❷

This museum features more than 500 exhibits relating to historical transportation. It includes a Forney tank-type locomotive that was used on elevated railways, a Union Pacific Big Boy locomotive, cable cars, and other pieces. The museum is open Monday through Saturday.

SITE LOCATION: 4303 Brighton Boulevard, Denver
PHONE: 303-297-1113
WEB SITE: www.forneymuseum.org
E-MAIL: museum@forneymuseum.org

Limon Heritage Museum ❸

This museum focuses on local history and the Union Pacific and Rock Island Railroads. Located in a restored 1910 depot, it includes a restored office and a lunch-counter diner. On display are several railcars including a saddle boxcar, a dining car, and a caboose.

SITE LOCATION: 899 First Street, Limon
PHONE: 719-775-8605
WEB SITE: www.townoflimon.com

Moffat Railway Car ❹

Tours of this 1906 Pullman car are available through the Moffat County Visitors Center, where it is on display. The car originally belonged to rail magnate David Moffat and was named for his daughter Marcia. It contains solid mahogany woodwork and sleeping quarters for 12.

SITE LOCATION: 360 E. Victory Way, Craig
PHONE: 800-864-4405 or 970-824-5689
WEB SITE: www.craig-chamber.com
E-MAIL: info@craig-chamber.com

Pikes Peak Historical Street Railway ❺

Located in an 1888 Rock Island Railroad roundhouse, the Pikes Peak Historical Street Railway Foundation offers a trolley ride on a short demonstration line. The roundhouse features a trolley museum with model displays and a restoration shop. A Southern Pacific baggage car holds a museum of Rock Island Railroad artifacts and models. The museum and grounds are open to the public on Saturdays.

SITE LOCATION: 2333 Steel Drive, Colorado Springs
PHONE: 719-475-9508
WEB SITE: www.coloradospringstrolleys.org
E-MAIL: cstrolley@juno.com

Pueblo Railway Museum ❻

Concentrating on the golden age of railroading, the museum displays steam and diesel locomotives, including AT&SF no. 2912, and rolling stock in the yard behind Union Depot. Artifacts and rotating displays are in the Southeastern Colorado Heritage Center located across from the depot. Locomotive cab, caboose, and coach rides are offered during special events.

SITE LOCATION: 132 W. B Street, Pueblo
PHONE: 719-251-5024
WEB SITE: www.pueblorailway.org
E-MAIL: info@pueblorailway.org

Ridgway Railroad Museum ❼

Known as the birthplace of the Rio Grande Southern Railroad, Ridgway is home to a museum that focuses on local railroading history. It displays an assortment of railcars, and its indoor collection includes artifacts, photos, and tools. The museum holds special events and work sessions throughout the year. It is currently restoring Galloping Goose no. 4.

SITE LOCATION: 150 Racecourse Road, Ridgway
PHONE: 970-626-5181
WEB SITE: www.ridgwayrailroadmuseum.org

Rio Grande Southern Railroad Museum ❽

The Rio Grande Southern Railroad Museum is located in a replica of the original Dolores depot. It is home to the restored Galloping Goose no. 5, which now operates twice a year on the Cumbres & Toltec Scenic Railroad and the Durango & Silverton Narrow Gauge Railroad. The museum is open Mondays through Saturdays during summer.

SITE LOCATION: 421 Railroad Avenue, Dolores
PHONE: 970-882-7082
WEB SITE: www.gallopinggoose5.com
E-MAIL: gghs5@centurytel.net

Windsor Museum ❾

Located in Boardwalk Park, this 1880s Colorado & Southern depot houses an exhibit of steam-era railroading history with an emphasis on local operations. You can walk through a freight room, waiting room, and station agent's room. A caboose is also on site. The museum is open Tuesdays through Saturdays during summer.

SITE LOCATION: Sixth Street and Ash Street, Windsor
PHONE: 970-674-2439
WEB SITE: www.ci.windsor.co.us
E-MAIL: form on Web site

Colorado Railroad Museum ⑩

SITE LOCATION: 17155 W. 44th Avenue, Golden
PHONE: 800-365-6263 or 303-279-4591
WEB SITE: www.crrm.org
E-MAIL: info@crrm.org

Jim Wrinn

When you think of Colorado railroading, you think of mountain-climbing, narrow gauge trains of the Denver & Rio Grande Western. And that is exactly what you'll see at this museum just outside Denver in Golden. But that's not all – the museum features 100 pieces of equipment from many other Colorado railroads.

CHOICES: The museum features narrow gauge and standard equipment, from a steam locomotive once used on the Pikes Peak Cog Railway to a 317-ton Burlington Route steam locomotive and even a set of streamlined 1950s passenger diesels from the Rio Grande. You'll see examples of the famous Galloping Goose self-propelled rail buses that ran on the narrow gauge Rio Grande Southern in southwestern Colorado and the only preserved standard gauge Rio Grande steam locomotive, no. 687, a 2-8-0 built in 1890 and retired in 1955.

WHEN TO GO: The museum is open year-round, except for several holidays. Go during one of the special events when a vintage steam or diesel locomotive powers passenger trains on a short ride around the 15-acre property.

GOOD TO KNOW: Be sure to see the monument that once stood along the Rio Grande tracks to commemorate the creation of the dome car – a bubble-top passenger car that became famous in the 1950s and 1960s for its superb views.

WORTH DOING: The MillerCoors Brewery is adjacent to the museum and offers tours Thursday through Monday.

DON'T MISS: Visit the five-stall roundhouse that houses the museum's restoration shop and features an operating turntable. A viewing gallery gives you a peek at the work it takes to maintain the collection.

GETTING THERE: The Colorado Railroad Museum is located 12 miles west of downtown Denver and is easily reached from I-70. Take Exit 265 westbound or Exit 266 eastbound and it is just off Highway 58 between I-70 and Golden.

DISCOUNT: $2 off adult passage; not valid for Day Out with Thomas.

Durango & Silverton Narrow Gauge Railroad ⏷

SITE LOCATION: 479 Main Avenue, Durango
PHONE: 877-872-4607 or 970-247-2733
WEB SITE: www.durangotrain.com
E-MAIL: info@durangotrain.com

Mike Danneman

The Durango & Silverton is one of the most spectacular narrow gauge steam train rides in North America. Traveling through the Rockies, coal-fired locomotives pull trains through the rugged Animas River Gorge on a railroad built in the 1880s to reach southwest Colorado silver mines.

CHOICES: The Durango & Silverton offers several options for passengers. If you like the great outdoors, ride in an open car but come prepared with jackets. Coaches with windows are also available, but on the day-long trip, the seats may be uncomfortable for those taller than six feet. If you want to splurge, book space on one of the line's three private cars, which are available on at least two trains during the busy summer months – do so and you'll live like a robber baron for a few hours, complete with a glass of champagne. If you can, when outbound from Durango, ride the right side of the train. It provides the best view of the Animas River Gorge at 350 feet above the water.

WHEN TO GO: Winter provides incredible snowy vistas. Summer offers the excitement of up to four trains running each way, but it is also the busy season. September has the best nature show when Aspen trees turn a brilliant yellow and quiver in the autumn breeze. Unique special events, such as the Cowboy Poet Train, take place throughout the year.

GOOD TO KNOW: Durango is a well-developed city with every amenity available to tourists, including at least two historic hotels. Several restaurants in Silverton cater to passengers, providing a quick meal and a taste of the old West.

WORTH DOING: Take part in the other activities that abound near Durango, such as whitewater rafting, hiking, and fly fishing. A visit to Mesa Verde National Park is a must.

DON'T MISS: Take the shop tour to see how the locomotives are maintained and restored in a working roundhouse, a C-shaped structure whose form was once found in rail yards coast-to-coast but now only in a few spots. There is a two-hour layover in Silverton, which gives you time to visit the freight yard museum in the depot.

GETTING THERE: The station is located in downtown Durango. The drive to the Four Corners area on Highway 550 is a scenic delight, as long as you don't mind heights.

DISCOUNT: $3 off adult ticket, up to four; new reservations only, excludes special events.

Fort Collins Municipal Railway 🖸

SITE LOCATION: Roosevelt Street and Oak Street, Fort Collins
PHONE: 970-224-5372
WEB SITE: www.fortnet.org/trolley
E-MAIL: fcmrs@netzero.net

Bryan Bechtold

Fort Collins was the last city in the United States to operate the tiny four-wheel trolley cars known as Birneys, running its trolley system until 1951. A volunteer group of citizens rebuilt the original Mountain Avenue track and restored Car 21 to like-new condition, returning it to operation on its authentic tree-lined route in 1984.

CHOICES: The three-mile, round-trip trolley ride runs along Mountain Avenue from City Park to Howe Street, two blocks west of downtown. A round trip lasts 30 minutes. Other boarding stops are at Shields Street and Loomis Street. There are free rides on special days and for moms on Mother's Day and dads on Father's Day.

WHEN TO GO: The trolley operates on weekend afternoons and holidays from May to September.

GOOD TO KNOW: The original trolley barn is just two blocks north on Howe Street at the downtown end of the line. Long-range plans call for reconnecting track to the carbarn. Inside is Birney Car 25, which is undergoing restoration. Car 25 is one of five remaining cars that ran in Fort Collins.

WORTH DOING: Both ends of the route are family friendly. Downtown Fort Collins has an outstanding variety of restaurants and shopping just a short walk from the trolley. You can also pack a picnic and enjoy the City Park end of the line. For outdoor enthusiasts, Rocky Mountain National Park is less than two hours away by car.

DON'T MISS: BNSF freight trains run right down the center of nearby Mason Street for almost a mile providing the best mainline street-running railroad action Colorado has to offer.

GETTING THERE: Fort Collins is 65 miles north of Denver on I-25. Exit I-25 at Colorado 14 and then drive west through town to City Park. A small depot is next to the tennis courts at Roosevelt and Oak Streets.

Georgetown Loop Railroad 🔟

SITE LOCATION: Loop Drive, Georgetown
PHONE: 888-456-6777
WEB SITE: www.georgetownlooprr.com
E-MAIL: info@railstarusa.com

Jim Wrinn

This railroad shows how engineering overcame mountains when it came to reaching precious minerals in the Colorado Rockies. As the name states, the railroad's highlight is a full loop, where the tracks cross over themselves to gain elevation. The reconstructed Devil's Gate viaduct stands no less spectacular than when it was built in the late 1800s.

CHOICES: You can board at the Devil's Gate station in Georgetown or at Silver Plume. Either way, you experience the same trip, but riding up grade first is always the better show. As you ride the train, scan the mountain slopes for bighorn sheep. Be sure to spot the grade of the abandoned Argentine Central Railroad, which went even higher than Silver Plume.

WHEN TO GO: Because of the climate and elevation the season is short - Memorial Day through mid-October. Interstate traffic from Denver over the July 4th holiday can be a major headache when everyone heads to Grand Lake, at the west entrance of Rocky Mountain National Park, for its dazzling fireworks display.

GOOD TO KNOW: Built in 1884, Colorado & Southern Mogul-type steam locomotive no. 9 plied this route for many years until the line was abandoned in 1938. The route was rebuilt in 1984.

WORTH DOING: The town of Georgetown is quaint and quiet with little influences of the modern world – with the exception of nearby I-70. Its National Historic Landmark District features unique shops, restaurants, and small museums in restored Victorian buildings.

DON'T MISS: After riding the train, travel on I-70 between Georgetown and Silver Plume and watch another train tackle the mountain, with not only the loop but also with a series of zigzags. At Silver Plume, you can take a guided walking tour through the 1870s Lebanon Silver Mine.

GETTING THERE: The railroad is about 50 miles west of Denver off I-70. Exit 226 takes you to Silver Plume and, a few miles away, Exit 228 takes you to Georgetown.

Leadville, Colorado & Southern Railroad 🔳

SITE LOCATION: 326 E. Seventh Street, Leadville
PHONE: 866-386-3936 or 719-486-3936
WEB SITE: www.leadville-train.com
E-MAIL: form on Web site

Jim Wrinn

In a state with many spectacular scenic railroads, this line doesn't disappoint. Leaving from the charming mining town of Leadville, the LC&S marches up the side of the Rockies near the tree line. Upon departure from the depot, the train leaves the 10,200-foot elevation for a 900-foot climb along the southern side of the upper Arkansas River Valley to a point close to Climax at Fremont Pass. The train passes through forests of lodgepole pine, spruce, and aspen.

CHOICES: On the 22-mile trip, you can ride in an open car or a car with a roof. Especially for train fans, there are several seats available in the locomotive or in the caboose. If it's a beautiful day in Colorado, as it often is, stick to the open cars for unobstructed views. Stay on the right side of the train for spectacular views of the mountains and the molybdenum mine at the end of the line. Along the way, the conductor provides narration and answers questions. Packages are also available for raft trips on the Arkansas River.

WHEN TO GO: The trains run late May through late September when the aspen trees put on a magnificent show of yellow. In mid-summer, the Wildflower Special lets you view alpine flowers at their peak.

GOOD TO KNOW: Incorporated in 1878, Leadville is the highest incorporated city in the continental United States at 10,152 feet above sea level. Downtown Leadville is home to many shops, galleries, restaurants, and lodging establishments and makes an easy base camp from which to explore the central Rockies.

WORTH DOING: Be sure to explore Leadville's National Historic Landmark District, which includes many buildings built between 1880 and 1905.

DON'T MISS: On the return trip, the train pauses for a break at French Gulch, where a wooden water tank that once supplied steam locomotives with water still stands. The break is a great chance to walk forward to the locomotive, where you can inspect the cab, meet the crew, and get a snapshot.

GETTING THERE: From Denver, take I-70 west and then Highway 91 south to Leadville. From Vail, take I-70 west to Highway 24 and then Highway 24 south to Leadville.

DISCOUNT: Group discount given for every adult ticket.

Pikes Peak Cog Railway 15

SITE LOCATION: 515 Ruxton Avenue, Manitou Springs
PHONE: 800-745-3773 or 719-685-5401
WEB SITE: www.cograilway.com
E-MAIL: info@cograilway.com

Jim Wrinn

The Pikes Peak Cog Railway offers a unique Swiss Alpine experience on rails. Diesel-powered, self-propelled passenger cars navigate unbelievably steep grades with the help of a cog to ascend the 14,110-foot high peak. The view at the top is beautiful, but the journey is awe inspiring as well with trains going beyond the timberline, passing herds of bighorn sheep, and arriving at a station that includes a high-altitude research center.

CHOICES: The railroad offers three-hour round trips that allow you 30 minutes at the summit. It also provides a one-way trip to the top for anyone who would like to hike back down (about six hours) or ride a mountain bike with an outfitter service. During the first part of the trip, the train travels through boulder fields, where you may see some interesting "faces" in the giant boulders. You'll also see some wildlife and a bristlecone pine forest with trees believed to be 2,000 years old.

WHEN TO GO: The railroad, unbelievably, operates year-round, thanks to a homemade snow plow that operates like a giant snow blower on rails. During summer, the railroad runs up to eight trains a day with departures every 80 minutes. During winter, November through March, the railway runs a limited schedule that is subject to a minimum number of passengers.

GOOD TO KNOW: The railroad uses modern Swiss-built trains of a type used in the Alps. These units tackle grades of up to 25 percent – meaning the track rises 25 feet for every 100 feet of forward travel.

WORTH DOING: At the base of Pikes Peak, about an hour's drive away, lie the historic gold-mining towns of Cripple Creek and Victor. You may still find gold in Cripple Creek – at the town's casinos - or ride the Cripple Creek & Victor Narrow Gauge Railroad. In Colorado Springs, explore the many red sandstone formations in the Garden of the Gods.

DON'T MISS: At the peak, make sure to walk around the summit and look for Denver. Just be careful. On the north side is a drop-off called the Bottomless Pit.

GETTING THERE: Manitou Springs is six miles from Colorado Springs. Take Exit 141 off I-25 and go west (toward the mountains) on Highway 24 four miles to the Manitou Avenue (Manitou Springs) exit. Go west on Manitou Avenue for 1.5 miles to Ruxton Avenue. Turn left and go to the top of Ruxton Avenue.

Platte Valley Trolley 16

SITE LOCATION: 15th Street and Platte Street, Denver
PHONE: 303-458-6255
WEB SITE: www.denvertrolley.org
E-MAIL: pvt@denvertrolley.org

Bryan Bechtold

The Platte Valley Trolley is often referred to as one of Denver's best-kept secrets. The trolley runs through the South Platte River Greenway Park linking several of the city's most popular attractions. The trolley is a faithful replica of a turn-of-the-century, open-air "breezer," which is ideally suited for enjoying the sightseeing trip.

CHOICES: The route starts at Confluence Park beside the REI store. The riverfront ride lasts 25 minutes. Stops are made at the Downtown Aquarium, Children's Museum, and Invesco Field at Mile High. The trolley only makes intermediate stops southbound, and runs end-to-end northbound.

WHEN TO GO: The trolley operates Friday, Saturday, and Sunday afternoons April through October. From Memorial Day through Labor Day, the trolley also operates on Mondays. It departs continuously every half hour from REI. During Denver Bronco home games, fans can catch a shuttle to the game.

GOOD TO KNOW: Confluence Park is the site of Denver's original settlement and is now a hub for paved bicycle trails that serve the city. There are several good restaurant choices nearby.

WORTH DOING: The Platte River area is a great place to take the family. Combine a trolley ride with nearby attractions, such as the Children's Museum, Elitch Gardens Amusement Park, or the aquarium, or just enjoy the great views of the downtown skyline.

DON'T MISS: The flagship REI store is housed in the former Denver Tramway powerhouse building. The Starbucks there has a collection of photos showing the interior as it looked in 1901, quite a difference from the three-story climbing rock there now. Give it a try!

GETTING THERE: The route is located in downtown Denver. By car, take I-25 to Exit 211 (23rd Street), turn east on Water Street, and follow the signs to the Children's Museum or continue straight to the REI store for your best parking options. RTD buses operate within a short walk. The trolley is about a 15-minute walk from Amtrak and RTD light rail service at Union Station.

Rio Grande Scenic Railroad 🔟

SITE LOCATION: 601 State Avenue, Alamosa
PHONE: 877-726-7245
WEB SITE: www.riograndescenicrailroad.com
E-MAIL: info@riograndescenicrailroad.com

Bryan Bechtold

The Denver & Rio Grande built an incredibly scenic route into the San Luis Valley and its biggest city, Alamosa, in the late 1880s. The standard gauge line of today replaced a much more difficult narrow gauge line but lost nothing as far as its engineering marvels or trackside splendor.

CHOICES: The railroad offers two routes, and steam locomotives 18 and 1744 power most excursion trains. The *San Luis Express* crosses famous LaVeta Pass over the Sangre de Cristo Mountains. The *Toltec Gorge Limited* takes you through the San Luis Valley to Antonito, where a connection can be made to the famous narrow-gauge Cumbres & Toltec Scenic Railroad. In addition, the railroad offers standard coach seating as well as dome-car seating. Hint: take the dome, as this glass bubble-top car provides unparalleled views of the mountains.

WHEN TO GO: The Rio Grande Scenic runs Memorial Day weekend through mid-October.

GOOD TO KNOW: There are more than 40 restaurants and a dozen lodging options near Alamosa. The railroad offers longer trips including half-day trips to Fir, at the top of the mountain on the LaVeta Pass route, as well as a trip to Great Sand Dunes National Park.

WORTH DOING: During the summer, the railroad offers its High Altitude Concert Series in a mountain setting reachable only by train. Listen to the music under the stars, surrounded by aspen and pines, in a natural meadow amphitheater.

DON'T MISS: For a unique rail experience, try riding the Monte Vista Mixed: a diesel-powered train made up of both freight and passenger cars that runs between Alamosa and Monte Vista.

GETTING THERE: Located in south-central Colorado, Alamosa is about 200 miles south of Denver and 90 miles west of Pueblo. Highway 160 is the key route in and out of the San Luis Valley. The highway becomes Main Street in Alamosa, and the depot is just off Main Street on State Avenue.

Royal Gorge Route Railroad 18

SITE LOCATION: 401 Water Street, Cañon City

PHONE: 888-724-5748 or 719-276-4000

WEB SITE: www.royalgorgeroute.com

Ghislain Gerard

Nowhere else in America can you ride a train through a very narrow mountain gorge with a fast-flowing river and look straight up at one thousand feet of cliff. The railroad offers a range of service on its 24-mile round trip through the Royal Gorge.

CHOICES: Service classes on the two-hour excursions begin with coach, which seats you in comfortable air-conditioned cars with access to the concession car and an open-air car. Vista-dome class provides panoramic views under glass, food service, and a full-service bar. Wine express class offers a selection of wine and accompanying appetizers. The Lunch Train offers a three-course gourmet lunch. The three-hour Dinner Train has a four-course gourmet dinner, and the Wine Dinner Train adds wine to its five-course dinner. The popular Murder Mystery Train presents an entertaining whodunit while you enjoy dinner.

WHEN TO GO: Summer offers more schedule options and more dinner trains, sometimes running up to 13 cars in push-pull fashion with a locomotive on each end. While the scenery is gorgeous year-round, Colorado is known for its brilliant yellow Aspen trees in September.

GOOD TO KNOW: Originally part of the historic Denver & Rio Grande Western Railroad, passenger service through the magnificent Royal Gorge ended in 1967 and was resumed in 1999 by the Royal Gorge Railroad. Cañon City has a generous array of motels and restaurants, and the railroad offers overnight packages with area hotels and B&Bs.

WORTH DOING: In summer, raft-and-rail packages include a nine-mile raft trip down the Arkansas River in Bighorn Canyon. Also available for would-be engineers is a cab ride in an F7 locomotive.

DON'T MISS: Riding through the Royal Gorge in one of the former Milwaukee Road or AT&SF full-length dome cars, where you can also enjoy lunch or dinner, is the best way to see the world's highest suspension bridge that spans the gorge 1,053 feet above the river.

GETTING THERE: Cañon City is 115 miles from Denver and 45 minutes from Colorado Springs via Highway 115. Colorado Springs has the nearest airport.

Ski Train

SITE LOCATION: 17th Street at Wynkoop Street, Denver
PHONE: 303-296-4754
WEB SITE: www.skitrain.com
E-MAIL: askskitrain@skitrain.com

Steve Patterson

Climbing up almost 4,000 feet through the Rocky Mountains, the Ski Train offers one of the most scenic rides in North America. It traverses 28 tunnels in 17 miles, including the 6.2-mile-long Moffat Tunnel, which is the third-longest tunnel in the United States and sixth-longest in the world.

CHOICES: Observe some of the most beautiful Rocky Mountain scenery not accessible by a highway, particularly on snowy days. Both coach and club classes offer reserved seating and group rates. Club seating features a continental breakfast buffet in the morning and snacks and beverages on the trip home. Coach passengers may purchase those items in the lounge cars. A full train can carry more than 750 passengers.

WHEN TO GO: The train starts running on its 56-mile trip just after the Christmas holidays and usually operates Saturdays and Sundays until April. It also operates on Thursdays and Fridays during February and March. In summer, it runs Saturdays from mid-July to the end of August.

GOOD TO KNOW: In bad weather, the ski train is often the only transportation that makes it to the ski slopes. There are free shuttle buses to the nearby towns of Winter Park and Fraser. All fares are based on same-day, round-trip travel, so if you are planning to stay overnight, you will have to purchase two round-trip tickets. The Ski Train sells out quickly, especially the limited club seats, so reservations are recommended.

WORTH DOING: Even if you don't ski, there is plenty to do in Winter Park including snowshoeing, snowboarding, and daily Snowcat tours. Summer ski trains are popular for family fun such as hiking and biking (you can bring your own bike aboard the train), and the alpine slide is a must-do activity.

DON'T MISS: Sit on the right side to watch the train climb the Front Range around the famous Big 10 curves and look back at the Denver skyline on the plain. After negotiating curved Tunnel 8, the train enters dramatic South Boulder Canyon.

GETTING THERE: Denver International Airport is served by most major airlines and is 20 miles from Union Station. Amtrak also serves Denver. I-25 and I-70 intersect about a mile from the depot.

CONNECTICUT

Connecticut Antique Machinery Association ❶

The association features an operating three-foot-gauge railroad that is powered by a 1925 Baldwin locomotive that was used in the sugar cane fields of Hawaii. A variety of other locomotives and rolling stock fill out this collection. The site contains six other exhibits dedicated to antique industrial and agricultural machinery.

SITE LOCATION: Route 7, Kent
PHONE: 860-927-0050
WEB SITE: www.ctamachinery.com
E-MAIL: camainfo@ctamachinery.com

Connecticut Trolley Museum ❷

Founded in 1940, this museum offers a narrated three-mile, round-trip trolley ride. Its collection contains passenger and freight streetcars, interurban cars, elevated railway cars, service cars, and other rail equipment. The 17-acre site includes a power substation, a restoration shop, and storage barns.

SITE LOCATION: 58 North Road, East Windsor
PHONE: 860-627-6540
WEB SITE: www.ceraonline.org
E-MAIL: office@ceraweb.org

Danbury Railway Museum ❸

This museum contains 50 pieces of equipment representing 11 different northeastern railroads and includes unique pieces such as a New Haven Railroad Mack FCD railbus. Vintage train rides in the yard go to the only operating turntable in Connecticut. The 1903 station features displays and a model layout of the Danbury yard. It is open year-round except for holidays.

SITE LOCATION: 120 White Street, Danbury
PHONE: 203-778-8337
WEB SITE: www.danbury.org/drm
E-MAIL: info@danburyrail.org
DISCOUNT: Receive $1 off each regular admission.

Shore Line Trolley Museum ❹

A visit to the museum is a unique sensory journey into the past as you hear trolley motors growl, smell the electric arc, and feel rattan seats. The museum operates a three-mile round trip along the scenic shore over the last remaining portion of Branford Electric Railway. It boasts a collection of almost 100 vintage vehicles.

SITE LOCATION: 17 River Street, East Haven
PHONE: 203-467-6927
WEB SITE: www.bera.org

SoNo Switch Tower Museum ❺

This 1896 New Haven Railroad switch tower has been restored, complete with an original 68 Armstrong lever mechanical machine. Located next to the Northeast Corridor main line, the unique museum is open Saturdays and Sundays May through October.

SITE LOCATION: 77 Washington Street, South Norwalk
PHONE: 203-246-6958
WEB SITE: www.sonotower.org
E-MAIL: info@westctnrhs.org

Connecticut Eastern Railroad Museum ⑥

SITE LOCATION: 55 Bridge Street, Willimantic
PHONE: 860-456-9999
WEB SITE: www.cteastrrmuseum.org
E-MAIL: info@cteastrrmuseum.org

Robert LaMay

For anyone interested in seeing what a 1900s-era railroad complex consisted of, this would be the place to visit. Located on the original site of the Columbia Junction freight yard, the Connecticut Eastern Railroad Museum is one of the few railroad operations in the United States to have a roundhouse and an operating standard gauge 60-foot Armstrong turntable.

CHOICES: The museum features a variety of restored buildings including a station, section house, and freight house. Numerous working projects occur every week throughout the museum's operating season. It houses several diesel locomotives and railcars. Tour guides are also on hand to show and explain the Ghost Train story and other tales of railroad history.

WHEN TO GO: The museum is open weekends from the first Saturday in May to the last weekend in October. A variety of events take place during the season, such as music concerts, night photo shoots, and Metal Fest – a full day of blacksmithing events and demonstrations.

GOOD TO KNOW: Kids of all ages can operate a replica 1850s-style pump car along a section of rail.

WORTH DOING: Willimantic is situated in the "Last Green Valley," designated as the Quinebaug and Shetucket Rivers Valley National Heritage Corridor. The valley contains seven state forests and five state parks. During Walktober, there are more than 100 guided walks and special events, including one at the Connecticut Eastern Railroad Museum.

DON'T MISS: Watch as a locomotive or rail bus is turned on the museum's turntable and then put into the Columbia Junction six-stall roundhouse. During Metal Fest, smell the burning embers and feel the heat as blacksmiths demonstrate their skills.

GETTING THERE: Located about 30 miles east of Hartford in downtown Willimantic, the museum can be easily reached via numerous state roads such as Routes 6, 66, 32, 195, and 2. Once downtown, turn onto Bridge Street (Route 289 south), take a quick right, and follow the railroad tracks down a dirt road to the museum entrance.

Essex Steam Train & Riverboat 7

SITE LOCATION: 1 Railroad Avenue, Essex
PHONE: 800-377-3987 or 860-767-0103
WEB SITE: www.essexsteamtrain.com
E-MAIL: valley.railroad@snet.net

Valley Railroad Company

The Essex Steam Train is unusual in offering a train ride that can be combined with a riverboat excursion, providing scenic views of the Connecticut River from both rail and water. The 12-mile rail round trip from Essex Station to Deep River takes about an hour while the rail-water package lasts more than two hours.

CHOICES: The Essex Steam Train is hauled by either locomotive 2-8-2 no. 40 or 2-8-0 no. 97, while the *Becky Thatcher*, a replica of a three-deck Mississippi-style riverboat, handles the water excursion. Beyond basic train and train-and-riverboat tours, the Valley Railroad Company offers a number of special events, including the annual Hot Steamed Jazz Festival and a dinner train. On some weekends, a caboose is available for riding. For the ultimate rail experience, the Your-Hand-on-the-Throttle program lets you actually run a locomotive.

WHEN TO GO: The railroad operates May through October, with Day Out with Thomas weekends in November and the North Pole Express – with Santa, holiday stories, and caroling – weekends during the Christmas season. Spring and fall are fine times to visit, with the leaves either a new green or in brilliant autumn colors.

GOOD TO KNOW: Essex is a historic seaport village, with lots of white-clapboard New England charm. The charmingly Victorian Goodspeed Opera House in nearby East Haddam presents excellent productions of classic musical comedies.

WORTH DOING: Nearby Gillette Castle is a whimsical faux-medieval mountaintop estate built of local fieldstone and completed in 1919 for actor and playwright William Gillette, most famous for his portrayal of Sherlock Holmes. Visit it on your own or as a train-ferry-hiking package offered by the railroad.

DON'T MISS: The diesel-hauled Essex Clipper Dinner Train, which operates seasonally and offers a four-course dinner, actually makes the longest run of any of the trains, going beyond Deep River and up to Haddam. One of its two dining cars is a special treat: the heavyweight Pullman parlor car *Wallingford*, built in 1927 for the New York, New Haven & Hartford Railroad.

GETTING THERE: Essex is located on Route 9 just three miles from I-95. The nearest major airports are in New Haven and Hartford, roughly equidistant.

Naugatuck Railroad

SITE LOCATION: 242 E. Main Street, Thomaston
PHONE: 860-283-7245
WEB SITE: www.rmne.org
E-MAIL: info@rmne.org

Scott Hartley

Today's Naugatuck Railroad runs over 19.6 miles of former New Haven Railroad, between Waterbury and Torrington, a line built by the original Naugatuck in 1849. The tracks follow the railroad's namesake river for the entire route. The Naugatuck Railroad, part of the Railroad Museum of New England, offers excursions over a nine-mile portion of its line.

CHOICES: Departing the 1881 Thomaston station aboard 1920s heavyweight coaches built for Canadian National, you cross two trestles over the Naugatuck River, see century-old New England brass mills, and roll high across the face of giant Thomaston Dam. Santa specials run weekends in December, a Day Out with Thomas provides family fun, and evening music and wine-tasting trains are also scheduled. Operating locomotives include U23B 2203 (the last domestic "U-Boat" built by General Electric) and Alco RS3 New Haven 529.

WHEN TO GO: Excursions run on Sundays and Tuesdays from Memorial Day through August. In September and October, Saturday departures are added. The fall colors peak in early to mid-October, and this is the most popular time to ride the Naugatuck's trains.

GOOD TO KNOW: Built in 1881 by the original Naugatuck Railroad, the Thomaston station is being restored as are several outbuildings and an operating control tower. The station features a display track of historic New England railroad rolling stock.

WORTH DOING: Thomaston offers a pleasant New England downtown with historic mills, a picturesque opera house, and other buildings. Nearby Litchfield has shops and restaurants as well. Waterbury's Mattatuck Museum shows visitors the history of Connecticut's brass industry.

DON'T MISS: Naugatuck's Engineer-for-an-Hour program provides the opportunity to run one of the railroad's diesels over the challenging north portion of the railroad with its many curves and grades.

GETTING THERE: Take I-84 to Waterbury, then Exit 20 to Route 8, and follow Route 8 north to Exit 38.

DELAWARE

Wilmington & Western Railroad ▪

SITE LOCATION: 2201 Newport-Gap Pike, Wilmington
PHONE: 302-998-1930
WEB SITE: www.wwrr.com
E-MAIL: schedule@wwrr.com

Jim Wrinn

The Wilmington & Western is one of the premier tourist railroads on the East Coast. Attractive equipment, historic steam locomotives, and a scenic route through Delaware's Red Clay Valley make this line a must-see when visiting the mid-Atlantic

CHOICES: The Wilmington & Western offers two basic trip options from Greenbank Station: a 90-minute round trip to the Mount Cuba picnic grove or a 2.5-hour round trip covering the entire 10-mile line to Hockessin. The train is comprised of vintage steel coaches with adjustable windows, and an open-air car is available during the warmer months. Special trains offer onboard dining, evening runs, and holiday-themed events.

WHEN TO GO: The W&W is open from April through December, but steam operates on only select dates for much of the season. Fall foliage and winter holidays see steam excursions nearly every weekend. Mid-October through early November is prime season for autumn leaves in the Red Clay Valley. December is Santa Claus Express time, with the focus on families and fun.

GOOD TO KNOW: Built by the American Locomotive Company in 1909 for the Mississippi Central, 4-4-0 American no. 98 returned to service after extensive restoration in 2004. Today, it's one of the few American Standard types operating.

WORTH DOING: Nearby attractions include the Hagley Museum & Library, a museum of American industrial history, and Winterthur, a magnificent estate showcasing rare collections of antiques and Americana amidst a 979-acre private garden.

DON'T MISS: On Pufferbelly Days, both the railroad's steam locomotives, 4-4-0 no. 98 and 0-6-0 no. 58, operate double-headed. On Speeder Days, you can ride a vintage track inspection vehicle in addition to the train.

GETTING THERE: Greenbank Station is about four miles southwest of downtown Wilmington on Route 41, close to I-95. Amtrak's Northeast Corridor provides frequent service to downtown Wilmington. Worldwide air connections are available 35 miles away at Philadelphia International Airport.

DISCOUNT: $1 off each adult ticket, up to four adults; excludes specials.

DISTRICT OF COLUMBIA

Smithsonian National Museum of American History ❶

SITE LOCATION: 14th Street and Constitution Avenue, Washington
PHONE: 202-633-1000
WEB SITE: www.americanhistory.si.edu
E-MAIL: info@si.edu

National Museum of American History

Newly reopened after a major renovation, the National Museum of American History features the landmark transportation exhibition America on the Move. Eighteen multimedia dioramas, each recreating a specific time and place using artifacts, images, and sound, demonstrate how road and rail transportation have shaped the American nation.

CHOICES: Must-see exhibits include the massive Southern Railway no. 1401, a 280-ton 4-6-2 passenger locomotive built in 1926; *Jupiter*, a stunning Baldwin-built narrow gauge 4-4-0; and a 19th century streetcar. Though not part of America on the Move, the museum also displays the *John Bull*, one of the oldest surviving steam locomotives in North America. This 1831 English-made locomotive is displayed on a vintage iron truss bridge that once served the Philadelphia and Reading Railroad.

WHEN TO GO: The museum is open every day of the year except Christmas Day. Spring sees the renowned Cherry Blossom trees in bloom at the nearby Tidal Basin. The Smithsonian Folklife Festival, a huge outdoor exposition of living cultural heritage, takes place each year around Independence Day on the National Mall.

GOOD TO KNOW: The National Museum of American History is only one of a dozen world-class Smithsonian museums located on or near the National Mall, exhibiting everything from art to aviation and natural history. All Smithsonian museums feature free admission.

WORTH DOING: Explore the National Mall and all it has to offer. In this national park, you can visit the Washington Monument, Lincoln Memorial, Jefferson Memorial, and several war memorials.

DON'T MISS: Listen to the re-created conversation between the fireman and engineer of Southern no. 1401 as they discuss their upcoming run. Take a full-immersion multimedia journey around Chicago's famous loop as it was in 1959 aboard "L" car 6719.

GETTING THERE: Parking is limited in the area, so public transportation is encouraged. Washington's Metrorail subway offers convenient access to the museum from its Smithsonian and Federal Triangle stations. Amtrak provides service from many points. Washington Reagan National Airport is conveniently located on Metrorail.

FLORIDA

Central Florida Railroad Museum ❶

Located in a former 1913 Tavares & Gulf Railroad station, the museum features a Clinchfield caboose and a 1938 Fairmont motor car. Exhibits focus on central Florida railroads, including the "Tug and Grunt." The museum is operated by the Winter Garden Heritage Foundation. That organization also operates the nearby Heritage Museum, which is housed in an Atlantic Coast Line depot and exhibits some railroad memorabilia and a Chessie caboose.

SITE LOCATION: 101 S. Boyd Street, Winter Garden
PHONE: 407-656-0559
WEB SITE: www.wghf.org
E-MAIL: museum@wghf.org

Flagler Museum ❷

The home of Henry Flagler, who developed the Florida East Coast Railway, is now a museum of the Gilded Age. Docent-led tours are offered, or you can tour the 55-room Whitehall on your own. The Flagler Kenan Pavilion, designed in the style of a 19th century Beaux Arts railway palace, houses Henry Flagler's private railcar.

SITE LOCATION: 1 Whitehall Way, Palm Beach
PHONE: 561-655-2833
WEB SITE: www.flaglermuseum.us
E-MAIL: mail@flaglermuseum.us

Inland Lakes Railway ▊

Operating from Eustis and Mount Dora in central Florida, the Inland Lakes Railway offers a variety of rail excursions to Orlando, Tavares, and other destinations. Murder mystery, theme trains, and dinner trains are offered. Dining options range from four-course dinners to lunch and pizza. Aboard dinner trains, you can enjoy your meal in a restored dining car or in a dome car.

SITE LOCATION: 51 W. Magnolia Avenue, Eustis
PHONE: 352-589-4300
WEB SITE: www.inlandlakesrailway.com
E-MAIL: info@inlandlakesrailway.com

Southwest Florida Museum of History ❹

Housed in the former Atlantic Coast Line Railroad depot, the museum displays a 1929 Pullman railcar. You can tour the *Esperanza* and get a glimpse of travel aboard a private car. The museum features exhibits from prehistoric times to modern day that showcase southwest Florida. It is open Tuesday through Saturday.

SITE LOCATION: 2300 Peck Street, Fort Myers
PHONE: 239-321-7430
WEB SITE: www.swflmuseumofhistory.com
E-MAIL: museuminfo@cityftmyers.com

Florida Railroad Museum ⑤

SITE LOCATION: 12210 83rd Street E, Parrish
PHONE: 877-869-0800
WEB SITE: www.frrm.org
E-MAIL: form on Web site

Scott Hartley

The Florida Railroad Museum operates diesel-powered trains on a 13-mile round trip in southwest Florida. Leisurely rides on air-conditioned and open-air coaches through farmland, piney woods, and palmetto flats, give riders a glimpse of Florida before Disney and interstate highways.

CHOICES: Variety is the order for the day with the Florida Railroad Museum's equipment. Passenger equipment comes from a wide range of railroads, including the Lackawanna, Union Pacific, and Louisville & Nashville. Regardless of the time of year, you'll want to opt for the air-conditioned rolling stock instead of open air – after all, air-conditioning was invented by Florida physician John Gorrie in 1851 for good reason! Get there well before train time to get a cool seat. Cab rides are also available. Special events include a World War II reenactment, a train robbery, and Halloween and Christmas trains.

WHEN TO GO: The Florida Railroad Museum operates weekends only, year-round. Mid-December through Easter is Florida's high season. The Florida Railroad Museum is at its busiest then, but the high season also boasts Florida's mildest weather, making it the perfect time to combine a ride on the railroad with a canoe trip or a picnic at nearby Little Manatee River State Park.

GOOD TO KNOW: The museum is located in the small town of Parrish. Parrish is quiet, but it's hardly remote, situated between Tampa and the Sarasota-Bradenton area, not far from the Gulf of Mexico and its beaches.

WORTH DOING: The Florida Railroad Museum's locomotive rental program allows you to operate one of three diesel-electrics from the 1950s (Alco, EMD, or GE) for a fee. You'll need to make a reservation in advance.

DON'T MISS: Packing a lunch for the museum's picnic area makes for an enjoyable break. No. 12, a Porter 0-6-0T steam locomotive is on display at the museum's picnic grove in Parrish. The engine was built in 1916 for the Brooklyn Navy Yard and later served with the Brooklyn Eastern District Terminal.

GETTING THERE: You have plenty of choices. Tampa International Airport and Sarasota Bradenton International Airport are fairly close by. Amtrak serves Tampa by train and Sarasota and Bradenton by dedicated connecting motor coach. By car, take I-75 for speed or Highway 301 to see more of the real Florida.

Gold Coast Railroad Museum ⑥

SITE LOCATION: 12450 SW 152nd Street, Miami
PHONE: 888-608-7246 or 305-253-0063
WEB SITE: www.gcrm.org
E-MAIL: webmaster@gcrm.org

Gold Coast Railroad Museum

With its impressive collection of rolling stock and locomotives – featuring the *Ferdinand Magellan*, a Pullman office car used by Presidents Roosevelt, Truman, Eisenhower, and Reagan – and its historic location at the site of a World War II airship base, the Gold Coast Railroad Museum is a fascinating place to visit.

CHOICES: Interested in former Florida East Coast Railway or *California Zephyr* passenger equipment? You'll find it here, along with diesels and steam locomotives from various railroads. But the museum isn't just a display of restored or preserved equipment. On weekends, the Gold Coast offers a 20-minute standard gauge train ride, using a diesel-electric (sometimes an EMD E8 or E9) and the *Belle Glade*, a former Florida East Coast stainless coach. Also on weekends, it runs a two-foot gauge children's train.

WHEN TO GO: The Gold Coast Railroad Museum operates year-round, Tuesday through Sunday and on holidays. Mid-December through Easter is when the Sunshine State is most popular with tourists. Florida summers are typically hot, but the reward for travelers is shorter lines at attractions and better hotel rates.

GOOD TO KNOW: It's no secret that the greater Miami area is a tourist mecca, with its area beaches, shops, deep-sea fishing, and nightclubs. But it's also a railroad buff's paradise, with extensive commuter rail service offered by Tri-Rail, vibrant freight operations by both the Florida East Coast and CSX, and significant Amtrak service.

WORTH DOING: The Gold Coast offers cab rides on its weekend diesel-hauled passenger trains for an additional fee. Make sure, however, you call ahead for reservations. And consider combining your trip to the Gold Coast with a visit to the Miami Metrozoo, which is located next to the railroad museum.

DON'T MISS: Florida East Coast Railway 4-6-2 steam locomotive no. 153, like the *Ferdinand Magellan*, is a National Historic Landmark. Used on "the railroad that died at sea," the 153 pulled a rescue train that delivered evacuees safely to Miami just before a hurricane destroyed the Key West line in 1935.

GETTING THERE: Miami is served by all major airlines, Amtrak, and major highways. The museum is located between Miami and Homestead, off the Florida Turnpike.

DISCOUNT: $1 off regular admission, up to four; excludes special events.

Seminole Gulf Railway 7

SITE LOCATION: 2805 Colonial Boulevard, Fort Myers
PHONE: 800-736-4853 or 239-275-8487
WEB SITE: www.semgulf.com
E-MAIL: reservations@semgulf.com

Scott Hartley

Seminole Gulf is a regional railroad with about 118 miles of track that provides freight and tourist service to Gulf communities in the Fort Myers area.

CHOICES: The railroad offers both standard excursions as well as murder mystery trains. The 90-minute, narrated daytime excursions take you across the Caloosahatchee River over a railroad drawbridge. The views from this and other numerous bridges are especially scenic. A variety of themed murder mysteries take place on a dinner train that serves five-course meals along its entertaining journey.

WHEN TO GO: Trips take place year-round, but of course, Florida is always best enjoyed in winter! The Christmas rail-boat train combines a train trip with a boat ride through Punta Gorda Isles' lighted holiday festivities.

GOOD TO KNOW: The railroad operates on the tracks of the former Atlantic Coast Line and Seaboard Air Line, which joined in 1969 to become Seaboard Coast Line.

WORTH DOING: Walk along Fort Myers Beach or on a beach on a nearby barrier island, such as Sanibel or Captiva, and go shelling. For more adventure, Everglades National Park is 90 minutes away. You can visit the park's Gulf Coast Visitor Center at Everglades City, where you can take a boat tour or rent a canoe. You can enter the heart of the park from the east, which is about a three-hour drive.

DON'T MISS: Try one of the railroad's special events, including trips during Halloween, Thanksgiving, and Christmas.

GETTING THERE: The railway is located in suburban Fort Myers, which is on the western Florida coast 40 miles north of Naples. The depot is located 1.5 miles from Highway 41 and three miles from I-75.

Florida

TECO Line Streetcar System 8

SITE LOCATION: St. Pete Times Forum Drive, Tampa
PHONE: 813-254-4278
WEB SITE: www.tecolinestreetcar.org
E-MAIL: riveral@gohart.org

Jim Wrinn

Nostalgic-looking streetcars take passengers along a 2.4-mile route that connects downtown Tampa, Channelside, and the Ybor City entertainment district.

CHOICES: Board anywhere along the line's 10 stops. Get off, enjoy the neighborhood, and catch a later car. Five stops are located in Tampa's Channel District, four are in historic Ybor City, and one is downtown. The TECO fleet includes a restored original Birney streetcar, replicas of Birney safety streetcars, and an open-air streetcar. Fares are charged per person per trip, but one-day unlimited rides cards are also available. The streetcar system also offers guided group tours.

WHEN TO GO: Cars operate year-round. They run every 15 to 20 minutes from morning through the evening with extended hours on Saturdays.

GOOD TO KNOW: Tampa's streetcar line dates back to 1892 when it carried workers between downtown and the cigar factories on the city's west side. The line peaked in the 1920s with some 24 million riders and then closed in 1946.

WORTH DOING: In Ybor City, within walking distance of the streetcar line, you can visit a cigar maker and even see craftsmen roll fresh cigars by hand. The Florida Aquarium and the Ybor City Museum are accessible from the line.

DON'T MISS: Check out the carbarn where the streetcars are serviced between Sixth and Seventh Avenues in Ybor City. You can't go into it, but it's easily visible from the sidewalk and features quite a display of colorful equipment.

GETTING THERE: If starting in Ybor City, which is east of downtown Tampa, take I-4 and follow the signs to Ybor City. At the Dick Greco Plaza downtown, you can connect to trolleys, buses, and taxis.

GEORGIA

Agrirama Museum of Culture & Historic Village ❶

At Agrirama, Georgia's Museum of Agriculture, you can tour 35 buildings that represent the state's past, including a railroad depot and sawmill. A ride aboard a logging train takes you around the historic site. The living museum is open Tuesday through Saturday year-round. Special events are scheduled throughout the year.

SITE LOCATION: 1392 Whiddon Mill Road, Tifton
PHONE: 800-767-1875 or 229-386-3344
WEB SITE: www.agrirama.com
E-MAIL: form on Web site

Stone Mountain Scenic Railroad ❷

A 1950s locomotive with open-air cars takes you on a five-mile, 30-minute excursion around Stone Mountain. Narration provides a look at rail history, beginning in the mid-1800s when the rail line was first built, and provides interesting facts about the mountain. And tune up your singing voice, as sing-alongs take place during the ride. Special Halloween and Christmas trains also run. The park has plenty of other fun events and attractions including a mini golf course themed around the Great Locomotive Chase.

SITE LOCATION: Highway 78, Stone Mountain
PHONE: 800-401-2407 or 770-498-5690
WEB SITE: www.stonemountainpark.com

Thronateeska Heritage Center ❸

The Thronateeska Heritage Center contains several historic railroad structures including an original 1857 freight depot and Railway Express Agency building, and its history museum is located in the 1912 Union Depot. Its transportation annex displays a variety of railcars and Georgia Northern Railway steam locomotive no. 107. The complex also includes a planetarium and science center.

SITE LOCATION: 100 W. Roosevelt Avenue, Albany
PHONE: 229-432-6955
WEB SITE: www.heritagecenter.org
E-MAIL: info@heritagecenter.org

Blue Ridge Scenic Railway

SITE LOCATION: 241 Depot Street, Blue Ridge

PHONE: 800-934-1898 or 706-632-9833

WEB SITE: www.brscenic.com

E-MAIL: info@brscenic.com

Jim Wrinn

The Louisville & Nashville's original route from Knoxville to Atlanta covered some rugged territory, and today it makes for a scenic ride into the wilderness. Following the unspoiled Toccoa River, this 26-mile round trip takes riders between the 1905 depot at Blue Ridge and McCaysville near the Tennessee border.

CHOICES: Trains depart downtown Blue Ridge from the depot, which was constructed in 1906 and is listed on the National Register of Historical Places. You can ride in either a closed-window car or an open-air car. As the diesel-powered train climbs through the north Georgia mountains, commentary is piped into the cars, and a conductor may add his own perspective to the trip.

WHEN TO GO: Trains run March through December, and spring and fall are great seasons for travel in the Southeast. The region's lush vegetation has a tendency to create a tunnel effect. But during spring and autumn, you have the chance to see into the forest as well as take in the scenery. Pumpkin pickin' and Santa trains offer family fun.

GOOD TO KNOW: This railroad started out as a narrow gauge line in the late 1880s with the tracks being three feet wide. Later investors changed it to standard gauge. The railway is the only mainline railroad excursion service based in Georgia.

WORTH DOING: The railroad offers a combination rail-and-raft package that is good for the Toccoa River, which the railroad crisscrosses, or for the nearby Ocoee River. The Toccoa is a slow run, while the Ocoee is a wild whitewater ride. Both options include return transportation to Blue Ridge. There is also a rest-and-rail package that allows you to rent a vacation cabin in the mountains.

DON'T MISS: During your layover, take the opportunity to walk around McCaysville, have lunch, and visit some of the town's antique shops.

GETTING THERE: Blue Ridge is about 90 miles north of Atlanta and about 80 miles from Chattanooga, Tenn. From Atlanta, take I-75 north to I-575, which turns into Highway 515, and continue on Highway 515 to Blue Ridge. The depot is on the left side of Depot Street.

Roundhouse Railroad Museum ❺

SITE LOCATION: 601 W. Harris Street, Savannah
PHONE: 912-651-6823
WEB SITE: www.chsgeorgia.org/roundhouse/home.htm
E-MAIL: roundhouse@chsgeorgia.org

Roundhouse Railroad Museum

Part of the multi-site Coastal Heritage Society museum complex, Savannah's Roundhouse Railroad Museum is a must-see for those interested in early American railroading technology. Located on the edge of Savannah's renowned historic district, the museum encompasses 13 structures from the original Central of Georgia shops complex, several of which date back to the early 1850s.

CHOICES: The 1926 roundhouse contains a collection of Georgia steam locomotives, passenger cars, and freight cars, including the 1886 0-6-0T shop switcher no. 8 and a rare 1878 wooden business car. A self-guided tour provides information about the history and technology of the site and the impact of the railroad on the local economy. Special events include a spring antiques and garden show and a fall blues festival. The operating turntable in the roundhouse is a must-see.

WHEN TO GO: The museum is open year-round. Savannah's near-tropical climate offers a welcome relief from northern cold throughout the winter months.

GOOD TO KNOW: The underground smoke-management system made the Central of Georgia shops one of the cleanest coal-fired industrial complexes in the 19th century. Buildings throughout the complex are connected to the central smokestack by hidden ducts. Smoke from the main boiler and dozens of individual forges and furnaces was sucked through the ducts, routed to the stack, and discharged away from the workers 125 feet in the air.

WORTH DOING: The Savannah Historic District, a National Historic Landmark, is one of America's premier urban historic neighborhoods. You'll find fine examples of buildings in the Georgian, Greek Revival, and Gothic styles.

DON'T MISS: Expand your tour with a visit to the other sites in the complex. The Savannah History Museum is housed in the 1850s Central of Georgia passenger station and train shed one block north of the roundhouse. Old Fort Jackson, a brick fort built before the War of 1812, presents a cannon-firing demonstration daily during summer. Battlefield Memorial Park commemorates a Revolutionary War battle.

GETTING THERE: Amtrak's *Palmetto*, *Silver Meteor*, and *Silver Star* all call at Savannah's suburban station. A number of major airlines or their regional affiliates serve Savannah International Airport.

SAM Shortline

SITE LOCATION: 105 E. Ninth Avenue, Cordele
PHONE: 877-427-2457 or 229-276-0755
WEB SITE: www.samshortline.com

SAM Shortline

The SAM Shortline offers a relaxing trip through the small towns of southwest Georgia. The train leaves from Cordele, and the main objective is to reach Archery. Along the way, you travel through Georgia Veterans State Park and the towns of Leslie, Americus and Plains, the home of President Jimmy Carter.

CHOICES: There are six different excursion trains, each one laying over in different towns on the route. If you would like to explore a location longer, you may be able to catch the train on its return trip. Both coach and lounge cars are available, and you can board at any of the depots along the route.

WHEN TO GO: Trains run Fridays and Saturdays as well as on select Mondays and Thursdays March through December. Special excursions operate throughout the season.

GOOD TO KNOW: Why SAM? The original railroad was the Savannah, Americus and Montgomery Railroad built during the 1880s and headed by Col. Samuel Hugh Hawkins of Americus.

WORTH DOING: Many of the excursions, such as the Peanut Express, stop in Plains and Archery, where you can visit Jimmy Carter's childhood home. In Plains, the Seaboard Coast Line depot was his campaign headquarters during the 1976 election. While you're there, make sure to buy a bag of peanuts.

DON'T MISS: In Americus, you can visit Habitat for Humanity's Global Village, and if you want to make a longer trip, the Andersonville National Historic Site and National POW Museum is 11 miles northeast.

GETTING THERE: Cordele is about 140 miles south of Atlanta. From I-75, take Exit 101 and go west on Highway 280. At Highway 41, turn north to Cordele.

Southeastern Railway Museum ❼

SITE LOCATION: 3595 Buford Highway, Duluth
PHONE: 770-476-2013
WEB SITE: www.srmduluth.org
E-MAIL: admin@southeasternrailwaymuseum.org

Jim Wrinn

The museum showcases railroading in Georgia and the Southeast with displays and more than 90 pieces of rolling stock. Among the highlights are a business car used to help convince leaders to bring the 1996 Olympics to Atlanta, a private car once used by President Warren G. Harding, and one of the famous green and gold Southern Crescent passenger diesels. It also offers short train rides.

CHOICES: The 34-acre museum features a variety of buildings and displays. Building One, the main exhibit hall, contains Southern Railway E8 passenger diesel-electric no. 6901 and the 1911 Pullman private car *Superb*, which was used by President Harding and is on the National Register of Historic Places. The museum's collection includes passenger coaches, private cars, trolleys, baggage cars, freight cars, cabooses, and maintenance-of-way equipment. The diesel-powered train rides take you around the museum's site aboard vintage cabooses.

WHEN TO GO: The museum is open Thursdays, Fridays, and Saturdays April through early December. It is also open Saturdays during January, February, and March. Train rides are offered in season, and a special railroad festival takes place each September.

GOOD TO KNOW: In 2008, the former Southern Railway Duluth depot was moved to the museum and will be restored. When completed, it will house exhibits.

WORTH DOING: From professional sports to botanical gardens and the zoo, take a few days and see all that the Atlanta area has to offer.

DON'T MISS: View famous excursion engines Savannah & Atlanta Pacific type no. 750 and Atlanta & West Point Pacific type no. 290, the latter well known for appearing in the movie *Fried Green Tomatoes*.

GETTING THERE: The museum is located in Duluth, a northeast suburb of Atlanta. It is just south of downtown Duluth. From Atlanta, take I-85 to Exit 104 and take Pleasant Hill Road to Buford Highway. Turn right on Buford Highway and then left onto Peachtree Road to the museum.

Southern Museum of Civil War and Locomotive History ⑧

SITE LOCATION: 2829 Cherokee Street, Kennesaw
PHONE: 770-427-2117
WEB SITE: www.southernmuseum.org

Southern Museum of Civil War and Locomotive History

A museum of high-caliber exhibits and static displays, the Southern Museum of Civil War and Locomotive History traces its roots back to 1972, when the City of Kennesaw acquired the famed steam locomotive *General*. The *General*, a Western & Atlantic Railroad 4-4-0 built in 1855, was the star in one of the Civil War's greatest acts of intrigue – the Great Locomotive Chase. The museum (part of which is located in a former cotton gin) has widened its collections and focus, making it a must-see attraction for visitors to the Atlanta area.

CHOICES: While the story of the Andrews Raid and the *General* is still the biggest offering at the museum, more comprehensive Civil War history and the story of Georgia locomotive manufacturer Glover Machine Works are also now chronicled here. The Glover Machine Works manufactured steam locomotives, locomotive parts, and other industrial products from 1902 until the 1930s. Patterns from the casting shop are artfully displayed, and extensive exhibits cover the story of the locomotive manufacturer. The facility is also the home of the Southern Railway Historical Association's archival collection.

WHEN TO GO: The museum is open daily year-round, except for major holidays, and the weather is generally mild. The Atlanta area has lots of modern railroad action, and other museums, like the Atlanta History Center, help tell the story of the Civil War and railroading in Atlanta.

GOOD TO KNOW: The story of the Andrews Raid was thrilling and unique enough to attract the attention of the Walt Disney Company, which released the film *The Great Locomotive Chase* in 1956.

WORTH DOING: Take a walking tour of historic Kennesaw (once known as Big Shanty) after exiting the front door of the museum and view a 1908 Western & Atlantic Railroad depot, numerous 19th century residences, and an 1887 grocery store.

DON'T MISS: The Atlanta Cyclorama, located in Grant Park, houses the *Texas*, the Western & Atlantic Railroad locomotive used by Confederates to hunt down Andrews Raiders.

GETTING THERE: Kennesaw is located off I-75 and Highway 41, about a 45-minute drive from Hartsfield-Jackson Atlanta International Airport, the world's busiest. Amtrak's *Crescent* also serves the city twice daily.

HAWAII

Hawaiian Railway 1

SITE LOCATION: 91-1001 Renton Road, Ewa
PHONE: 808-681-5461
WEB SITE: www.hawaiianrailway.com
E-MAIL: rides@hawaiianrailway.com

Hawaiian Railway

The Hawaiian Railway is the only active railroad on the island of Oahu. It offers regularly scheduled 90-minute, fully narrated rides over 6.5 miles of track. Along the way, you'll pass a variety of interesting and historical sites, including Fort Barrette. The train stops at Kahe Point, so you can take in the extraordinary ocean views.

CHOICES: Regular excursions take place twice each Sunday afternoon, except for the second Sunday of each month. On these Sundays, the famous Dillingham parlor car *Ambassador* is added to the regular train of open cars, and reservations (and an additional fare) are necessary for riding in this car. Three side-rod diesel locomotives have been restored to operation, and several steam locomotives have been cosmetically restored. The railway also has a vast collection of locomotives, cars, and other equipment.

WHEN TO GO: The railway's train yard is open year-round except for certain major holidays.

GOOD TO KNOW: The *Ambassador* is the luxurious parlor car that Benjamin Dillingham, founder of the Oahu Railway & Land Company, had built for his personal use in 1900. Restored by the Hawaiian Railway Society, the *Ambassador* is worth the ride, and the fare for riding the car goes toward its upkeep.

WORTH DOING: No trip to Oahu would be complete without a heart-rending visit to Pearl Harbor. You can also wander over Oahu and other islands and literally discover pieces of Hawaii's railroading past, which included sugar plantation, military, and common carrier railways.

DON'T MISS: The railway, which is situated on what was part of the Oahu Railway & Land Company main line, is north of Pearl Harbor. The scenery is incredible. Wear comfortable shoes and wander through the train yard and then relax with lunch in the picnic area.

GETTING THERE: The Railway is minutes from Honolulu by bus or car. If you drive, take H1 west and exit on 5A Ewa. Then take Highway 76 south for 2.5 miles, turn right at Renton Road, and continue for 1.5 miles to the entrance.

Kauai Plantation Railway 2

SITE LOCATION: 3-2087 Kaumualii Highway, Lihue
PHONE: 808-245-7245
WEB SITE: www.kauaiplantationrailway.com
E-MAIL: train@hawaiilink.net

David Lustig

The Kauai Plantation Railway operates daily on a genuine Hawaiian plantation. Experience plantation life and learn about Kauai agriculture as the train travels through more than 100 acres of unspoiled Hawaii on a three-foot-gauge train. Passengers enjoy a 40-minute journey through fields of sugar, pineapple, banana, papaya, coffee, tropical flowers, and hardwood trees.

CHOICES: Train rides leave from a Hawaiian train depot, and you can ride in a reproduction of a railway car from the time of King Kalakaua or an open-sided excursion car. In addition, there is a ride-hike-lunch-orchard tour. Currently, motive power is a pair of small diesels, including a restored 1939 Whitcomb diesel engine. Two Baldwin steam locomotives are being rebuilt to power excursions. These engines were built for plantation service on the Island of Oahu and are some of the few Hawaiian engines that remain.

WHEN TO GO: The train operates daily, and any day is a good day in Hawaii, and there are up to five runs a day. Hawaii is in the tropics, and that suggests suntan lotion, a hat, and comfortable clothing.

GOOD TO KNOW: The three-foot-gauge railway was the first railroad built on Kauai in almost 100 years. More than 2.5 miles of roadbed was constructed with rails hand-spiked onto 6,000 wooden ties. More than 50 varieties of fruits and vegetables can be found on the plantation, from avocado and bananas to rambutan and sugar cane. The plantation also features a restaurant and shops.

WORTH DOING: A public luau is scheduled on Tuesday and Friday evenings, and a special train can take you there.

DON'T MISS: On the tour package, after riding the train, you can hike in the rainforest and sample fresh fruit picked right off the tree. You also have the opportunity to feed goats, sheep, and pigs.

GETTING THERE: The Kauai Plantation is just off Route 50 (Kaumualii Highway) approximately one mile south of Lihue, which is the main city on Kauai. The railway is located at Kilohana Plantation next to Kauai Community College. Just look for the white picket fence.

Lahaina Kaanapali Railroad ▣

SITE LOCATION: 975 Limahana Place, Lahaina
PHONE: 800-499-2307 or 808-667-6851
WEB SITE: www.sugarcanetrain.com
E-MAIL: form on Web site

Matt Austin

The Sugar Cane Train travels between the historical whaling town of Lahaina to the lush Kaanapali Resort on the Hawaiian island of Maui. Narrow gauge steam engines transport visitors in open-air cars through the Kaanapali golf courses, along the ocean, and across a scenic railroad trestle.

CHOICES: You can board the Sugar Cane Train from either the Lahaina station or the Puukolii station. On the round trip, the conductor entertains you with narration about the history of the train and the sugar cane industry as well as fun Hawaiian facts. Don't miss the beautiful views of the Pacific Ocean and of the neighboring islands, Molokai and Lanai, from the 325-foot curved wooden trestle.

WHEN TO GO: Steam trains operate daily, all year round. While the most popular time is summer, if you visit between December and April, you just might see a breaching humpback whale from the train. During this time, many whales are active off the west Maui coast.

GOOD TO KNOW: While few Hawaiian railroads remain today, for more than 100 years, they hauled sugar cane to the mills and transported workers. You can learn more about the industry at the Alexander & Baldwin Sugar Museum.

WORTH DOING: There are a variety of luaus offered on the island, and you should experience at least one of these unique Hawaiian activities. West Maui is a premier Hawaii tourist destination, featuring five-star hotels and exquisite dining and shopping experiences. You'll be able to take a glass-bottom boat cruise, snorkel, try assorted water sports, and even dive into a tank of sharks at the Maui Ocean Center.

DON'T MISS: By sitting in the same seat, you will be able to experience both an ocean view and a mountain view. The views alternate depending on the direction of the train.

GETTING THERE: Many large airlines offer direct flights to Maui from mainland, West Coast cities. Once on Maui, both of the railroad's stations are located off Honoapiilani Highway (Highway 30), the coast's main, and only, highway.

IDAHO

Canyon County Historical Museum ❶

Built in 1903, the building served as the Oregon Short Line depot until 1925, when it was used as offices for the Union Pacific. The building now houses artifacts relating to the Union Pacific and local history. Outside, you can tour a UP caboose. The museum is open year-round Tuesday through Saturday.

SITE LOCATION: 1200 Front Street, Nampa
PHONE: 208-467-7611
WEB SITE: www.canyoncountyhistory.com
E-MAIL: info@canyoncountyhistory.com

Northern Pacific Depot Railroad Museum ❷

Listed on the National Register of Historic Places, this building served as a station until the 1980s. The elegant chateau-style depot was built at the turn of the 20th century from brick transported from China and concrete panels made from mine tailings. It now serves as a railroad museum that features exhibits on railroading in the area's mining district. Depot Day takes place in May.

SITE LOCATION: 219 Sixth Street, Wallace
PHONE: 208-752-0111
WEB SITE: wallace-id.com/business.html#tourist

Thunder Mountain Line Railroad 3

SITE LOCATION: 120 Mill Road, Horseshoe Bend
PHONE: 877-432-7245 or 208-331-1184
WEB SITE: www.thundermountainline.com
E-MAIL: form on Web site

Jim Wrinn

This is one of the most scenic trips in the northern part of the Rocky Mountains. The train parallels the Payette River for most of the journey through sagebrush-covered hills, fir trees, and mountain meadows. Often visible are fox, deer, elk, blue heron, osprey, and bald eagles. Much of the river is excellent for whitewater rafting, so you not only get entertainment from the scenery but from the rafters as well.

CHOICES: Three different trips are possible. The *Horseshoe Bend Express* makes a two-hour round trip between Horseshoe Bend and Banks and travels along an old wagon road. The *Cabarton Flyer* leaves from the mountain town of Cascade and follows the Payette River. The *Cascade Limited* is a five-hour, one-way trip from Horseshoe Bend to Cascade that passes through Boise National Forest and includes lunch and a return bus trip. The railroad also operates theme trains that allow you to experience a reenacted train robbery, murder mystery, or elegant dinner. Some special trains run from Horseshoe Bend to the town of Montour.

WHEN TO GO: The countryside is rugged and beautiful to travel through any time of the year. The *Horseshoe Bend Express* and *Cascade Limited* operate mid-March through November, and the *Cabarton Flyer* runs mid-May through September. Themed train rides and special events take place throughout the year.

GOOD TO KNOW: The *Cabarton Flyer* boards at the Ashley Inn in Cascade.

WORTH DOING: Experience the scenic Payette River and Boise National Forest up close. You can raft or kayak through Class IV rapids or just float along the river. The forest offers over 1,300 miles of hiking trails and more than 70 camping and picnic spots.

DON'T MISS: Ride the *Cabarton Flyer* through what is believed to be the world's shortest railroad tunnel at 38 feet in length.

GETTING THERE: The Horseshoe Bend depot is located about 25 minutes north of Boise. Take Highway 55 from Boise to Horseshoe Bend and once there turn right on Mill Road. Cascade is about another 40 miles north of Horseshoe Bend on Highway 55, and the Ashley Inn is on Main Street (Highway 55).

ILLINOIS

Amboy Depot Museum ❶

Built in 1876, this former Illinois Central division headquarters building has been restored, inside and out. It is now a local museum that presents the history of Amboy and its relationship to the Illinois Central Railroad. The museum also contains a freight house with additional artifacts, a retired steam engine, and a caboose. It is open year-round.

SITE LOCATION: 50 S. East Avenue, Amboy
PHONE: 815-857-4700
WEB SITE: www.amboydepotmuseum.org
E-MAIL: information@amboydepotmuseum.org

Fox River Trolley Museum ❷

Passengers ride the historic remnant of an 1896 interurban railroad on a four-mile trip along the banks of the Fox River and the Blackhawk Forest Preserve. The museum operates a variety of antique Chicago-area trolleys. The museum is open May through early November, and a number of special events are also scheduled including the museum's Trolleyfest.

SITE LOCATION: 361 S. LaFox Street, South Elgin
PHONE: 847-697-4676
WEB SITE: www.foxtrolley.org
E-MAIL: info@foxtrolley.org

Galesburg Railroad Museum ❸

The Galesburg Railroad Museum's display of artifacts and memorabilia includes a 1930 Burlington Route Hudson steam locomotive, a Railway Post Office/Railway Express Agency Car, a 1930 caboose, a Pullman parlor car, and two inspection cars. The museum is open April through November.

SITE LOCATION: 211 S. Seminary Street, Galesburg
PHONE: 309-342-9400
WEB SITE: www.visitgalesburg.com/attractions.html

Great Western Railroad Museum ❹

This depot museum displays artifacts of the Chicago Great Western Railway. The depot serviced the nearby Winston Tunnel, the longest railroad tunnel in Illinois. The museum features a Milwaukee Road caboose, a working telegraph, and operating model railroads. It is open weekends May through October.

SITE LOCATION: 111 E. Myrtle Street, Elizabeth
PHONE: 815-858-2343
WEB SITE: www.elizabethhistoricalsociety.org
E-MAIL: ehs@internetni.com

Greenup Depot ❺

The historic Greenup depot is a museum that displays artifacts of railroad and telegraph history. The preserved 1870 Vandalia Line depot also maintains a collection of audio, visual, and written materials related to these subjects. It is open year-round.

SITE LOCATION: 216 Cumberland Street, Greenup
PHONE: 217-923-9306
WEB SITE: www.greenupdepot.org
E-MAIL: historic@rr1.net

Historic Pullman Foundation ❻

The Historic Pullman Foundation operates the Pullman Visitor Center, which features artifacts, photos and a video that informs visitors about George Pullman, the Pullman Company, and Pullman's 1880s model industrial town. You can take a self-guided tour of the historic area or a guided walking tour, which are offered the first Sunday of the month from May through October.

SITE LOCATION: 11141 S. Cottage Grove Avenue, Chicago
PHONE: 773-785-8901
WEB SITE: www.pullmanil.org
E-MAIL: foundation@pullmanil.org

Kankakee Railroad Museum ❼

Kankakee's restored train depot displays railroad memorabilia and a model train layout of Kankakee in the 1950s. A 1947 Pullman coach is displayed outside the depot. The museum is open Tuesday through Sunday.

SITE LOCATION: 197 S. East Avenue, Kankakee
PHONE: 815-929-9320
WEB SITE: www.kankakeerrmuseum.com

Museum of Science and Industry ❽

Board the *Silver Streak* and step into history. The showpiece of the museum's rail collection, the *Pioneer Zephyr* completed a record-setting run in 1934 by traveling from Denver to Chicago in just over 13 hours at an average speed of 77.5 mph. The museum's 3,500-square-foot layout shows a train's journey from Chicago to Seattle. Touring the German submarine *U-505* and the coal mine are a must.

SITE LOCATION: 57th Street and Lake Shore Drive, Chicago
PHONE: 800-468-6674 or 773-684-1414
WEB SITE: www.msichicago.org
E-MAIL: contact@msichicago.org

Trolley Car 36 ❾

Departing from downtown's Riverview Park, a 45-minute trolley ride transports you along Rockford's historic riverfront, with a 10-minute stopover at Sinnissippi Gardens and Lagoon. Excursions take place during the summer. After being severely damaged in a carbarn fire, Trolley Car 36 should be back in service for the 2009 season.

SITE LOCATION: 324 N. Madison Street, Rockford
PHONE: 815-987-8894
WEB SITE: www.rockfordparkdistrict.org

Union Depot Railroad Museum ❿

The railroad museum is housed in the remaining portion of the 1888 depot. Fully restored, it contains materials related to the Chicago, Burlington & Quincy, Illinois Central, and Milwaukee Road. You can tour a 1923 Mikado type 2-8-2 steam locomotive and a Milwaukee Road combine car. Grab a bite at the nearby Whistle Stop restaurant in the renovated Illinois Central freight house.

SITE LOCATION: 683 Main Street, Mendota
PHONE: 815-538-3800
WEB SITE: www.mendotamuseums.org
E-MAIL: mmhs@mtco.com

Illinois Railway Museum ⑪

SITE LOCATION: 7000 Olson Road, Union
PHONE: 800-244-7245 or 815-923-4000
WEB SITE: www.irm.org

Kathi Kube

Just 90 minutes northwest from downtown Chicago, and about half an hour from Union Pacific's Geneva Subdivision, lies the Illinois Railway Museum, which prides itself on running more diesel trains than other comparable museums. The museum also pays homage to its beginnings as an electric railway museum by operating streetcars and interurban cars daily.

CHOICES: As an operating museum, there are many choices of trains to ride, including streetcars, interurbans, and other commuter cars pulled by vintage diesels. You can even ride a trolley or electric bus from one equipment barn to another. When you're not riding trains, explore the 80 acres of land and 400 pieces of equipment, including almost 90 freight cars, plus signals, tools, signage, and other artifacts. Six barns contain rail equipment, and another has bus equipment. Admission includes unlimited rides.

WHEN TO GO: The museum is open weekends in April and October and daily from May through September. During July and August, remember that not all the cars and none of the barns are air-conditioned. The museum operates a variety of special events including Terror on the Railroad, Christmas on the Railroad, and a Take-the-Throttle experience.

GOOD TO KNOW: After a three-year absence for restoration work, the Chicago, Burlington & Quincy *Nebraska Zephyr* has returned to IRM's grounds and should be back in service.

WORTH DOING: Union is centrally located between Rockford and suburban Chicago. It also offers tourists Donley's Wild West Town with gunslinger shows, pony rides, and gold panning. Nearby Marengo has several restaurants, and about a dozen hotels are within a half-hour drive from the museum.

DON'T MISS: Diesel Days in July and Museum Showcase Weekend in September are great times to see a lot of equipment running. Typically, 14 vintage locomotives are put to work pulling freight and commuter trains on Diesel Days. On Museum Showcase Weekend, the staff operates less-frequently run equipment.

GETTING THERE: If driving from Chicago, take I-90 to Highway 20, the Marengo exit. Drive northwest about 4.5 miles to Union Road and then take Union Road north.

DISCOUNT: $1 off each adult, 50 cents off each child; cannot combine with any other offer.

Monticello Railway Museum ⑫

SITE LOCATION: 992 Iron Horse Place, Monticello
PHONE: 877-762-9011 or 217-762-9011
WEB SITE: www.mrym.org
E-MAIL: info@mrym.org

Jim Wrinn

In the midsection of Illinois, this museum offers one of the best collections of rolling stock and a good train ride to boot. All decked out in their original attires, two streamlined diesel locomotives of the 1950s, one from Canadian National and the other from the Wabash Railroad, are among the most popular locomotives.

CHOICES: Although the museum has several steam engines, it has one of the Midwest's premier diesel locomotive collections. The collection features a Milwaukee Road SWX and a former Illinois Central RS3 and displays more than 80 pieces of rolling stock. You can board the eight-mile round trip over former Illinois Central and Illinois Terminal trackage from two historic depots, one at the museum and the other in downtown Monticello. At either location, you can make a layover for additional exploration and then catch a later return trip.

WHEN TO GO: The museum is open on weekends and holidays May through October. Special events are scheduled throughout the year for both train buffs and families alike.

GOOD TO KNOW: The Illinois Central depot at the museum was originally built in 1919 at Deland, and the Wabash depot located in Monticello dates to 1899.

WORTH DOING: Just a short drive away, on Allerton Road, is one of the Seven Wonders of Illinois. The Allerton Park and Retreat Center was once a private mansion. And you can now walk through 14 miles of wooded trails and gardens that contain 100 sculptures.

DON'T MISS: For a fee, you can operate a locomotive for 30 minutes under the supervision of a regular member of the train crew during spring and fall throttle times.

GETTING THERE: The museum is located between Champaign and Decatur, just off I-72. At Exit 166, take Market Street to Iron Horse Place and follow the frontage road to the end. The town of Monticello is just a few miles away via Highway 105.

DISCOUNT: $1 off each adult ticket, up to four adults.

Rochelle Railroad Park ⑬

SITE LOCATION: 124 N. Ninth Street, Rochelle
PHONE: 815-562-7031
WEB SITE: www.rochellerailroadpark.org
E-MAIL: tourism@rochelle.net

Erik Bergstrom

With more than 80 trains passing through daily, the Rochelle Railroad Park is one of the most popular railroad-watching destinations in North America thanks to a perfect blend of heavy railroad action and a safe, well-appointed place to watch the passing trains.

CHOICES: BNSF Railway and Union Pacific double-track main lines cross right in the middle of Rochelle. Recognizing the popularity of the location to railfans, the city of Rochelle built a railroad park adjacent to the tracks that features picnic tables and a scanner tuned to railroad radio frequencies. The park is an excellent place to watch trains around the clock. However, if you're interested in shooting photos or videos, the sun can be troublesome at times. At those times, you can venture out to other railroad hot spots in the area like the BNSF Mendota Subdivision in Mendota or the heavily trafficked BNSF Trancon at Toluca. Regardless of where your day takes you, the park is a great place relax and watch trains.

WHEN TO GO: Since the park is always open, you can visit at any time of the day or any time of the year. Braving the cold winter months provides special viewing opportunities.

GOOD TO KNOW: There are a handful of hotels to choose from in the Rochelle area. Also, if you'd like a preview of the action in Rochelle, visit *Trains* magazine's Web site and watch from a live Web cam perched above the park's pavilion. Go to www.trainsmag. com and click on the Web cams link. (The site requires registration, which is free.)

WORTH DOING: The Illinois Railroad Museum in Union has one of the greatest collections of railroad equipment in the United States, and at only an hour's drive away, it's well worth the trip.

DON'T MISS: For photographers looking for a unique old-meets-new vantage point, a drive west to Nelson is a must. There, a steam-era coal tower still straddles the very active Union Pacific double-track main line.

GETTING THERE: Rochelle is conveniently located at the junction of I-88 and I-39 in north central Illinois, a little more than an hour from Chicago's O'Hare International Airport. Once off the Interstate, Highway 38 or Highway 251 will take you to the railroad park.

Silver Creek & Stephenson Railroad

SITE LOCATION: 2954 S. Walnut Road, Freeport
PHONE: 815-235-2198
WEB SITE: www.thefreeportshow.com
E-MAIL: thefreeportshow@thefreeportshow.com

Jim Wrinn

This railroad offers a four-mile ride behind a 1912 geared Heisler steam engine. Trains leave from a reproduction of the original Illinois Central depot in Elroy, and the building houses a large collection of railroad memorabilia. Special theme trains run during the year and during special events at the Silvercreek Museum.

CHOICES: A Heisler steam locomotive pulls several cabooses and an open-air car through farmlands and across Yellow Creek on a 30-foot-high cement and stone pier bridge. The Silvercreek depot houses the ticket office and railroad displays.

WHEN TO GO: The train ride operates on various weekends and holidays between Memorial Day and the end of October.

GOOD TO KNOW: Volunteers created this railroad on the abandoned right-of-way of the Chicago, Milwaukee, St. Paul & Pacific Railroad. Because rails and ties were removed prior to purchase, members had to haul rail in from as far away as Minnesota, and ties were salvaged from across Illinois. Members of the Stephenson County Antique Engine Club laid their first tracks in May 1985.

WORTH DOING: Ride the train on one trip and photograph the engine at work on a following outing.

DON'T MISS: Give the 36-ton Heisler a close inspection. Unlike most steam locomotives, it is driven with a V-2 arrangement of the cylinders on either side of the boiler; they run a crankshaft that moves a gearbox and wheels. Fewer than 1,200 of these locomotives were built, and only a handful remain in operation today.

GETTING THERE: Freeport is about 20 miles west of Rockford on Highway 20, and the museum is on the corner of Walnut and Lamm Roads.

INDIANA

Carthage, Knightstown and Shirley Railroad ❶

After departing from the old New York Central station, the CKS takes you on a 10-mile, 75-minute round trip from Knightstown to Carthage. When you pull back into the station, you can look over the railroad's assortment of antique railroad equipment. The CKS offers special events, including train robberies, during its season. It operates Fridays, Saturdays, and Sundays May through October.

SITE LOCATION: 112 W. Carey Street, Knightstown
PHONE: 765-345-5561
WEB SITE: www.cksrail.com
E-MAIL: cksrrinc@netzero.net

Hoosier Valley Railroad Museum ❷

The museum's collection consists of 30 pieces of rolling stock, former Chesapeake & Ohio 2-8-4 steam locomotive no. 2789, and a variety of signals. The museum is open Saturdays, and it offers train rides featuring cabooses and an open air car. A guest engineer program is also available.

SITE LOCATION: 507 Mulberry Street, North Judson
PHONE: 574-896-3950
WEB SITE: hvrm.railfan.net
E-MAIL: hvrm@yahoo.com

Linden Railroad Museum ❸

The Linden Railroad Museum contains memorabilia from the two railroads it served, the Nickel Plate Road and the Monon Railroad. It displays a caboose from each railroad and several other pieces of equipment. Built in 1907, it is listed on the National Register of Historic Places. It is open May through September.

SITE LOCATION: 520 N. Main Street, Linden
PHONE: 765-339-7245
WEB SITE: www.lindendepot.com
E-MAIL: information@lindendepot.com

Madison Railroad Station ❹

This restored 1895 Pennsylvania Railroad station is known for its unique octagon waiting room with stained glass windows. Exhibits describe the Madison Railroad Station and the Madison Railroad Incline. You can visit an agent's office, try the functional telegraph key, and walk through a restored, wooden caboose.

SITE LOCATION: 615 W. First Street, Madison
PHONE: 812-265-2335
WEB SITE: www.jchshc.org
E-MAIL: form on Web site

Monon Connection Museum ❺

The museum features a completely furnished, full-size replica of an Illinois Central depot and outdoor displays. Exhibits include a large collection of dining car china, hundreds of hand-held lanterns, and restored brass steam locomotive bells and whistles. It is open Tuesday through Sunday.

SITE LOCATION: 10012 N. Highway 421, Monon
PHONE: 219-253-4101
WEB SITE: www.mononconnection.com
E-MAIL: mononconnection@urhere.net

National New York Central Railroad Museum ❻

At this museum, you begin your journey through the history of the New York Central by entering through a 1915 passenger coach. In the main gallery, which is a 100-year-old freight house, hands-on exhibits let you construct track and operate a steam locomotive. Outside, the museum features a collection of locomotives and rolling stock including an NYC Mohawk 4-8-2.

SITE LOCATION: 721 S. Main Street, Elkhart
PHONE: 574-294-3001
WEB SITE: www.nycrrmuseum.org
E-MAIL: info@nycrrmuseum.org
DISCOUNT: Buy one adult admission and get one admission of equal or lesser value free.

Princeton Railway Museum ❼

The Princeton Railway Museum contains artifacts of the railroads that served the area. It is located in the recently restored Chicago & Eastern Illinois passenger depot, which was built in 1875. The museum shares the depot with the Gibson County visitors bureau and is open Monday through Friday.

SITE LOCATION: 702 W. Broadway Street, Princeton
PHONE: 888-390-5825
WEB SITE: www.gibsoncountyin.org/attractions.htm

Wabash Valley Railroaders Museum ❽

The museum features two interlocking towers with operating machines, a depot, and a viewing platform adjacent to CSXT main lines. Haley Tower was one of the last manned interlocking towers in the Midwest, and the 1910 Spring Hill Tower was the last lever interlocking machine on the Canadian Pacific. It is open weekends May through October.

SITE LOCATION: 1316 Plum Street, Terre Haute
PHONE: 812 238-9058
WEB SITE: www.haleytower.org
E-MAIL: hytwr1@joink.com

Indiana

Hesston Steam Museum ❾

SITE LOCATION: County Road 1000 N, La Porte
PHONE: 219-778-2783 or 219-872-5055
WEB SITE: www.hesston.org

Jim Wrinn

This unique museum runs steam trains of two narrow gauges, two-foot and three-foot, in a parklike setting. It also offers miniature live steam operations and other steam-powered attractions including a sawmill and a steam crane.

CHOICES: Ride a steam locomotive, in your choice of gauges, through the museum's 155-acre site. Each train travels over a different route. Wander through a unique collection of steam equipment. Be sure to look for an 1889 Scottish-built locomotive and a Czech 0-4-0 built in 1940. The annual Hesston Steam & Power Show takes place over Labor Day weekend. Beside trains, the event features the operation of antique farm equipment, cars, and other machinery.

WHEN TO GO: Trains run weekends and holidays Memorial Day through Labor Day and Sundays-only from Labor Day through October. On Memorial Day weekend, additional steam equipment runs, and the sawmill operates over the July 4th weekend. In fall, you can enjoy apple cider made from an antique press.

GOOD TO KNOW: The railroad's geared Shay locomotive, New Mexico Lumber Company no. 7, was the last narrow gauge model built back in 1929. After years of restoration due to fire damage, the Shay is back in operation.

WORTH DOING: If you like college football, less than an hour away is South Bend, where you can attend a Notre Dame game, if tickets are available, and tour the College Football Hall of Fame.

DON'T MISS: Watch the 92-ton, steam-powered log crane feed logs to the steam-powered lumber mill. Take a walk down by the pond near the depot for a scenic photo of a steam train.

GETTING THERE: The museum is in northern Indiana near the Michigan border and is about a 90-minute drive from Chicago. It is easily accessible from either I-94 (Exit 1) or the Indiana toll road (Exit 49) on County Road 1000.

Indiana Railway Museum ⑩

SITE LOCATION: 1 Monon Street, French Lick
PHONE: 800-748-7246 or 812-936-2405
WEB SITE: www.indianarailwaymuseum.org
E-MAIL: museumstore@indianarailwaymuseum.org

Jim Wrinn

For many years, the Southern Railway and the Monon Railroad brought scores of vacationers to the mineral spring baths in the southern Indiana hill country. Today, the museum offers a 20-mile round trip that leaves from the historic 1907 depot that served both railroads and travels through beautiful forested country and the 2,200-foot Burton tunnel.

CHOICES: Located in a historic passenger depot, the museum operates the French Lick, West Baden & Southern Railway. Two-hour excursions through the Hoosier National Forest travel along lakes and limestone cuts. Train robbery specials occur throughout the season, and Santa trains and haunted trains also run. The museum features an impressive collection of equipment with exhibits housed in the depot as well. The collection includes steam and diesel locomotives and more than 65 passenger and freight cars.

WHEN TO GO: The museum is open year-round Monday through Friday and on weekends April through November. Trains operate weekends April through November and on several holidays. Between June and October, Tuesday and Thursday runs are added. Trips in October feature beautiful fall colors of the scenic Hoosier National Forest.

GOOD TO KNOW: You can stay at (or tour) the restored, historic French Lick Springs Resort, listed on the National Register of Historic Places, or the West Baden Springs Hotel, which features a 200-foot domed atrium and is a National Historic Landmark.

WORTH DOING: Southern Indiana is home to a variety of caves ready for exploring, such as Squire Boone Caverns, Wyandotte Caves, and Marengo Cave.

DON'T MISS: Be sure to check out the former Louisville, New Albany & Corydon Railroad boxcar no. 14023 repainted as a Pluto water car that shipped Pluto mineral water that was bottled by the French Lick Springs Hotel.

GETTING THERE: French Lick is in southern Indiana, easily accessible from Bloomington (60 miles), Columbus (90 miles), and Indianapolis (110 miles). From Indianapolis or Bloomington, take Highway 37 to Highway 56. Take Highway 56 west to French Lick and the museum. From Columbus, take I-65 to Highway 56.

DISCOUNT: $1 off a regular adult ticket, up to four adults.

Indiana Transportation Museum ⑪

SITE LOCATION: Forest Park Drive, Noblesville
PHONE: 317-773-6000 or 317-776-7887
WEB SITE: www.itm.org
E-MAIL: itmfishers@hotmail.com

David Wilcox

Located in Forest Park in Noblesville, the Indiana Transportation Museum offers a wide variety of historic displays and a selection of rail excursions over different track segments. Passengers have an array of riding and dining options.

CHOICES: The Weekend Express, which operates on most Saturday and Sunday afternoons, departs from the museum and gives you the opportunity to travel either north to Atlanta or south to Fishers. Leaving from Fishers on select Friday evenings, the Hamiltonian Dinner Train stops in Noblesville and Cicero, and you can disembark at either location to enjoy a range of cuisine at local restaurants. For more casual dining, you can ride the Pizza Train, which departs the museum on select Saturday evenings and travels north to Tipton for pizza at a choice of restaurants. Also operating on Saturdays, Dinner in the Diner offers patrons a four-course meal aboard the *Cross Keys Tavern*, a restored Louisville & Nashville dining car.

WHEN TO GO: Indiana Transportation Museum's operating season begins in mid-April and continues through October, and operations conclude with the Polar Bear Express in December. The museum grounds are open Saturdays and Sundays through the season. In August, the museum runs trains from Fishers to the state fair.

GOOD TO KNOW: Museum admission fees cover the grounds and are included in train fares purchased at the museum.

WORTH DOING: Plan to spend the day at the Indiana Transportation Museum's complex and enjoy Forest Park. Bring a picnic lunch and enjoy the beautiful setting. For the kids, there is an aquatic center, a carousel, a playground, and miniature golf. For the adults, walking trails cover the park, and two golf courses are nearby.

DON'T MISS: By making advance arrangements, you can view some of the museum's restoration projects and see firsthand the inner workings of both steam and diesel locomotives. Work continues on Nickel Plate Road 587, a 1918 Baldwin 2-8-2, and also undergoing restoration is former Milwaukee Road F7 no. 72.

GETTING THERE: The museum is located in Forest Park, which is just north of State Road 32 on State Road 19 in Noblesville. Just 20 miles north of Indianapolis, the area is easily accessible from I-69 and Highway 31. Amtrak serves Indianapolis from both Chicago and Washington, D.C.

TrainTown ⑫

Indiana

SITE LOCATION: 15808 Edgerton Road, New Haven
PHONE: 260-493-0765
WEB SITE: www.765.org
E-MAIL: contact@765.org

Jim Wrinn

TrainTown, operated by the Fort Wayne Railroad Historical Society, is home to one of the nation's largest operating steam locomotives, Nickel Plate Road 2-8-4 no. 765, which runs occasionally.

CHOICES: On weekends, you can tour TrainTown and check out the 400-ton no. 765 and other historic rail equipment. Make sure to visit the shops and talk with the volunteers who restore everything from baggage carts to locomotives. Several times a year, the society conducts operating days with rides aboard a vintage caboose.

WHEN TO GO: TrainTown is open on Saturdays and Sundays. Excursions on the 765 are scheduled as the opportunities to run the locomotive become available, such as at Trainfestival 2009 (in July) at the Steam Railroading Institute in Owosso, Mich. Santa trains run in December.

GOOD TO KNOW: The 765, a 1944 Berkshire type, is one of the most modern and powerful steam locomotives still capable of operation. It has pulled excursion trains in 16 states and was rebuilt at a cost of more than $800,000.

WORTH DOING: The group offers an Engineer-for-an-Hour program with a 44-ton diesel. For a fee, you can operate the engine under supervision.

DON'T MISS: Get a conductor's eye-view from the recently restored Nickel Plate caboose 141.

GETTING THERE: TrainTown is just east of Fort Wayne in the village of New Haven. From Fort Wayne, take I-469 to Exit 21. Turn right on Harper Road, then right on Ryan Road, and left on Edgerton Road.

93

Whitewater Valley Railroad 13

SITE LOCATION: 455 Market Street, Connersville
PHONE: 765-825-2054
WEB SITE: www.whitewatervalleyrr.org
E-MAIL: form on Web site

Jim Wrinn

This surprising 19-mile line travels from Connersville to Metamora with much of the trip near the Whitewater Canal. The scenic route features excellent views of the forests and farms.

CHOICES: The railroad offers standard, open-window coaches as well as caboose rides on its 32-mile, five-hour round trip. A two-hour layover gives you a chance to tour Metamora, a restored canal town.

WHEN TO GO: Regular excursion trains operate on Saturdays and Sundays from May through October. During the year, watch for special event trains, such as the one to Metamora Canal Days, the Civil War Train, and fall foliage trains. Other events are themed around holidays and children's activities.

GOOD TO KNOW: The railroad has an ongoing restoration program and has recently completed a variety of projects including a Nickel Plate caboose.

WORTH DOING: Metamora is a popular getaway spot with plenty of art galleries, shops, and restaurants. Take time to explore the city's historic buildings. You can also watch its water-powered grist mill in action and take a boat ride along the canal.

DON'T MISS: Inspect the operating diesel built by the Lima Locomotive Works of Lima, Ohio. Believed to be the last of its kind in operation today, locomotive no. 25 was one of only 174 diesels built by this company, one of the most famous steam locomotive manufacturers of all time. The museum also owns three others from this builder.

GETTING THERE: Connersville is about 65 miles southeast of Indianapolis and is accessible from all directions. If coming from the north, take Highway 1 off I-70 into Connersville. The depot is on your left between Fourth and Fifth Streets.

IOWA

Marquette Depot Museum ❶

Housed in a renovated Milwaukee Road depot, the museum contains Milwaukee Road exhibits and general railroad artifacts. A restored caboose is on display. The museum is open daily May through October, and the depot also contains a travel information center.

SITE LOCATION: 216 Edgar Street, Marquette
PHONE: 563-873-1200
WEB SITE: www.mcgreg-marq.org

Boone & Scenic Valley Railroad 2

SITE LOCATION: 225 10th Street, Boone
PHONE: 800-626-0319 or 515-432-4249
WEB SITE: www.scenic-valleyrr.com
E-MAIL: info@bsvrr.com

Jim Wrinn

Iowa isn't known for rolling terrain, but this fascinating railroad provides a scenic ride with interesting landscape through the Des Moines River Valley. The railroad runs across two impressive bridges, with the 156-foot-tall Bass Point Creek High Bridge being the highlight of a 15-mile round trip. The railroad's dinner, dessert, and picnic trains run on a slightly longer route.

CHOICES: The railroad is among the few in the country that offer steam-, diesel-, and electric-powered trains. You can ride a standard excursion in coach class or opt for the *Valley View* car, which was formerly a C&NW transfer caboose. There is also limited seating in the train's caboose. Hop the restored 1915 Charles City & Western electric trolley for an interurban run through downtown Boone. And browse the railroad equipment displayed on the grounds or inside the depot's museum. Picnic trains travel the same route as the dinner or dessert trains, you just have to supply the lunch.

WHEN TO GO: Between Memorial Day through the end of October, excursion trains run daily, while trolleys operate on weekends. Dinner trains are scheduled on various Fridays and Saturdays. The museum grounds are open year-round. The indoor museum is open daily during the summer season and weekdays November through May.

GOOD TO KNOW: The railroad's Chinese steam engine, built in 1989, is one of two built at that time and imported to the United States for tour and excursion service.

WORTH DOING: Boone celebrates its railroad heritage during Pufferbilly Days, an annual event with train rides, a model train display, a parade, and a spike-driving contest.

DON'T MISS: On the dinner, dessert, and picnic trains, step outside on the *City of San Francisco*'s rear observation deck to experience the sights and smells.

GETTING THERE: The railroad is in central Iowa, an hour's drive northwest of Des Moines. Take I-35 to Ames and travel west on Highway 30 to Boone. Go north on Story Street through the business district to 10th Street and then go west six blocks to the depot.

DISCOUNT: $2 off each adult ticket, up to two adults.

Midwest Central Railroad ▣

SITE LOCATION: 405 E. Threshers Road, Mount Pleasant
PHONE: 319-385-2912
WEB SITE: www.mcrr.org
E-MAIL: jwcrouch@iowatelecom.net

Jeff Terry

The Midwest Central Railroad was established when volunteers built a 1.25-mile of track around the Midwest Old Threshers Reunion site and acquired several steam locomotives and cars. Later, to bring visitors and exhibitors into the grounds, a counter-clockwise trolley loop line was built, dubbed the Midwest Electric Railway. On this loop line, streetcars from around the world operate frequently, often with standing room only.

CHOICES: Both the Midwest Central Railroad and the Midwest Electric Railway are in full operation during the Old Threshers Reunion, which takes place over the Labor Day weekend. The Museum and Education Center houses the railroad's antique equipment. Both the railroad and the electric line operate during Midwestern Haunted Rails each October, and the railroad also runs a steam North Pole Express. A steam train also operates during Mount Pleasant's annual July 4th celebration.

WHEN TO GO: The Midwest Old Threshers Reunion begins the Thursday before Labor Day and ends on Labor Day. The railroad begins operating on the Wednesday prior to the reunion, and the trolleys begin running on the Saturday before the reunion.

GOOD TO KNOW: The Midwest Old Threshers Reunion is the largest gathering of agricultural and tractor enthusiasts in the United States. It's like an old-fashioned state fair with tractor pulls, a steam-powered merry-go-round, and other fun activities. But its emphasis is on living agricultural history, and there are demonstrations of steam tractors, early gas tractors, and other period farm implements.

WORTH DOING: If you're a camper, stay at the Old Threshers campground and take the trolley into the grounds and then ride the train. You can take in the whole show without the hassle of parking and enjoy the sights and sounds of steam as you camp. Just be sure to make campground (or hotel) reservations early.

DON'T MISS: Take an international trolley ride. Midwest Electric Railway international streetcars include two open-air cars, one from Rio de Janeiro, Brazil, and car no. 1945 from Milan, Italy.

GETTING THERE: Probably the best way to visit Mount Pleasant is by driving. Located in southeastern Iowa, Mount Pleasant is south of Iowa City on Highway 218. The city is also served daily by Amtrak's *California Zephyr*.

Union Pacific Railroad Museum ❹

SITE LOCATION: 200 Pearl Street, Council Bluffs
PHONE: 712-329-8307
WEB SITE: www.uprr.com/aboutup/history/museum
E-MAIL: upmuseum@up.com

Union Pacific Railroad

Few railroads have gone to the great lengths of the Union Pacific to preserve and document their past. The Union Pacific Railroad Museum houses one of the oldest corporation collections of any kind in the country. Visitors will not find lines of steam locomotives, diesels, or rolling stock. Rather, they will be inundated with a tasteful display of artifacts, photographs, and documents that trace the development of the UP and the role it played in American West.

CHOICES: The museum can be taken in whole or digested by specific eras depending on your interests. The Union Pacific's history is a history of the American West. The collection dates from the mid-1800s and features original manuscripts such as reports from survey teams searching for the best land route to lay tracks. Surveying equipment, early rail equipment, and other artifacts fill the building. Docents are available to show and explain everything within the museum's walls.

WHEN TO GO: With the exception of a raging snowstorm, even winter is a good time to visit the museum. It is open Tuesdays through Saturdays. Events and special exhibits are changed periodically during the year.

GOOD TO KNOW: Council Bluffs is a quiet, modern city across the Missouri River from Omaha, Neb. There are numerous motels, hotels, restaurants, and parks in both cities.

WORTH DOING: Take time to tour both Council Bluffs and Omaha. Both are culturally rich cities with much to offer visitors. Council Bluffs has several casinos and is Iowa's leading gaming spot. The Henry Doorly Zoo in Omaha is a world-class zoo that appeals to adults as well as children.

DON'T MISS: The museum has a combination of static and interactive displays. The working locomotive simulator will fuel your thirst in thinking about a career in railroading. Plan to spend many hours here.

GETTING THERE: Omaha is an important regional airline hub with numerous flights from all directions daily, and Amtrak serves Omaha. Located on the east side of Council Bluffs, the museum is easily accessible for motorists from I-80 or I-29.

KANSAS

Abilene & Smoky Valley Railroad ❶

A 90-minute, 10-mile round trip takes you through the Smoky Hill River Valley from historic Abilene to Enterprise. The diesel-powered excursion train crosses the river on a high-span steel bridge. You can ride in a 1902 wooden passenger/dining car or an open-air gondola car. Dinner and special trains also run. Santa Fe no. 3415, a 1919 Baldwin 4-6-2 steam locomotive, has been restored to operating condition.

SITE LOCATION: 200 S. Fifth Street, Abilene
PHONE: 888-426-6687 or 785-263-1077
WEB SITE: www.asvrr.org
E-MAIL: info@asvrr.org

Great Plains Transportation Museum ❷

The museum features an outdoor display of locomotives, cabooses, and cars, including Santa Fe steam locomotive no. 3768 and Santa Fe FP45 diesel no. 93. Indoor exhibits feature railroad signs, lanterns, tools, and other artifacts. It is open year-round on Saturdays and also on Sundays from April to October.

SITE LOCATION: 700 E. Douglas Avenue, Wichita
PHONE: 316-263-0944
WEB SITE: www.gptm.us
E-MAIL: info@gptm.us

Santa Fe Depot ❸

Dating to 1911, the former Santa Fe depot is on the National Register of Historic Places. It contains railroad memorabilia, some found within the depot itself, and a model train display. The stylish brick building also houses the Cannonball Welcome Center. It is open year-round Monday through Friday.

SITE LOCATION: 201 E. Sherman Avenue, Kingman
PHONE: 620-532-2142
WEB SITE: skyways.lib.ks.us/towns/Kingman/depot
E-MAIL: sfdepot@sbcglobal.net

Midland Railway 🄴

SITE LOCATION: 1515 W. High Street, Baldwin City
PHONE: 800-651-0388 or 913-371-3410
WEB SITE: www.midland-ry.org

Deek Deitrick

The Midland Railway offers 20-mile round trips in the pleasant Kansas countryside between Baldwin City and Ottawa. The Midland has a roster of first-generation diesels that includes an Alco RS-3 in its original New York Central livery, a Burlington NW-2 in Midland Railway green, and a rare Katy RS-3m in Deramus red.

CHOICES: Regular service includes one-hour excursions from Baldwin City to Norwood that cross two 200-foot trestles and two-hour trips to the end of the line at Ottawa Junction, where the line meets BNSF's Transcon. Midland also offers a mystery train, Thomas the Tank Engine, and other specials.

WHEN TO GO: The Midland operates primarily on weekends from May to October, with seasonal trains around Easter and Christmas. The annual Railfan Weekend is a big draw, with rides offered in diesel cabs, on track speeders, or in a Railway Post Office car. The Midland also participates in a variety of community festivals, including the annual Planes, Trains, and Automobiles celebration on Father's Day weekend and the Maple Leaf Festival, the third weekend in October.

GOOD TO KNOW: Baldwin City has a pair of B&Bs, plus a host of restaurants, all within two miles of the Midland station. More extensive offerings can be found 30 minutes away in Lawrence, Ottawa, or Olathe.

WORTH DOING: Visit the bridge near the Douglas-Franklin County line, which is a favorite photo location. Directions can be obtained at the Baldwin City station.

DON'T MISS: Look through the Midland's 1906 Baldwin City depot, which is on the National Register of Historic Places.

GETTING THERE: The closest Amtrak stops are in Lawrence and Kansas City, Mo., and the closest major airport is in Kansas City. Baldwin City is 45 miles southwest of Kansas City on Highway 56. The Midland depot is on High Street, just west of the town square.

DISCOUNT: $1 off adult ticket; not valid on specials.

KENTUCKY

Bluegrass Scenic Railroad 1

The railroad offers a six-mile round trip through the heart of Kentucky's Bluegrass region. The diesel-powered train is made up of vintage coaches from the 1920s and '30s, and it departs from Woodford County Park. Indoor and outdoor displays include a watchman's shanty, a working telegraph set, and Kentucky railroading artifacts. The museum grounds are open year-round, and excursions run on weekends from mid-May through October.

SITE LOCATION: 175 Beasley Road, Versailles
PHONE: 800-755-2476 or 859-873-2476
WEB SITE: www.bgrm.org
E-MAIL: form on Web site

Paducah Railroad Museum 2

Operated by the Paducah Chapter of the National Railway Historical Society, the museum displays equipment and memorabilia from railroads including the three that served Paducah. It features replicas of a waiting room and freight office as well as section cars, tools, and an operating signaling system. A steam engine, a caboose, and a baggage car are displayed a block away.

SITE LOCATION: 200 Washington Street, Paducah
PHONE: 270-519-7377
WEB SITE: www.paducahrr.org

Railway Museum of Greater Cincinnati 3

The museum collects, restores, and displays equipment that belonged to the seven railroads then served Cincinnati. The outdoor yard contains more than 70 cars and locomotives. It includes a large number of Pullman cars, several switchers, and a Pennsylvania Railroad E8A diesel locomotive. It is open Wednesdays and Saturdays year-round.

SITE LOCATION: 315 W. Southern Avenue, Covington
WEB SITE: www.cincirailmuseum.org
E-MAIL: questions@cincirailmuseum.org

Big South Fork Scenic Railway 4

SITE LOCATION: 100 Henderson Street, Stearns
PHONE: 800-462-5664 or 606-376-5330
WEB SITE: www.bsfsry.com
E-MAIL: info@bsfsry.com

Big South Fork Scenic Railway

In the 20th century, short lines and branches brought forth coal for use nationwide, and one of the primary locations was Stearns, home of the Kentucky & Tennessee short line. The coal is gone now, but the K&T has been reborn as a scenic railroad.

CHOICES: The railway offers three-hour trips through the Big South Fork National River and Recreation Area on the former Kentucky & Tennessee Railway. The train follows mountain streams, passes through a tunnel, and crosses a bridge as it descends 600 feet to the floor of the river valley. The ride includes a layover at the restored mining camp of Blue Heron.

WHEN TO GO: The railroad runs on a varied schedule from the end of March through December. Spring is especially beautiful in this part of the Appalachians because of all of the blooming plants that inhabit the mountains.

GOOD TO KNOW: The bridge over Roaring Paunch Creek is a unique structure. It was constructed in 1937 from a used railroad bridge. The girders of the bridge needed to be offset because the line crossed the creek at an angle. The bridge's girders were offset in the opposite direction, so it was placed upside down, and the ties and track were then added.

WORTH DOING: Train fares include admission to the McCreary County Museum, which is housed in the Stearns Coal and Lumber Company headquarters that was built in 1907.

DON'T MISS: Take the walking tour of the Blue Heron Mine at the end of the run. Built in 1937, this mine and coal tipple operated until it was abandoned in 1962. It was restored with ghost structures (representations of where the actual buildings stood) and oral history exhibits by the National Park Service as part of the Big South Fork River and Recreation Area. You can also camp, hike, fish, and raft the river.

GETTING THERE: Stearns is 70 miles from Knoxville, Tenn., and 120 miles from Lexington. From Knoxville, take I-75 north to Exit 141. Take Route 63 west to the junction with Route 27. Take Route 27 north to Stearns. Turn left on Route 92 and travel west one mile to the depot.

DISCOUNT: $2 off each regular adult admission; excludes specials.

Kentucky Railway Museum ⑤

SITE LOCATION: 136 S. Main Street, New Haven
PHONE: 800-272-0152 or 502-549-5470
WEB SITE: www.kyrail.org
E-MAIL: info@kyrail.org

Becky Csborne

Housed in a replica of the original New Haven station, the Kentucky Railway Museum has more than 50,000 items in its collection and more than 120 pieces of rolling stock and engines. The museum also operates excursions on 17 miles of former Louisville & Nashville track.

CHOICES: The museum's excursion trains take you on a 22-mile, 90-minute round trip through the scenic, historic Rolling Fork River Valley between New Haven and Boston. The museum operates ex-L&N 4-6-2 no. 152, built in 1905 and listed on the National Register, on steam engine weekends. Other operating power includes ex-Monon BL2 no. 32 and ex-AT&SF CF-7 no. 2546.

WHEN TO GO: The museum is open year-round, and excursions take place April through December. Trains run on weekends throughout the season with several weekday runs added during summer. Spring and fall scenery is nice, with temperatures in the 70s and low 80s. Open-air and air-conditioned coaches are available.

GOOD TO KNOW: Hotels and inns are available in Bardstown and Elizabethtown, both about 20 minutes away. The Sherwood Inn, a B&B, is adjacent to the museum.

WORTH DOING: Abraham Lincoln was born nearby, and historical sites to visit include his birthplace, boyhood home, and the Lincoln Museum. Mammoth Cave National Park, Fort Knox, the Patton Museum of Cavalry and Armor, and My Old Kentucky Home State Park are also close by. My Old Kentucky Dinner Train is 15 miles away.

DON'T MISS: The museum also offers dinner trains, murder mystery trains, engine and caboose rides, train holdups, Santa trains, and days out with Thomas the Tank Engine.

GETTING THERE: The museum is about 45 miles from Louisville and 65 miles from Lexington. If driving from Louisville, take I-65 south to Exit 105, Route 61 to Boston, and then Route 52 to New Haven. From Lexington, take Route 60 west to the Blue Grass Parkway. Take the parkway to Exit 21 and then take Route 31E to New Haven.

DISCOUNT: Receive 10% off train fares.

My Old Kentucky Dinner Train 6

SITE LOCATION: 602 N. Third Street, Bardstown
PHONE: 866-801-3463 or 502-348-7500
WEB SITE: www.kydinnertrain.com
E-MAIL: info@kydinnertrain.com

Impact Photography

My Old Kentucky Dinner Train operates in 1940s dining cars on 15 miles of former Louisville & Nashville track between Bardstown and Limestone Springs. The passenger waiting room is located in Bardstown's former limestone freight house, which dates from 1860 and is on the National Register of Historic Places.

CHOICES: The train operates year-round, and it offers both lunch and dinner trips, as well as occasional special events such as a mystery train. It offers two-hour lunch excursions on Saturdays. Other lunch and dinner excursions run Tuesday through Sunday on a varied schedule. Menu selections for the four-course meal include prime rib, seafood, and poultry. There are also vegetarian dishes and children's items. Trains are pulled by two ex-Southern FP-7a's. The Budd-built lightweight cars are of AT&SF, C&O, and PRR ancestry, including the former C&O 1921 that operated on President Dwight Eisenhower's funeral train. Two distilleries, several warehouses, and two restored depots, Deatsville and Limestone Springs, are on the line.

WHEN TO GO: The scenery is especially nice in spring and fall, and the temperatures are in the 70s and low 80s. Tobacco is grown from June through August and can be viewed along the route.

GOOD TO KNOW: Founded in 1780, Bardstown is Kentucky's second-oldest city and features a mix of old and new inns, restaurants, and shops. There are also accommodations in Elizabethtown, about 20 minutes away.

WORTH DOING: The area is rich in history and includes Civil War museums as well as Abraham Lincoln's birthplace and his boyhood home. Several local distilleries give tours, and the Kentucky Railway Museum is 15 minutes away.

DON'T MISS: The train passes through part of the Bernheim Forest, a private 14,000-acre nature preserve, a habitat for a variety of trees, vegetation, and wildlife. While in the forest, the train passes slowly over the 310-foot-long, 60-foot-high Jackson Hollow timber trestle built for predecessor Bardstown & Louisville Railroad in 1860.

GETTING THERE: Bardstown is about 40 miles south of Louisville and 55 miles southwest of Lexington. Air service is available to Louisville International Airport and Blue Grass Airport in Lexington. When driving from Louisville, take Route 31E, and from Lexington, take Route 60 west and then the Blue Grass Parkway.

LOUISIANA

DeQuincy Railroad Museum ❶

Home to the DeQuincy Railroad Museum, the former Kansas City Southern depot is an outstanding example of Mission Revival architecture and is on the National Register of Historic Places. It displays a 1913 Alco steam locomotive, a caboose, and a passenger coach as well as artifacts and memorabilia. The annual Louisiana Railroad Days Festival is held here in April.

SITE LOCATION: 400 Lake Charles Avenue, DeQuincy
PHONE: 337-786-2823
WEB SITE: www.visitlakecharles.org

Old Hickory Railroad ❷

The Old Hickory Railroad features a live steam locomotive pulling two open coaches on a six-mile trip through the town of Jackson, which has more than 100 historic buildings. It operates Saturdays and Sundays from late March through November. Special events include the Battle of Jackson Crossroads, an attack on the train by Civil War reenactors. The site also houses the G scale Little Hickory Railroad and Republic of West Florida Museum.

SITE LOCATION: 3406 College Street, Jackson
PHONE: 225-634-7397
WEB SITE: www.louisianasteamtrain.com
E-MAIL: Harv707@aol.com

Southern Forest Heritage Museum ❸

At this museum, a guided tour takes you around a 57-acre historic sawmill complex, where you'll see a roundhouse and other industrial structures, three early logging locomotives, two McGiffert loaders, a Clyde skidder, and other steam equipment. Motor car rides on original Red River & Gulf railroad track are also available.

SITE LOCATION: Route 497, Long Leaf
PHONE: 318-748-8404
WEB SITE: www.forestheritagemuseum.org
E-MAIL: longleaf@centurytel.net

MAINE

Boothbay Railway Village ❶

A two-foot-gauge steam train ride takes you around a re-created historic village. Rail buildings include several stations, an engine house, a water tower, and a crossing tower. Exhibits include a history of Maine narrow gauge railroads, and various pieces of rolling stock and equipment are on display, as are more than 50 antique or classic automobiles and other vehicles.

SITE LOCATION: 586 Wiscasset Road, Boothbay
PHONE: 207-633-4727
WEB SITE: www.railwayvillage.org
E-MAIL: staff@railwayvillage.org

Cole Land Transportation Museum ❷

The museum houses 200 antique land transportation vehicles and 2,000 photographs of life in early Maine. Its railroad collection includes one of the first Bangor & Aroostook diesels, a Canadian Pacific section shack, a Maine Central caboose, and a relocated station.

SITE LOCATION: 405 Perry Road, Bangor
PHONE: 207-990-3600
WEB SITE: www.colemuseum.org
E-MAIL: mail@colemuseum.org

Oakfield Railroad Museum ❸

Exhibits in the restored Oakfield station include hundreds of photographs dating to the beginning of the Bangor & Aroostook Railroad in 1891, vintage signs and advertising pieces, signal lanterns, original railroad maps, and telegraph equipment. A restored caboose, handcar, and motor car are also displayed. It is open Saturday and Sunday afternoons.

SITE LOCATION: Station Street, Oakfield
PHONE: 207-757-8575
WEB SITE: www.oakfieldmuseum.org
E-MAIL: oakfieldmuseum@pwless.net

Maine

Sandy River and Rangeley Lakes Railroad ❹

You can ride along the original narrow gauge roadbed of the SR&RL Railroad in 1884 Laconia Coach no. 18, powered by a replica of SR&RL no. 4 or another locomotive. You can also tour the eight-stall roundhouse to see ongoing restoration projects. Trains operate on select weekends June through October.

SITE LOCATION: 128 Bridge Street, Phillips
PHONE: 207-778-3621
WEB SITE: www.srrl-rr.org

Seashore Trolley Museum ❺

The museum offers a 25-minute ride through the countryside aboard a restored early 1900s electric streetcar. There are more than 50 streetcars on display in three carbarns. Almost every state is represented as well as Canada, Japan, and several European countries. Special events, including a sunset ride with ice cream, are scheduled throughout the year.

SITE LOCATION: 195 Log Cabin Road, Kennebunkport
PHONE: 207-967-2712
WEB SITE: www.trolleymuseum.org
E-MAIL: form on Web site

Maine Eastern Railroad

SITE LOCATION: 4 Union Street, Rockland
PHONE: 866-637-2457
WEB SITE: www.maineeasternrailroad.com
E-MAIL: info@maineeasternrailroad.com

Bob Johnston

The Maine Eastern offers scenic coastline views from big-windowed, stainless steel coaches pulled by former New Haven Railroad FL9 locomotives. The railroad operates on a 57-mile branch line between Brunswick and Rockland. Along the line, there are 33 bridges and more than 100 curves.

CHOICES: Beginning in late May, one two-hour round trip runs on Saturday and Sunday out of Rockland. Then in late June through October, service expands with two round trips Wednesday through Saturday. In addition to riding in the rebuilt 1940s and '50s coaches, passengers can also reserve a parlor-class seat in a vintage lounge car for a nominal extra fare. A dining car serves food café-style, and narration describes the area's scenery and history. If you travel Wednesday through Saturday, it is possible to ride the entire line from either end point, stopping en route to explore the villages of Bath and Wiscasset. If you would like to extend your trip, you can arrange to have your ticket match the dates of your vacation.

WHEN TO GO: Riding to Rockland's North Atlantic Blues Festival in July, the multi-day Lobster Fest in August, or other special events in the fall color season provide a great way to beat traffic jams on two-lane Route 1. For summer festivals, a single round trip leaves from Brunswick each weekend day.

GOOD TO KNOW: The Maine Eastern features several travel packages for those wishing some singular experiences. They include a train, plane, and lighthouse package with a 30-minute airplane ride and various rail and sail options that include trips aboard a sailboat or a working lobster boat.

WORTH DOING: Stay in the area several days and explore the extraordinary coast, which is dotted with unique lighthouses including Pemaquid Point in Bristol. Making the trip up the coast to Acadia National Park or taking a whale-watching trip are excellent activities.

DON'T MISS: Putter around recently restored train stations at Bath (built in 1941) and Rockland (1919). Aboard the train, keep your eyes open as you may spot a moose that has wandered south.

GETTING THERE: Brunswick is about a 30-minute drive from Portland and 2.5 hours from Boston. Rockland is 90 minutes from Portland and about 3.5 hours from Boston. Route 1 can get crowded, especially on summer weekends, but it offers many scenic views.

Maine Narrow Gauge Railroad & Museum ⑦

SITE LOCATION: 58 Fore Street, Portland
PHONE: 207-828-0814
WEB SITE: www.mngrr.org
E-MAIL: mngrr@maine.rr.com

Arthur Hussey II

The Maine Narrow Gauge Railroad & Museum operates along the Eastern Promenade fronting Casco Bay. Excursions provide spectacular views of ferries, sailboats, cruise ships, lobster boats, and freighters as well as the many islands that dot the bay.

CHOICES: The railroad operates diesel and steam locomotives with authentic open-window coaches and open-sided excursion cars. Tour the museum and see several beautifully restored passenger coaches, including *Rangeley*, the only two-foot gauge private car ever built. Also on display is a railbus used on the Sandy River and Bridgton & Harrison Railroads.

WHEN TO GO: The museum is open year-round, and trains run daily mid-May through mid-October and on weekends during the rest of the schedule. Various special events, including a Polar Express train, take place throughout the year. The railroad's schedule shows when steam trains operate.

GOOD TO KNOW: Most of the railroad's equipment once operated on two famed Maine two-footers: the Sandy River & Rangeley Lakes and the Bridgton & Harrison. The equipment was saved from the scrappers in the 1940s by industrialist Ellis D. Atwood and operated at the Edaville Railroad in Massachusetts until 1994, when it returned to Maine.

WORTH DOING: The Portland waterfront is a busy area for tourists, and there are many other attractions in the area, including much of the original Federal-style architecture found in Maine's second largest city.

DON'T MISS: Ride on the water side of the train for the best views. A walking and bike path follows the line for its entire length, which makes taking action photos easy.

GETTING THERE: Portland International Airport is nearby, and Boston's Logan Airport is about two hours south. Amtrak's "Down Easter" trains run between Boston's North Station and Portland. I-95 passes just west of Portland.

Wiscasset, Waterville & Farmington Railway 8

SITE LOCATION: 97 Cross Road, Alna
PHONE: 207-882-4193
WEB SITE: www.wwfry.org
E-MAIL: info@wwfry.org

Steve Hussar

The railway is a faithful recreation of a portion of the original two-foot gauge Wiscasset, Waterville & Farmington Railway, which was abandoned following a wreck in 1933. This line follows the original right-of-way, and the museum operates several pieces of preserved rolling stock from the original railway.

CHOICES: Trains operate between the Sheepscot station and Alna Center. Be sure to ride in Wiscasset & Quebec coach no. 3, a gem built by Jackson & Sharpe in 1894. Then visit the railway's newly expanded shop, where museum volunteers rebuild and maintain rolling stock using traditional skills and techniques.

WHEN TO GO: The museum is open every Saturday year-round, as well as on Sundays beginning Memorial Day weekend through mid-October. Trains operate Saturdays and Sundays June through September and just on Saturdays the rest of the operating season. September and October are the best months to visit, after the summer crowds have diminished and the insects are dormant.

GOOD TO KNOW: Maine was famous for its two-foot gauge railways, a thrifty New England response to the expense of building and maintaining a railroad. Five two-foot gauge railways once operated in Maine, but all were closed by 1941.

WORTH DOING: The mid-coast region of Maine features plenty of attractions, lodging choices, and restaurants. Be sure to sample the bounty of the sea, especially lobsters, clams, and fish. Room rates are highest in July and August, and reservations are a must. Traffic on Route 1, the main coastal artery, is very heavy and slow moving on summer weekends.

DON'T MISS: Visit the museum during the spring and fall "track meets." On these long weekends, volunteers from all over the country arrive to construct track, extending the railway a thousand feet or more during each session. You can even join in if you like.

GETTING THERE: The closest airports are in Portland and Augusta. The museum itself is on a rural road just off Route 218 about four miles from Wiscasset and Route 1.

MARYLAND

Bowie Railroad Station ❶
The 1910 Pennsylvania station has been restored and now contains local history and rail exhibits. An interlocking switch tower, waiting shed, and caboose are also on site. The station is open to the public Tuesday through Sunday.

SITE LOCATION: 8614 Chestnut Avenue, Bowie
PHONE: 301-809-3089
WEB SITE: www.cityofbowie.org/museums/museums.asp

Chesapeake Beach Railway Museum ❷
From 1900 until 1935, the Chesapeake Beach Railway brought people to the resorts of Chesapeake Beach and North Beach. Housed in the railway's original station, the museum exhibits photographs, artifacts, and memorabilia from both the railroad and the resort. A parlor car is also on display. The museum is open daily April through October and on weekends the rest of the year.

SITE LOCATION: 4155 Mears Avenue, Chesapeake Beach
PHONE: 410-257-3892
WEB SITE: www.cbrm.org
E-MAIL: cbrailway@co.cal.md.us

Ellicott City Station ❸

Located on the B&O Railroad's historic Old Main Line, Ellicott City Station could be the oldest surviving railroad station in the country. The main depot building was completed in 1831, and the freight house was built in 1855. The museum displays a replica of the first horse-drawn passenger railcar, the *Pioneer*, and a 1927 caboose. It is now a unit of the B&O Railroad Museum, and you can purchase a joint admission.

SITE LOCATION: 2711 Maryland Avenue, Ellicott City
PHONE: 410-461-1945
WEB SITE: www.ecborail.org
E-MAIL: form on Web site

Gaithersburg Community Museum ❹

Located in the restored 1884 B&O railroad station, the museum includes permanent and rotating history exhibits. An outdoor display features a 1918 Buffalo Creek & Gauley steam locomotive, a B&O bay window caboose, a troop kitchen car, and other equipment. It is open Thursday through Saturday.

SITE LOCATION: 9 S. Summit Avenue, Gaithersburg
PHONE: 301-258-6160
WEB SITE: www.gaithersburgmd.gov/museum

Hagerstown Roundhouse Museum ❺

Located in a historic building, the museum presents local rail history through artifacts, photos, and model train layouts. A Baldwin diesel, two Western Maryland cabooses, and a Hagerstown & Frederick trolley are on display. It is open Friday through Sunday year-round.

SITE LOCATION: 300 S. Burhans Boulevard, Hagerstown
PHONE: 301-739-4665
WEB SITE: www.roundhouse.org
E-MAIL: form on Web site

Baltimore & Ohio Railroad Museum ⑥

Site Location: 901 W. Pratt Street, Baltimore
PHONE: 410-752-2490
WEB SITE: www.borail.org
E-MAIL: info@borail.org

Alexander Mitchell IV

Known as the birthplace of American railroading, the B&O Railroad Museum combines a diverse collection of railroad artifacts and rolling stock with a landmark setting and a unique focus upon a single railroad (the Baltimore & Ohio) and its subsidiaries and successors.

CHOICES: The museum occupies several vintage buildings, and it houses the largest collection of 19th century locomotives in North America. Its fully covered roundhouse and turntable, built in 1884, is a distinctive feature of Baltimore's skyline. The museum features B&O locomotives dating back to 1836 and operable replicas of the 1831 *Tom Thumb* and the *Lafayette*. Later steamers and diesels are also well represented, and many passenger cars and freight cars round out the collection. Allow at least a half day for a full tour, including a train ride down the first mile of American intercity railroading (included with admission).

WHEN TO GO: The museum is open year-round, but late spring and fall are recommended. Summer months are not only high tourist season in Baltimore but also months of high humidity. Special events are spread throughout the year, and train rides are not offered during February and March.

GOOD TO KNOW: The B&O museum is located in a residential neighborhood just west of downtown and the city's major stadiums. You can walk from downtown's Inner Harbor district, but a taxi or MTA transit bus is suggested. Combined admission to the nearby Ellicott City Railroad Museum, the oldest railroad station in America, is also available.

WORTH DOING: Baltimore has a host of other attractions, including the Baltimore Streetcar Museum, the National Aquarium, the Maryland Zoo, the Walters Art Gallery, and Fort McHenry.

DON'T MISS: If time permits, stop at the museum's restoration facility and observe craftsmen restoring vintage rolling stock.

GETTING THERE: Baltimore is served by many airlines, Amtrak, and mass transit, and the museum is only a few minutes off I-95 by car.

Baltimore Streetcar Museum ❼

SITE LOCATION: 1901 Falls Road, Baltimore
PHONE: 410-547-0264
WEB SITE: www.baltimorestreetcar.org

Alexander Mitchell IV

Relive a piece of Baltimore's history by hopping on one of the city's original streetcars for a one-mile ride. The trip takes you along the former right-of-way of the Maryland & Pennsylvania in the Jones Falls Valley and passes a former freight house and roundhouse before turning on a loop for the return ride.

CHOICES: In Trolley Theatre, you can view a short presentation about trolleys and streetcars that ran in Baltimore from 1859 to 1963. Guides will also lead you on a tour of the car house, where you can view 13 Baltimore streetcars, ranging from a horse car to the last PCC that ran in Baltimore, and several buses and "trackless trolleys." The visitor center houses museum displays and a research library. There is a family admission plan as well as individual admissions. Admission includes unlimited rides, the car house tour, and museum access.

WHEN TO GO: The museum is open on Sunday afternoons year-round and additionally on Saturday afternoons June through October. If visiting Baltimore in summer, it can be excessively hot and muggy.

GOOD TO KNOW: Since 1968, the Baltimore Streetcar Museum has operated its distinctive and unique collection of streetcars and other transit equipment, one of the only transit museum collections to focus exclusively on a collection from one city. In recent years, the collection's scope has expanded to include three cars from Philadelphia.

WORTH DOING: Baltimore is full of interesting things to see including the picturesque Inner Harbor, National Aquarium, and the USS *Constellation*. The historic Mount Vernon neighborhood, with the Walters Art Gallery, Meyerhoff Symphony Hall, Peabody Institute, eclectic shops and restaurants, is a short rail or bus ride to the south.

DON'T MISS: In the car house, look for Baltimore Transit Company's rare crane car 3715. It is the only known piece of Baltimore Transit's work equipment on rail saved from the '50s. For railfans, the B&O Railroad museum is 10 minutes away.

GETTING THERE: The museum is two blocks west of Charles Street and Maryland Avenue, major north-south streets. Baltimore has plenty of transportation alternatives. From Amtrak's Penn Station, it is a few minutes' walk. The MTA Light Rail – spiritual successor to the streetcars – also serves Penn Station with connections to downtown and Baltimore-Washington International Airport.

National Capital Trolley Museum ❽

SITE LOCATION: 1313 Bonifant Road, Colesville
PHONE: 301-384-6088
WEB SITE: www.dctrolley.org

Erik Ledbetter

In summer 2009, the National Capital Trolley Museum will debut a new multi-million dollar visitor center, carbarn, and demonstration railway. For the first time, visitors will have access to the majority of the museum's collection of 14 historic street railway cars and associated artifacts.

CHOICES: Take a 20-minute ride aboard a vintage American streetcar or European tram on the museum's mile-long demonstration railway. Learn how streetcars shaped the development of Washington and its suburbs through hands-on exhibits in the visitor center. View streetcars from the 1890s to the 1950s in the carbarn. In addition to streetcars from the United States – including DC Transit car 1101, one of the very last to operate in Washington – the collection also includes vintage trams from several European cities.

WHEN TO GO: Following the museum's reopening, it will be open weekends year-round as well as on Thursdays and Fridays during select months. Opening hours vary by day and by season.

GOOD TO KNOW: The museum's new facilities incorporate architectural elements of past electric railway buildings in Washington. Art Deco design aficionados can see three generations of streamlined PCC cars, from an original 1937 car to a 1971 Belgian-built car, side by side in the carbarn.

WORTH DOING: Bring a picnic basket and enjoy lunch in Northwest Branch Park, the museum's home, while you watch the trolleys roll by. Downtown Washington, with its wealth of cultural and historic attractions, is just 14 miles away.

DON'T MISS: Take a ride aboard one of the European trolleys for a rare opportunity to experience Old World as well as American streetcar craftsmanship.

GETTING THERE: The museum is located in Northwest Branch Park, about a 20-minute drive from the Capital Beltway. Bonifant Road is 5.5 miles north of I-495 (the Capital Beltway). Glenmont is the closest Washington Metrorail subway station. From there, Montgomery County Ride-On Bus no. 26 leaves for the museum at 30-minute intervals on Saturdays and Sundays. This bus also serves the White Flint and Twinbrook Metrorail stations.

Walkersville Southern Railroad ⑨

SITE LOCATION: 34 W. Pennsylvania Avenue, Walkersville
PHONE: 877-363-9777 or 301-898-0899
WEB SITE: www.wsrr.org
E-MAIL: admin@wsrr.org

Alexander Mitchell IV

The Walkersville Southern Railroad takes you on a pleasant eight-mile, 70-minute round trip through woods and farmland, past a restored century-old lime kiln, and crosses the Monocacy River over a rebuilt bridge. A museum occupies a former ice plant and features rail artifacts from the line and a model railroad.

CHOICES: Trains depart from Frederick's original station, pulled by one of the railroad's collection of four-wheeled switchers, which include a 1939 Davenport gas mechanical, a rare 1942 EMD type 40 diesel, and a 1942 Plymouth gas mechanical. Passengers may ride in a former Long Island Railroad coach, a sheltered open flatcar with benches, a caboose, or a refurbished troop carrier. Parks and picnic stands are located at both ends of the line.

WHEN TO GO: From May through October, there are three Saturday departures. In addition, the railroad operates two trips on Sundays in May, June, September, and October (but not July and August). Special events include mystery dinner trains, holiday trains, teddy bear picnics, and Jesse James robberies.

GOOD TO KNOW: In 1972, Hurricane Agnes washed out the Monocacy River bridge and halted service over the river until the bridge was rebuilt in 1996. The railroad has a working relationship with the Chesapeake Railway Association, which owns several pieces of rolling stock on the line including the 1930-built Pullman *Meadow Lark* that is currently being restored for service.

WORTH DOING: For Civil War buffs, Gettysburg and Harpers Ferry are little more than an hour away.

DON'T MISS: The railway line between Walkersville and Frederick was built in 1869. Take in the railroad's station, built by the Pennsylvania Railroad in the late 1800s, and the freight house, which also dates from that period.

GETTING THERE: The railroad is 50 miles from Baltimore or Washington, D.C. From Baltimore, take I-70 west to Exit 53B near Frederick. Follow Route 15 north for six miles and then turn right onto Biggs Ford Road. Travel about two miles and look for a grain elevator, which is adjacent to the station.

Western Maryland Scenic Railroad

SITE LOCATION: 13 Canal Street, Cumberland
PHONE: 800-872-4650 or 301-759-4400
WEB SITE: www.wmsr.com
E-MAIL: trainmaster@wmsr.com

Jim Wrinn

Of all the Appalachian freight railroads, the Western Maryland was one of the most beloved because of its excellent steam power, which tackled difficult mountain grades. Today, the trip out of Cumberland on the roadbed of the main line, with a short detour the last few miles onto a branch into Frostburg, is one of the best parts of the Western Maryland.

CHOICES: Traveling through the mountains of western Maryland, this 32-mile round trip take takes you from Cumberland's restored Western Maryland Railway station to an 1891 Cumberland & Pennsylvania depot in Frostburg. You'll ride aboard restored coaches pulled by a 1916 Baldwin steam locomotive or a vintage diesel engine. First-class seating, which includes lunch, is available on some departures. The railroad also offers locomotive cab rides as well as murder mystery, Christmas, and other special trains.

WHEN TO GO: Trains run May through December. October, during the height of the fall color season, is especially beautiful but make reservations in advance because the trains can fill up quickly.

GOOD TO KNOW: The Western Maryland Station houses the Chesapeake & Ohio Canal National Historical Park's Cumberland Visitor Center, where you can learn more about the C&O Canal.

WORTH DOING: When the train arrives in Frostburg, you have a 90-minute layover. Be sure to walk forward and find a spot to watch the locomotive change directions on the turntable. You will also have time to walk down Main Street for shopping or dining.

DON'T MISS: Stick to the right side of the train. Leaving Cumberland, the train passes through the Narrows, a gap in the mountain that also allows the highway and paralleling CSX (the former B&O) an escape to the west. Just beyond is famous Helmstetter's Curve, a sharp turn in the railroad tracks. From here on, views remain mostly on the right side as the train makes its way higher into the mountains.

GETTING THERE: When driving, Cumberland is about two-and-a-half hours from Baltimore, Washington, or Pittsburgh. From either direction, the Western Maryland Station is easily reached from Exit 43C off I-68 in downtown Cumberland.

MASSACHUSETTS

Chatham Railroad Museum ❶

This restored country depot is situated on its original site. Museum exhibits feature hundreds of railroad artifacts from the Chatham Railroad Company and other railroads, including a restored 1910 New York Central caboose and telegraph instruments.

SITE LOCATION: 153 Depot Road, Chatham
PHONE: 508-945-5199

Edaville USA ❷

This is a family fun park with a two-mile train ride through a 1300-acre cranberry plantation. There are 11 amusement rides and an indoor play area. Special events include National Cranberry Festival, Holiday Festival of Lights, and many others.

SITE LOCATION: 7 Eda Avenue, South Carver
PHONE: 877-332-8455 or 508-866-8190
WEB SITE: www.edaville.com
E-MAIL: info@edaville.com

Lowell National Historical Park ❸

The park includes a variety of structures related to industry including 5.6 miles of canals and restored mill buildings. It displays a Boston & Maine 0-6-0 Manchester locomotive built in 1910, a combine/tool car, and two open-air trolleys. A trolley ride operates March through November.

SITE LOCATION: 246 Market Street, Lowell
PHONE: 978-970-5000
WEB SITE: www.nps.gov/lowe

Old Colony & Fall River Railroad Museum ❹

The museum, located in railroad cars that include a renovated Pennsylvania Railroad coach, features artifacts of New England railroads such as Penn Central, Conrail, Amtrak, and the New Haven.

SITE LOCATION: 2 Water Street, Fall River
PHONE: 508-674-9340
WEB SITE: www.ocandfrrailroadmuseum.com
E-MAIL: info@ocandfrrailroadmuseum.com

Shelburne Falls Trolley Museum ❺

The museum features a 15-minute trolley ride, complete with an interpretive talk by the motorman. Examine the excellent restoration work on car no. 10, which has been in the area since being built in 1896 (including 65 years as a chicken coop). The museum also displays railroad and trolley artifacts, a steam locomotive, a caboose, and other items.

SITE LOCATION: 14 Depot Street, Shelburne Falls
PHONE: 413-625-9443
WEB SITE: www.sftm.org
E-MAIL: trolley@sftm.org

Berkshire Scenic Railway ⁶

SITE LOCATION: 10 Willow Creek Road, Lenox
PHONE: 413-637-2210
WEB SITE: www.berkshirescenicrailroad.org
E-MAIL: marketing@berkshirescenicrailroad.org

Scott Hartley

The Berkshire Scenic Railway Museum operates excursion trains that follow the scenic Housatonic River over part of the onetime New Haven Railroad's route to Pittsfield. Operations are based out of the railway's beautifully restored New Haven station at Lenox, and trains run to Stockbridge. The adjacent museum includes many pieces of rolling stock.

CHOICES: Berkshire Scenic operates on Saturdays, Sundays, and major holidays from Memorial Day to late October. There are two departure times for a 90-minute, 20-mile round trip to Stockbridge. Well-suited for younger riders, there is also a 45-minute, narrated trip to Lee and back. Trains consist of former Delaware, Lackawanna & Western coaches from the 1920s. Operating locomotives include a former New York Central EMD SW8, an ex-Maine Central Alco S1, a GE 50-ton switcher, and a Housatonic modified EMD RS3.

WHEN TO GO: New England's famed fall foliage peaks in this region in early October. During that time, expect full trains, high lodging rates, and crowded roads. It is less congested at other times.

GOOD TO KNOW: There is abundant lodging in Lenox, Lee, and Pittsfield. The Berkshire Hills are known for skiing, but the area is a year-round tourist destination. Fine dining as well as fast-food chains can be found throughout the region.

WORTH DOING: The museum's Lenox station contains an impressive collection of local railroad historical artifacts. Housed in an old coach on the museum grounds, the Gilded Age exhibit displays the history of this era in Berkshire County.

DON'T MISS: Nearby attractions include weekend concerts at Tanglewood (the summer home of the Boston Symphony), the Hancock Shaker Village, and the Norman Rockwell Museum.

GETTING THERE: The Berkshire Scenic Railway is located near Routes 7 and 20, five miles north of Massachusetts Turnpike (I-90) Exit 2. Amtrak's *Lake Shore Limited* stops daily at nearby Pittsfield. The nearest commercial air service is at Albany, N.Y., or Hartford, Conn.

Cape Cod Central Railroad 7

SITE LOCATION: 252 Main Street, Hyannis
PHONE: 888-797-7245 or 508-771-3800
WEB SITE: www.capetrain.com
E-MAIL: form on Web site

Cape Cod Central

The Cape Cod Central Railroad operates diesel-powered scenic excursions and dinner trains, which also include lunch and brunch outings. It runs from Hyannis over 23 miles of the former Old Colony Railroad that became part of the New York, New Haven & Hartford. Along the way, you'll pass cranberry bogs, forests, and marshes. Boarding is also possible at Sandwich.

CHOICES: For evening dining, passengers can select either the Elegant Dinner Train, involving multiple courses served with all the flourishes, or the Family Supper Train, which offers less formal service, a shorter ride, lower fares, a clown, and special children's meals. The popular Murder Mystery Train, a variation on the Elegant Dinner Train, runs on occasional evenings.

WHEN TO GO: Trains run from mid-May through October in various combinations and with varying frequencies. Sea breezes mean that Hyannis typically remains temperate throughout the railroad's operating season but visiting out of high summer may minimize crowds.

GOOD TO KNOW: Hyannis is quintessential Cape Cod, with all the sun, sand, salt – and tourists. Whale watching, beaching, fishing, golfing, and biking are among the available outdoor activities. The John F. Kennedy Hyannis Museum is located in town. There are many lodging choices and a wide variety of fine restaurants.

WORTH DOING: The railroad offers a package with HyLine Cruises that includes a one-hour boat tour of Hyannis harbor and the Kennedy compound. The boats are little gems: Maine-style coastal steamers *Prudence* (the real McCoy, though now dieselized, built in 1911) and *Patience* (a convincing replica built in 1982).

DON'T MISS: The Elegant Dinner Train offers one decided advantage – in addition to the cuisine – over the other meal trains (and scenic excursions as well). While the other trains are all two hours in length and run briefly along the Cape Cod Canal, only the three-hour Elegant Dinner Train crosses it on a lift bridge into the town of Buzzards Bay. This bridge features outstanding aesthetics and was the longest of its kind when completed in 1935.

GETTING THERE: Hyannis is located on the Atlantic Ocean at the elbow of Cape Cod. Barnstable Municipal Airport hosts commercial flights from Boston and New York.

MICHIGAN

Clinton Northern Railway ❶

Housed in a historic Grand Trunk depot, the museum's artifacts include tools, signs, and station agent items. A 1902 Barney & Smith sleeper car, a 1903 post office-baggage car, and a 1926 Ann Arbor maintenance-of-way crew car are also on display.

SITE LOCATION: 107 E. Railroad Street, St. Johns
PHONE: 989-668-7246
WEB SITE: www.clintonnorthernrailway.org
E-MAIL: form on Web site

Coopersville & Marne Railway ❷

Powered by a 1950s-era diesel locomotive, this railway's 14-mile, 75-minute excursion travels through farmland and crosses an open-deck girder bridge, four creeks, and a highway bridge. Before making the return trip, the engine is uncoupled, run along a passing siding, and coupled to the other end, which makes for fascinating watching.

SITE LOCATION: 311 Danforth Street, Coopersville
PHONE: 616-997-7000
WEB SITE: www.coopersvilleandmarne.org

Durand Union Station ❸

This 100-year-old depot museum was the second busiest depot in Michigan, and its lower level has been restored to its former glory, with terrazzo floors and oak trim. Still functioning as a depot, the building also houses the Michigan Railroad History Museum. The museum contains exhibits showing railroading's role in lumber, mining, agriculture, and other industries.

SITE LOCATION: 200 Railroad Street, Durand
PHONE: 989-288-3561
WEB SITE: www.durandstation.org
E-MAIL: dusi@durandstation.org
DISCOUNT: Flash your *Trains* discount card and grab a goodie bag on your way out!

Flushing Area Museum ❹

The museum's collection includes permanent displays of railroad artifacts as well as local historical exhibits. It is housed in the Flushing depot, which was built in 1888 and provided passenger service until 1971. The building was restored by the Flushing Area Historical Society to its former appearance.

SITE LOCATION: 431 W. Main Street, Flushing
PHONE: 810-487-0814
WEB SITE: www.flushinghistorical.org
E-MAIL: fahs@att.net

Michigan

Houghton County Historical Museum ❺

The museum includes the restored Mineral Range depot, which contains a collection of Copper County railroad artifacts. The museum operates the Lake Linden & Torch Lake Railroad. A narrow gauge, 0-4-0 Porter steam locomotive takes you on a half-mile ride. It is open June through September.

SITE LOCATION: 53102 Highway M-26, Lake Linden
PHONE: 906-296-4121
WEB SITE: www.houghtonhistory.org
E-MAIL: president@houghtonhistory.org

Michigan Transit Museum ❻

The Michigan Transit Museum is housed in a depot restored to its 1900 appearance and includes railroading exhibits from that time. The museum's train leaves Joy Park for a 45-minute ride around the Selfridge Air Museum, which you can also visit. The train features a diesel switcher and South Shore car no. 11. The transit museum is open year-round, and trains run June through September.

SITE LOCATION: 200 Grand Avenue, Mount Clemens
PHONE: 586-463-1863
WEB SITE: www.michigantransitmuseum.org
E-MAIL: info@michigantransitmuseum.org

Old Road Dinner Train 🔳

The train provides fine dining and fun entertainment from two locations, Blissfield and Charlotte. The murder mystery dinner trains provide a five-course dinner as you participate in a comical, interactive mystery show. Saturday excursions out of Blissfield along a segment of the Erie & Kalamazoo Railroad are also offered.

SITE LOCATION: 301 E. Adrian Street, Blissfield
PHONE: 888-467-2451
WEB SITE: www.murdermysterytrain.com
E-MAIL: reservations@murdermysterytrain.com

Saginaw Railway Museum 🔳

Located in a restored 1907 Pere Marquette Railway depot, this museum displays GP-9, RS1, and GE 25-ton locomotives, three cabooses, a combine coach, and various boxcars. It includes an 1898 Armstrong interlocking tower as well as a variety of smaller artifacts.

SITE LOCATION: 900 Maple Street, Saginaw
PHONE: 989-790-7994
WEB SITE: www.saginawrailwaymuseum.org
E-MAIL: info@saginawrailwaymuseum.org

Southern Michigan Railroad 🔳

The railroad offers nostalgic train tours over the remaining track of the early Palmyra and Jacksonburgh Railroad. Train tours are offered through the late spring and fall seasons with holiday trips available. The museum, which focuses on the Clinton Branch, is open Saturdays from mid-May through September.

SITE LOCATION: 320 S. Division Street, Clinton
PHONE: 517-456-7677
WEB SITE: www.southernmichiganrailroad.org
E-MAIL: trains@southernmichiganrailroad.org

SS City of Milwaukee ❿

The SS *City of Milwaukee*, a national historic landmark, is the last surviving traditional Great Lakes railroad car ferry. Built in 1931, the *City of Milwaukee* served the Grand Trunk Western and Ann Arbor Railroads. The car deck houses five Ann Arbor boxcars that serve as exhibit spaces and a theater. Both 30- and 60-minute tours are offered.

SITE LOCATION: 99 Arthur Street, Manistee
PHONE: 231-723-3587
WEB SITE: www.carferry.com
E-MAIL: form on Web site

Train Travel ⓫

This group operates three different trains offering a variety of rail experiences. The Michigan Star Clipper Dinner Train prepares five-course meals onboard. The Steel Wheels Entertainment Train provides a unique venue for comedy, music, and dancing. The Walled Lake Scenic Railway offers excursions aboard open-air coaches.

SITE LOCATION: 840 N Pontiac Trail, Walled Lake
PHONE: 248-960-9440
WEB SITE: www.rail-road.com

Tri-Cities Historical Museum ⓬

The Tri-Cities Historical Museum operates out of two buildings including a former Grand Trunk Western depot. Located on the banks of the Grand River, the depot museum, built in 1871, contains two floors of railroad and local historical artifacts. On display is a Pere Marquette Railway steam locomotive.

SITE LOCATION: 1 North Harbor Drive, Grand Haven
PHONE: 616-842-0700
WEB SITE: www.tri-citiesmuseum.org

Greenfield Village at the Henry Ford ⑬

SITE LOCATION: 20900 Oakwood Boulevard, Dearborn
PHONE: 800-835-5237 or 313-982-6001
WEB SITE: www.thehenryford.org

Jim Wrinn

The Henry Ford claims to be America's greatest history attraction, and even though it's in the capital of, and shrine to, the automobile, railroads are well represented here. The centerpiece for this is the Detroit, Toledo & Milwaukee Roundhouse, a reconstruction of the original in Marshall, Mich., believed to be one of only seven 19th century roundhouses remaining. A steam railroad encircles the historic 90-acre village.

CHOICES: You can ride the train around the village in open-air cars on a 30-minute narrated trip. Departing from the 1859 Smiths Creek depot, the train also makes stops at strategic locations throughout the village. The roundhouse includes hands-on railroading displays and a 1902 Atlantic engine. A mezzanine provides an excellent vantage point from where you can see work going on. Also, be sure to go inside the Henry Ford museum to view railroad cars and locomotives, including an Alleghany type, one of the largest steam locomotives ever built.

WHEN TO GO: Greenfield Village is open daily mid-April through October. From November through December, it is open Friday through Sunday. It is closed the remainder of the year.

GOOD TO KNOW: Henry Ford had his own railroads: one to switch his car plant and another, the Detroit, Toledo & Ironton, to move parts as well as finished product.

WORTH DOING: Railroad Junction, where the roundhouse and depot are located, is one of seven different historic districts in Greenfield Village. In Henry Ford's Model T, District, you can tour a replica of Ford's first factory and ride in a Model T.

DON'T MISS: Get to the roundhouse early in the day to help the crew turn the steam engine on the turntable. It's so well balanced that two people can do it, but it's more fun when you get to push a giant engine around.

GETTING THERE: Just west of Detroit, the Henry Ford is located in Dearborn on the corner of Village Road and Oakwood Boulevard, just west of the Southfield Freeway and south of Michigan Avenue (Highway 12). There is easy access from I-94 or I-75. You may also ride an Amtrak train to the museum.

Huckleberry Railroad

SITE LOCATION: 6140 Bray Road, Flint
PHONE: 800-648-7275 or 810-736-7100
WEB SITE: www.geneseecountyparks.org
E-MAIL: parkswebteam@gcparks.org

Jim Wrinn

The Huckleberry Railroad is part of a historical village that is operated by Genesee County Parks in Flint. The narrow gauge railroad is built on an abandoned Pere Marquette Railway right-of-way. An eight-mile, 35-minute ride carries passengers through neighborhoods, by a lake, and into wooded areas.

CHOICES: Ride in one of the railroad's historic coaches or cabooses pulled by a Baldwin 4-6-0 or a Baldwin 2-8-2, two of the seven locomotives owned by the Huckleberry Railroad.

WHEN TO GO: Trains run Memorial Day weekend through Labor Day, with special trains throughout the year. During the railroad's railfan weekend, usually held in August, you can see all the trains, get good photos, and talk with the train crews.

GOOD TO KNOW: The Huckleberry Railroad was named because it ran so slow that a person could jump off the train, pick some huckleberries, and jump back on the train without breaking a sweat.

WORTH DOING: Look for Rio Grande 2-8-2 no. 464, one of a rare class of narrow gauge Mikado type steam locomotives on the Colorado railroad. Built in 1903 and restored in 2005, it was nicknamed *Mudhen* because it waddled like a chicken as it went down the tracks.

DON'T MISS: Take a stroll through Crossroads Village, which has 34 historic structures on 51 acres. Costumed interpreters welcome you to the homes, mills, and shops that date back to the 1800s. Special events are scheduled throughout the summer, and you can take a ride on a paddle-wheel riverboat.

GETTING THERE: The railroad is located just north of Flint, about an hour from Detroit. From Detroit, take I-75 to I-475. Follow I-475 north to Saginaw Street (Exit 13). Take Saginaw Street north to Stanley Road, turn east on Stanley Road, and then turn south on Bray Road to the village and railroad.

Little River Railroad 15

SITE LOCATION: 29 W. Park Avenue, Coldwater
PHONE: 260-316-0529
WEB SITE: www.littleriverrailroad.com
E-MAIL: customerservice@littleriverrailroad.com

Jim Wrinn

Whoever said bigger is better never visited the Little River Railroad. This railroad is home to one of the smallest standard gauge steam locomotives of its type ever built. No. 110 is a 57-ton Pacific that has all the charm of a ballerina, and the railroad offers 90-minute trips behind it from Coldwater to nearby Quincy.

CHOICES: Ride in a coach or open-air car. During the 30-minute layover in Quincy, be sure to exit the train and watch as the locomotive is switched to the other end of the train. At times, a second locomotive, 0-4-0T no. 1 is in service.

WHEN TO GO: Trains run weekends Memorial Day through September. During Train Fest, on Labor Day weekend, Little River runs both of its engines as well as a motor car. The railroad offers a variety of special events throughout the year including a photo run, pumpkin trains, haunted trains, and the Holiday Express.

GOOD TO KNOW: Engine no. 110 started out on the Little River Railroad in east Tennessee. An Indiana family, the Blooms, rescued and rebuilt it for excursion work in the 1970s, and members of that same family continue this tradition of preservation.

WORTH DOING: The area features many antique shops and preserved buildings. In Coldwater, take in a film at the Capri Drive-in, one of the last of its kind.

DON'T MISS: Take time to look over the exhibits in the Coldwater depot, an 1883 Lake Shore and Michigan Southern depot.

GETTING THERE: Coldwater is in south-central Michigan. Take I-69 to Exit 13 for Coldwater. Follow Highway 12 west, turn left onto Division Street, and then turn right onto Park Avenue to the depot.

Steam Railroading Institute ⓰

SITE LOCATION: 405 S. Washington Street, Owosso
PHONE: 989-725-9464
WEB SITE: www.mstrp.com
E-MAIL: mfolland@mstrp.com

Jim Wrinn

The Steam Railroading Institute is all about preserving steam locomotives, and there is always restoration work going on. The institute displays equipment and offers some train rides.

CHOICES: The seven-acre site includes a roundhouse and turntable. Weekends during the summer, Flagg Coal Company 0-4-0T no. 75 operates on short trips. Built in 1930, this small tank engine is typical of many industrial locomotives used across the land.

WHEN TO GO: In November and December, the North Pole Express is the big event, as the Pere Marquette no. 1225 takes visitors on a 24-mile round trip to the North Pole, where kids can enjoy a variety of activities. It is recommended that you reserve tickets far in advance as the trains sell out quickly. During TrainFestival 2009 (July 24-26), Pere Marquette no. 1225 will be joined by Nickel Plate Road steam locomotive no. 765, and both locomotives will pull excursions.

GOOD TO KNOW: The Pere Marquette 2-8-4 no. 1225 was the model and sound effects machine for the steam train in the movie *Polar Express*. It shows what a modern (1941) mainline steam locomotive is all about.

WORTH DOING: The Michigan Railroad History Museum is housed in historic Durand Union Station, 20 minutes away in Durand.

DON'T MISS: Look around the visitor center, which is housed in a renovated freight warehouse that was also a creamery. It now contains exhibits, artifacts, and a model train layout.

GETTING THERE: Owosso is about 30 miles northeast of Lansing and 30 miles west of Flint. From Flint, take Highway 21 west to Owosso. From Lansing, take I-69 to Highway 52 north to Owosso. In Owosso, the Steam Railroading Institute is on south Washington Street.

MINNESOTA

Depot Museum ❶

Located in the 1907 headquarters of the Duluth & Iron Range Railroad, this museum highlights the early history of Lake County. The Lake County Historical Society operates the museum and displays a Mallet steam locomotive and a Baldwin 3 Spot. The museum is open daily May through October and then on weekends through December.

SITE LOCATION: 520 South Avenue, Two Harbors
PHONE: 218-834-4898
WEB SITE: www.northshorehistory.com/sites/depot
E-MAIL: lakehist@lakenet.com

End-O-Line Railroad Park & Museum ❷

End-O-Line Railroad Park is a working railroad yard that includes a 1901 manually operated turntable, a rebuilt engine house on its original foundation, an original four-room depot, a water tower, an 1899 section foreman's house, a Grand Trunk Western caboose, and two steam locomotives. Open Memorial Day to Labor Day, it also includes other historical buildings.

SITE LOCATION: 440 N. Mill Street, Currie
PHONE: 507-763-3708
WEB SITE: www.endoline.com
E-MAIL: endoline@co.murray.mn.us

Iron Horse Central Railroad Museum ❸

Housed in an 1895 St. Paul & Duluth station, the museum displays more than 20 historic railcars. It is open Saturdays June through October. The *Bumblebee*, a homebuilt, yellow-and-black motor car, operates in a loop around the museum, and a steam locomotive runs on special occasions.

SITE LOCATION: 24880 Morgan Avenue, Chisago City
PHONE: 651-336-4531

Ironworld ❹

The center offers a 2.4-mile trolley ride to a re-created mine location. The round trip, aboard a 1928 Melbourne trolley, offers fascinating views of the Pillsbury mine. Preserving Iron Range history, Ironworld includes a museum, outdoor exhibits, and restored buildings. The site is open year-round, but trolleys operate May through October.

SITE LOCATION: 801 SW Highway 169, Chisholm
PHONE: 800-372-6437 or 218-254-7959
WEB SITE: www.ironworld.com
E-MAIL: beth.pierce@ironworld.com

Minnehaha Depot ❺

Located in Minnehaha Park, the tiny Minnehaha depot's architecture features delicate gingerbread details. Built in 1875, the building replaced an earlier Milwaukee Road depot on the first line into the Twin Cities from Chicago. Managed by the Minnesota Transportation Museum, the depot is open Sundays Memorial Day weekend through Labor Day.

SITE LOCATION: Highway 55 and Minnehaha Parkway, Minneapolis
PHONE: 651-228-0263
WEB SITE: www.mtmuseum.org
E-MAIL: admin@mtmuseum.org

Minnesota Streetcar Museum ❻

This museum operates two different streetcar lines from May through November. Located southwest of downtown Minneapolis, the Como-Harriet line runs between Lake Harriet and Lake Calhoun. The Excelsior line is about 15 miles west of downtown Minneapolis. The museum exhibits electric streetcars that ran in the state.

SITE LOCATION: 2330 W. 42nd Street, Minneapolis
PHONE: 952-922-1096
WEB SITE: www.trolleyride.org
E-MAIL: info@msmuseum.org

Old Depot Railroad Museum ❼

A former Great Northern depot, this museum contains two floors of artifacts and memorabilia. Displays include telegraph equipment, tools, signs, uniforms, and lanterns. Authentic railroad sounds add to your experience. You can also hop aboard a wooden caboose and sit in the brakeman's seat. The museum is open Memorial Day through September.

SITE LOCATION: 651 W. Highway 12, Dassel
PHONE: 320-275-3876
WEB SITE: www.theolddepot.com
E-MAIL: dasseldepot@hotmail.com

Jackson Street Roundhouse ⑧

SITE LOCATION: 193 E. Pennsylvania Avenue, St. Paul
PHONE: 651-228-0263
WEB SITE: www.trainride.org
E-MAIL: admin@mtmuseum.org

Steve Glischinski

The former Great Northern Jackson Street Roundhouse was built in 1907 to service passenger locomotives. Closed in 1959, the roundhouse was converted to nonrailroad use and the tracks removed. In 1985, it was purchased by the Minnesota Transportation Museum and renovations began. One of the highlights was the reinstallation of the turntable and installation of new roundhouse doors built to the 1906 blueprint specs.

CHOICES: Visitors can roam the roundhouse and the outdoor grounds, take a short caboose ride pulled by a switch engine, and participate in interactive exhibits. Tours of the roundhouse where equipment restoration takes place are also available. Included in the collection are three Northern Pacific steam locomotives and Great Northern no. 400, the first production SD45 owned by the GN Historical Society. On Saturdays, take a ride on the miniature *Rock Island Rocket*, a perfect replica of the *Twin Star Rocket*. It was built in 1947 by Larry Sauter, a high school industrial arts teacher.

WHEN TO GO: The museum is open Wednesdays and Saturdays year-round, but it can be chilly inside the roundhouse in the winter – and downright cold outside. Summer or early fall are the best times to visit.

GOOD TO KNOW: St. Paul and Minneapolis have a wide diversity of restaurants and hotels for any taste and budget.

WORTH DOING: Walk inside the cab of Dan Patch Lines no. 100, built in 1913 by General Electric, and you've walked into history. It is one of the first locomotives that used an internal combustion engine and is the granddaddy of today's diesel locomotives.

DON'T MISS: After taking in the roundhouse, you can learn more about the Great Northern Railway by visiting the St. Paul home of James J. Hill, who founded the Great Northern. His mansion was completed in 1891 and was the largest and most expensive home in Minnesota at the time. The Minnesota Historical Society now owns it.

GETTING THERE: The Twin Cities of Minneapolis and St. Paul have Amtrak, airline, and bus service. The roundhouse is located north of the Minnesota State Capitol. Take the Pennsylvania Avenue exit off I-35E and drive west two blocks to the roundhouse.

DISCOUNT: $2 off each adult ticket, up to four adults.

Lake Superior & Mississippi Railroad 9

SITE LOCATION: Grand Avenue and Fremont Street, Duluth

PHONE: 218-624-7549

WEB SITE: www.lsmrr.org

E-MAIL: info@lsmrr.org

Jim Wrenn

Here's a laid-back operation that is a great complement to the marshlands near Duluth. A 90-minute ride on this railroad is a great way to relax and enjoy nature along the St. Louis River estuary, Spirit Lake, and Mud Lake.

CHOICES: While taking in the scenery and wildlife when riding in a restored, open-window coach, you can listen to narration of the area's rich history. The coaches, built in 1912, operated between the Iron Range and Duluth. For a truly outdoor experience, ride the Safari Car, a converted flat car. Power is provided by a General Electric industrial switcher built in 1946.

WHEN TO GO: Excursions operate on Saturdays and Sundays, beginning in June and running until October.

GOOD TO KNOW: The railroad takes its name from the first line built between the Twin Cities and Duluth, and it uses some of that line's original track.

WORTH DOING: Visit the nearby Lake Superior Railroad Museum or some of the many other museums in the area.

DON'T MISS: Keep your eyes on the marshes for egrets.

GETTING THERE: Duluth is on Lake Superior, about 150 miles from the Twin Cities. In Duluth, exit I-35 at Cody Street, turn right onto 63rd Avenue, and then turn right onto Grand Avenue to Fremont Street.

Lake Superior Railroad Museum ⑩

SITE LOCATION: 506 W. Michigan Street, Duluth
PHONE: 800-423-1273 or 218-722-1273
WEB SITE: www.lsrm.org
E-MAIL: form on Web site

Jim Wrinn

This is a combination of a great railroad museum and a great train ride. The Lake Superior Railroad Museum is located in the historic depot in downtown Duluth. Its extensive rolling stock collection rests in the train shed, and just outside, excursion trains ply the route to Two Harbors, with outstanding views along the way.

CHOICES: The Lake Superior Railroad Museum has a large collection of railroad equipment that changes annually. It includes steam, diesel, and electric locomotives as well as passenger coaches, freight cars, and cabooses. Much of the equipment was used on Minnesota railroads, including the first locomotive operated in the state. The museum also operates the North Shore Scenic Railroad, which conducts regular excursions as well as special trains. A 90-minute excursion runs along the shores of Lake Superior to Lester River. The six-hour round trip through the countryside to Two Harbors takes you over seven bridges. Also operating are an elegant dinner train, a pizza train, and other specials.

WHEN TO GO: The museum is open year-round, with extended summer hours, and regular excursions are offered late May through mid-October.

GOOD TO KNOW: Soo Line 4-6-2 steam locomotive no. 2719 has been restored and is back in service. One of its runs is a fall foliage trip to Two Harbors.

WORTH DOING: Take time to tour historic Union Depot. Admission to the Lake Superior Railroad Museum also admits you to three other museums in the building: the Duluth Children's Museum, Duluth Art Institute, and St. Louis County Historical Society.

DON'T MISS: Take a close look at the *William Crooks*, the first locomotive operated in Minnesota. Built in 1861, it is one of a handful of engines remaining from before the Civil War. Climb into the cab of the Duluth, Missabe, and Iron Range Railroad Yellowstone type locomotive and pause a few minutes. The clever museum folks have set up the engine so that its massive drivers and running gear rotate periodically.

GETTING THERE: Situated on Lake Superior, Duluth is about 150 miles from the Twin Cities. To reach the museum, take Exit 256 off I-35 and follow Michigan Street to the depot.

Milwaukee Road 261 11

SITE LOCATION: 401 Harrison Street, Minneapolis
PHONE: 651-765-9812
WEB SITE: www.261.com

Ernie Mastroianni

The Friends of the 261 operate mainline excursion trips around the Midwest pulled by former Milwaukee Road steam locomotive no. 261, a 4-8-4 built by American Locomotive Company in 1944. The locomotive was donated to the National Railroad Museum in Green Bay, Wis., in 1956. Leased from the museum, the 261 was returned to active service in 1993 and has operated at least one excursion every year since restoration.

CHOICES: The Friends of the 261 offer several options for passengers. All trips include coach, first-class, and premium-class services. Premium-class includes hors d'oeuvres and gourmet meals prepared onboard and a ride in one of two former Milwaukee Road Hiawatha cars: Skytop lounge observation *Cedar Rapids* and full-length Super Dome no. 53. First-class includes an upscale meal plan with hors d'oeuvres and a ride in parlor or lounge cars. Both first- and premium-class include complimentary beverages.

WHEN TO GO: Generally, 261 pulls trips as early as May and as late as October. One of the most popular and scenic routes is along the Mississippi River between Minneapolis and Winona operated in early autumn when the leaves begin to change.

GOOD TO KNOW: Trains usually leave from the 261 shop facility in northeast Minneapolis. Head down to the shop in Minneapolis the evening before a trip just to take in the sights and sounds of a large steam engine at night. Usually the crew has a donation box out, and for a small price, you can have a look in the cab.

WORTH DOING: Downtown Minneapolis is near the 261 shop and has a variety of hotels and restaurants. For a complete Milwaukee Road experience, stay in one of the two hotels at the former Milwaukee Road Minneapolis passenger depot, built in 1898 and beautifully restored. Rail memorabilia and photographs can be found throughout the building.

DON'T MISS: Get a look at Skytop lounge observation car *Cedar Rapids*. Built by the Milwaukee Road in 1948, with their large glass area, the Skytops were unlike any other rail passenger car. The *Cedar Rapids* is the only Skytop still in operation.

GETTING THERE: Minneapolis-St. Paul has Amtrak, airline, light rail transit, and bus service. A short walk from the Metro Transit bus stop at Central Avenue and Broadway will get you to the shop, or you can take a taxi. Ample parking is available at the shop on excursion days.

MISSISSIPPI

Water Valley Casey Jones Railroad Museum ❶

The museum displays many of the artifacts from the defunct Casey Jones Railroad Museum State Park at Vaughan. The museum contains railroad memorabilia and photos and displays rolling stock. It is open Thursdays, Fridays, and Saturdays.

SITE LOCATION: 105 Railroad Avenue, Water Valley
PHONE: 662-473-1154
WEB SITE: www.watervalley.net/users/caseyjones/home.htm
E-MAIL: jgurner@watervalley.net

MISSOURI

Belton, Grandview & Kansas City Railroad 1

At this laid-back railroad, you can walk around the yard, look at displayed equipment, and talk to the crew before boarding a five-mile excursion. The 45-minute round trip runs south from Belton. Rides in the caboose with the conductor or in the locomotive with the engineer are also available.

SITE LOCATION: 502 E. Walnut Street, Belton
PHONE: 816-331-0630
WEB SITE: www.beltonrailroad.org
E-MAIL: info@beltonrailroad.org

Branson Scenic Railway 2

This railway operates a 40-mile round trip through the Ozark foothills and southwest Missouri wilderness. The train takes you over trestles and through tunnels into areas only accessible by rail, as narration describes landmarks, abandoned towns, and wildlife, before you return to the original 1905 Branson depot. The railway also operates dinner trains.

SITE LOCATION: 206 E. Main Street, Branson
PHONE: 800-287-2462 or 417-334-6110
WEB SITE: www.bransontrain.com
E-MAIL: form on Web site

Chicago & Alton Railroad Depot 3

Built in 1879, the restored, two-story Chicago & Alton Railroad depot features a four room stationmaster's residence on the second floor. Each room is furnished in the period. The first floor contains two original restored Railway Express baggage carts, railroad tools, equipment, and many other items. The depot is open April through October, and guided tours are available.

SITE LOCATION: 318 W. Pacific Avenue, Independence
PHONE: 816-325-7955
WEB SITE: www.chicagoalton1879depot.com

KC Rail Experience ❹

Located in historic Union Station, the KC Rail Experience features several vintage railcars, artifacts, and a locomotive simulator. Enhancing the experience are 20 ghostly figures from the station's past that tell the story of the men and women of the railroads.

SITE LOCATION: 30 W. Pershing Road, Kansas City
PHONE: 877-724-2489 or 816-460-2000
WEB SITE: www.unionstation.org
E-MAIL: visitor@unionstation.org

Railroad Historical Museum ❺

Located in Grant Beach Park, this train museum is an actual train. A locomotive, baggage car, commuter car, and caboose contain artifacts from the St. Louis-San Francisco and other railroads. After touring the museum, you can enjoy the park's pool, playground, and picnic area. It is open Saturdays May through October.

SITE LOCATION: 1300 N. Grant Street, Springfield
PHONE: 417-882-9106
WEB SITE: www.rrhistoricalmuseum.zoomshare.com

St. Louis Iron Mountain & Southern Railway ❻

From April through December, this railway offers a variety of trips including sightseeing excursions, murder mysteries, train robberies, and holiday-themed rides. Trains are pulled by a 1950 EMD E8 diesel.

SITE LOCATION: Highway 61 at Highway 25, Jackson
PHONE: 800-455-7245 or 573-243-1688
WEB SITE: www.slimrr.com
E-MAIL: cherjxmo@aol.com

Museum of Transportation ❼

SITE LOCATION: 3015 Barrett Station Road, St Louis
PHONE: 314-615-8668
WEB SITE: www.museumoftransport.org

Museum of Transportation

If you want to be surrounded by trains, this is the place. A visit here brings you in touch with more than 70 locomotives of steam, diesel, and electric power. You'll see scores of railcars and even see one of the first railroad tunnels west of the Mississippi. The 150-acre site also houses airplanes, cars, and riverboats.

CHOICES: The museum features miles of switching and exhibition track and includes 10 buildings. Its collection of more than 30 steam locomotives is one of the largest around, and stairs let you climb into the cabs of many of them. Many rare and unusual items grace the site, including the world's largest tank car, an Aerotrain, and even a cast-iron turntable. A miniature train also operates.

WHEN TO GO: The museum is open year-round. It is open daily during its summer schedule, which begins in May and runs through Labor Day. During the rest of the year, the museum is open Tuesday through Sunday.

GOOD TO KNOW: Operated as a county park, the museum is located on the site of a manmade railroad tunnel that was used by the Missouri Pacific Railroad from 1853 until 1944 and is now listed on the National Register of Historic Places.

WORTH DOING: Climb into the cab of the Union Pacific Big Boy no. 4006 and see what it felt like to be the engineer on one of the world's largest steam locomotives. And climb aboard Santa Fe no. 5011 and ring the engine's bell.

DON'T MISS: View the Union Pacific Centennial type diesel no. 6944. It's the modern equivalent of the Big Boy with two diesel engines, 6,600 horsepower, and a length of 98 feet. Also, be sure and check out the FT demonstrator no. 103. It was the first mainline diesel locomotive built for freight service in North America back in 1939. Its national tour proved the worth of diesel power and launched a full change of power from steam to diesel.

GETTING THERE: The museum is about 12 miles west of downtown St. Louis. When driving from I-270, either north or south, exit at Dougherty Ferry Road (Exit 8), go west about one mile to Barrett Station Road, and turn left. The museum is on the right.

MONTANA

Charlie Russell Chew-Choo Dinner Train ■

This dinner train takes you on a 3.5-hour excursion over the old Chicago, Milwaukee, St. Paul & Pacific Railroad line from Kingston Junction to Denton. The ride crosses three historic trestles, passes through a 2,000-foot tunnel, and travels through the land that inspired artist Charles Russell. Along the way, you'll enjoy a catered prime rib dinner. Just keep your eyes open for masked bandits! North Pole runs take place in December.

SITE LOCATION: 211 E. Main Street, Lewistown
PHONE: 866-912-3980 or 406-538-8969
WEB SITE: www.montanacharlierussellchewchoo.com
E-MAIL: lewchamb@midrivers.com

Historical Museum at Fort Missoula ❷

Located in Fort Missoula, the Historical Museum includes 13 structures that depict the area's history. One is the Drummond depot, which was constructed by the Chicago, Milwaukee, St. Paul & Pacific Railroad in 1910. Fort Missoula is on the National Register of Historic Places.

SITE LOCATION: South Avenue, Missoula
PHONE: 406-728-3476
WEB SITE: www.fortmissoulamuseum.org
E-MAIL: ftmslamuseum@montana.com

Alder Gulch Short Line [3]

SITE LOCATION: Wallace Street, Virginia City
PHONE: 406-843-5247
WEB SITE: www.virginiacitymt.com

Joe King

The Alder Gulch Short Line is one of three operating 30-inch gauge tourist railroads in the United States. This narrow gauge railroad connects the former gold mining towns of Virginia City and Nevada City. The line winds along Alder Creek, where you can view the remains of gold mining operations, dredge tailings, and a variety of wildlife. Grades approaching 4 percent challenge the little line.

CHOICES: Steam trains run weekends and holidays throughout the summer, while a gas-powered train operates on weekdays. Passengers may board the train at the depots in both Virginia City or Nevada City for either a one-way ride or a three-mile round trip. A round-trip ticket includes access to a walking tour of the historic collection of Western buildings and displays in Nevada City. Also, round-trip passengers can lay over at either terminal, look around, and complete their trips later in the day.

WHEN TO GO: The operating season runs between Memorial Day and Labor Day weekends. Occasional moonlight rides are scheduled during the season.

GOOD TO KNOW: The line was completely rebuilt in the late 1990s when heavier motive power arrived. If you are interested in the Old West, mining, architecture, and history, plan on spending several hours exploring each town. With more than 100 historic buildings, Virginia City is one of best-preserved mining towns in the West.

WORTH DOING: Visit the historic Livingston depot, built in 1902, that provided access to Yellowstone National Park. The Italianate-style depot has been restored as a local museum. If interested in mining, the World Museum of Mining in Butte is located on a mining site. It features more than 50 structures, including a re-created mining town.

DON'T MISS: The Alder Gulch Short Line is situated in scenic southwest Montana. Camping, fly-fishing, golf, day drives, hiking, biking, horse pack trips, nature watching, and gold-panning opportunities abound. The wonders of Yellowstone Park are also nearby.

GETTING THERE: Virginia City is located on Highway 287 approximately 80 miles south of Butte, and the Alder Gulch Short Line is located south of I-90 and east of I-15.

DISCOUNT: 10% discount at the gift store and 10% off each train ticket, up to four tickets.

Copper King Express 4

SITE LOCATION: 300 W. Commercial Avenue, Anaconda
PHONE: 877-563-5458 or 406-563-5458
WEB SITE: www.copperkingexpress.com
E-MAIL: copperkingtours@yahoo.com

Mike Harbour

The *Copper King Express* is an excursion through the Butte and Anaconda area, where you'll see structures and other reminders of early settlers. The world's largest smokestack on the Anaconda smelter can be seen 20 miles away.

CHOICES: The recently refurbished coach cars, fit for a copper king, offer a comfortable ride on the three-hour round trip that runs to Ramsay through rugged Durant Canyon. The story of the Butte, Anaconda & Pacific Railroad is shown in a video on the train and in the railroad's museum.

WHEN TO GO: The *Copper King Express* operates on Saturdays May though September. Going earlier or later in the season lessens the chance of having hazy skies from Western wildfires. From June to August, Big Sky Country often turns brown, both from lack of rain and smoke. In November and December, the North Pole Express operates.

GOOD TO KNOW: Anaconda has come a long way from the rough-and-tumble company town it used to be, and now visitors can find a nice assortment of shops and restaurants. It might seem out of place, but one of the top examples of Art Deco style can be found in Anaconda's Washoe Theater, which is filled with silver, gold, and, of course, copper furnishings and details.

WORTH DOING: There are plenty of camping and hiking opportunities in the nearby Beaverhead-Deerlodge National Forest, and fishermen can drop a line in Georgetown Lake a few miles west of Anaconda or in the numerous trout streams found throughout the area. Take a road trip west to Philipsburg and head up to the Granite Ghost Town State Park and step back in time.

DON'T MISS: Take a look through the railway's museum, which is housed in a working roundhouse, one of the few still in operation.

GETTING THERE: Regional jets fly into Butte, the closest airport of note, but flying into Missoula and Helena offer more choices, but with a longer drive to Anaconda. Anaconda is about 20 miles from Butte off I-90. Exit at Highway 1, which runs into Anaconda and becomes Commercial Avenue. The railroad is eight blocks past Main Street.

NEBRASKA

Durham Museum ❶

Built in 1931, Omaha's Union Station is a beautiful example of Art Deco style. This historic railroad station now houses permanent and traveling historical exhibits. Rail displays include an 1890 steam locomotive, a streetcar, and a variety of railcars. Be sure to have a malt, ice cream soda, or phosphate at the restored soda fountain as travelers did in 1931.

SITE LOCATION: 801 S. 10th Street, Omaha
PHONE: 402-444-5071
WEB SITE: www.durhammuseum.org
E-MAIL: info@durhammuseum.org

Fremont & Elkhorn Valley Railroad ❷

This excursion train runs over a route laid out in 1869. The railroad offers a 16-mile round trip from Fremont to Nickerson. Diesel locomotives pull vintage railcars across historic territory. Excursions operate on weekends May through October. The Fremont Dinner Train also operates over the railroad's track. Visit the Nebraska Railroad Museum, which is located on site.

SITE LOCATION: 1835 N. Somers Avenue, Fremont
PHONE: 402-727-0615
WEB SITE: www.fremontrailroad.com
E-MAIL: fevr@fremontrailroad.com

Golden Spike Tower ❸

You can experience the sights and sounds of the Union Pacific's Bailey Yard from two distinct views. As the world's largest reclassification yard, Bailey Yard handles 10,000 cars every day. You can watch from a fully enclosed area 95 feet above the ground or from an open viewing platform seven stories high. The tower also displays UP and local artifacts. It is open daily except for major holidays.

SITE LOCATION: 1249 N. Homestead Road, North Platte
PHONE: 308-532-9920
WEB SITE: www.goldenspiketower.com
E-MAIL: info@goldenspiketower.com
DISCOUNT: $1 off each adult ticket, up to four adults.

Rock Island Depot Railroad Museum ❹

The museum is located in one of the state's only remaining Rock Island depots. Built in 1914, the building also housed the railroad's Western Division Headquarters. The collection features Rock Island artifacts and a restored baggage room. The site also includes the original freight house and gardens.

SITE LOCATION: 910 Bacon Road, Fairbury
PHONE: 402-729-5131
WEB SITE: www.jeffersoncountyhistory.com
E-MAIL: fairburyridepot@alltel.net

Stuhr Museum of the Prairie Pioneer ❺

This interactive museum takes you back to an 1890s railroad town with more than 60 restored buildings. During the summer, townspeople dressed in period clothing demonstrate daily life on the Plains. A 1901 steam locomotive, a 1912 caboose, an 1871 coach, and other railcars are on display.

SITE LOCATION: 3133 W. Highway 34, Grand Island
PHONE: 308-385-5316
WEB SITE: www.stuhrmuseum.org
E-MAIL: info@sturhmuseum.org

Trails & Rails Museum ❻

The Rails portion of the museum includes an 1898 Union Pacific depot. The depot houses transportation exhibits, and its waiting room and ticket office have been restored. On display are a 2-8-0 Baldwin steam engine, a UP flatcar, a caboose, and other equipment. Open year-round, the museum features other historic buildings including the distinctive Freighters Hotel.

SITE LOCATION: 710 W. 11th Street, Kearney
PHONE: 308-234-3041
WEB SITE: www.bchs.us/museum.html
E-MAIL: bchs@bchs.us

NEVADA

Nevada Northern Railway ■

SITE LOCATION: 1100 Avenue A, East Ely
PHONE: 866-407-8326 or 775-289-2085
WEB SITE: www.nevadanorthernrailway.net
E-MAIL: info@nnry.com

Peter Hansen

The Nevada Northern is often hailed as the best-preserved standard gauge railroad in the country. The operating railway museum is headquartered on a 56-acre complex with 66 historic buildings, set amid the vastness of the Great Basin. The Nevada Northern was completed in 1906 to haul copper from area mines and smelters to the outside world. Most cars and locomotives have been on the railroad since the first day of their service lives, and they're maintained in the company's own shops.

CHOICES: The Nevada Northern offers something for everyone, railfan or not. Steam engines run weekends between April and October. The railroad operates a variety of special and seasonal trains, including barbecue trains, wine trains, and a Halloween ghost train that features stories from the region's colorful past. The railway's roster includes three steam engines, wooden passenger cars, a steam-powered rotary plow, and a steam-powered wrecking crane. Structures include the original depot, engine house, freight shed, coaling tower, and water tower. Diesels include everything from an SD9 to a Baldwin VO1000 and a trio of Alco RS-model road switchers.

WHEN TO GO: Summer is busy, with trains running daily, except on Tuesday. Temperatures are usually in the 80s. The railroad operates from mid-April through December.

GOOD TO KNOW: An annual highlight for photographers is the Winter Steam Spectacular that is held in January or February. Cold, dry desert air often makes for spectacular photos.

WORTH DOING: The shop tour, which is included with every train ticket, features any historic equipment that's not on the road at the time of your visit.

DON'T MISS: Visit Great Basin National Park, which is 60 miles from Ely. In this diverse environment, you'll see 13,000-foot-tall mountains, 5,000-year-old bristlecone pines, and Lehman Caves.

GETTING THERE: Ely is in east-central Nevada at the junction of Highways 6, 50, and 93. Amtrak's *California Zephyr* stops at Elko, 188 miles away.

DISCOUNT: Buy one adult ticket and get one free.

Nevada Southern Railway 2

SITE LOCATION: 600 Yucca Street, Boulder City
PHONE: 702-486-5933
WEB SITE: www.nevadasouthern.com

Nevada Southern Railway

The railway offers a train ride with a historical twist. This was part of the construction railway from Las Vegas to Hoover Dam, with tracks having been laid in 1931. It's a nice ride in the desert and a break from the hustle of Las Vegas.

CHOICES: Located within former Union Pacific rail yards, the site includes a platform built to resemble a past structure. Along the 45-minute round trip, you get an up-close look at desert plant life, especially when riding in the train's open-air car. The other cars are air-conditioned, restored Pullman coaches dating back to 1911. A generator car behind the locomotive supplies power to the coaches. Operated by the Nevada State Railroad Museum, the railway's outdoor interpretative area displays a variety of equipment, including steam locomotive no. 264 and its unique Vanderbilt tender.

WHEN TO GO: The railway operates February through mid-December. Summer in Nevada can be hot, with temperatures hitting triple digits.

GOOD TO KNOW: You'll save money in Boulder City. It's the only community in Nevada where gambling is not legal.

WORTH DOING: Take a trip to nearby Boulder Dam and tour this technological wonder. Boating on Lake Mead is a popular activity any time of the year.

DON'T MISS: Ride a train pulled by a historic diesel. One of the locomotives used, UP no. 844, is one of the last GP30 diesel locomotives – the early 1960s type of diesel that replaced the first generation of diesel locomotives that had themselves replaced steam power.

GETTING THERE: Boulder City is a 30-minute drive from Las Vegas and McCarran International Airport. It is an easy drive from Las Vegas along Highway 93 into Boulder City. Once there, turn left on Yucca Street to the museum.

Nevada State Railroad Museum ❸

SITE LOCATION: 2180 S. Carson Street, Carson City
PHONE: 775-687-6953
WEB SITE: www.nevadaculture.org
E-MAIL: form on Web site

Peter Hansen

Few states can claim as rich a railroading heritage as Nevada, and this museum does an admirable job of interpreting it. The first transcontinental railroad, the state's many mining railroads, and the historic Virginia & Truckee – which ran right past the museum property – are all represented here. The museum boasts a particularly fine collection of 19th century rolling stock, much of which originally came from the V&T and was used in dozens of Hollywood films and television shows.

CHOICES: Star of the museum's collection is *Inyo*, a wood-burning 4-4-0 built for the V&T in 1875, and the museum still steams it over the July 4th holiday. When *Inyo* isn't operating, it's on display along with other beautifully restored pre-1915 freight and passenger equipment. Other rolling stock can be seen in the restoration shop, including an ex-V&T McKeen motor car that is scheduled for completion in mid-2009.

WHEN TO GO: Steam trains or a 1926 motor car operate most weekends from May to October. Mid-summer highs are usually in the 80s, with little chance of precipitation.

GOOD TO KNOW: Carson City's downtown area is very walkable. The state capitol grounds and surrounding neighborhoods of historic homes are particularly pleasant. A wide variety of hotels, motels, and restaurants can be found nearby.

WORTH DOING: For those whose interests run toward scholarly pursuits, the museum has impressive static displays exploring such topics as the Central Pacific Railroad in Nevada railroading and the evolution of V&T motive power. Lectures by leading rail historians are offered several times a year, and the museum also hosts an annual symposium on Nevada railroad history.

DON'T MISS: For more insight on general Nevada history, the Nevada State Museum is located at 600 N. Carson Street, about a mile from the railroad museum.

GETTING THERE: The museum is on Highway 395 (Carson Street) on the south side of Carson City. Carson City is within a day's drive of most major cities on the West Coast. Amtrak's *California Zephyr* stops at Reno, about 35 miles away, and several major airlines also serve Reno.

Virginia & Truckee Railroad ▪

SITE LOCATION: Washington Street and F Street, Virginia City
PHONE: 775-847-0380
WEB SITE: virginiatruckee.com

Virginia & Truckee Railroad

The famous Comstock Lode yielded more than $400 million of silver and gold during a roughly 30-year period beginning in 1859 – and it led to the creation of both Virginia City and the Virginia & Truckee Railroad. The city saw up to 45 arrivals and departures a day. Today's V&T operates a 35-minute, five-mile round trip from Virginia City to Gold Hill.

CHOICES: Along the ride to Gold City, you'll view rugged mountain scenery and mine ruins accompanied by informative narration. The V&T also offers a longer 50-minute round trip to American Flat, and as the line continues to expand, so will the train rides. Special trains include a haunted Halloween train that is not only fun but offers spectacular stargazing on V&T's mountain right-of-way, far from city lights. The railroad powers its trains with either a 1916 Baldwin 2-8-0 steam locomotive from the Longview, Portland & Northern or a General Electric 80-ton diesel. Passenger cars include a restored 1914 Pullman coach and a 1907 private car.

WHEN TO GO: V&T operates daily from late May to the end of October. Temperatures are comfortable throughout the operating season, with average highs topping out in the low 80s during July and August.

GOOD TO KNOW: Virginia City boasts a variety of restaurants, hotels, and B&Bs that recall the town's frontier heritage, and many are within walking distance of the V&T station.

WORTH DOING: The historic Virginia City walking tour provides a good sense of the Comstock mining boom. It includes historic mansions, churches, the Piper Opera House, and the *Territorial Enterprise* newspaper, where young Mark Twain worked as a reporter.

DON'T MISS: The Nevada State Railroad Museum in nearby Carson City displays more than 30 pieces of equipment that operated on the V&T.

GETTING THERE: Virginia City is on Highway 341, 25 miles south of Reno and 15 miles north of Carson City. Amtrak's *California Zephyr* stops at Reno, and several major airlines also serve Reno.

NEW HAMPSHIRE

Ashland Railroad Station Museum ❶

The museum was built by the Boston, Concord & Montreal Railroad as a station around 1869. It is one of the state's best preserved examples of a 19th century passenger station. The museum contains rail artifacts and photo displays. Occasionally, an excursion train stops at the museum. It is open Saturdays during July and August.

SITE LOCATION: 69 Depot Street, Ashland
PHONE: 603-968-3902
WEB SITE: www.oldashlandnh.org

Café Lafayette Dinner Train ❷

Ride aboard a restaurant with a view of mountains and forests. This two-hour, 20-mile round trip follows the Pemigewasset River over a 100 year old spur of the Boston and Maine Railroad. Enjoy a five-course dinner in several restored Pullman cars, including the *Granite Eagle*, a dome car that rode on the *City of New Orleans*

SITE LOCATION: Route 112, North Woodstock
PHONE: 800-699-3501 or 603-745-3500
WEB SITE: www.cafelafayette.com

Gorham Historical Society Museum ❸

The 1907 former Grand Trunk Railroad station houses a museum that exhibits rail and local historical items. It displays a 1911 Baldwin steam locomotive, a 1949 F7 diesel locomotive, and several boxcars. Operated by the Gorham Historical Society, the museum is open Memorial Day weekend through mid-October.

SITE LOCATION: 25 Railroad Street, Gorham
PHONE: 603-466-5338
WEB SITE: www.aannh.org/heritage/coos/gorhamhist.php
E-MAIL: gorhamhistoricalsociety@gmail.com

Hobo Railroad 4

Located in the White Mountains, the excursion train goes over the Pemigewasset River, through the woods, and past Grandma's Crossing. For a unique meal on the 80-minute ride, grab a hobo lunch, complete with bindle stick. The railroad operates May through October, and it features fall foliage runs, Santa trains, and other special events.

SITE LOCATION: 64 Railroad Street, Lincoln
PHONE: 603-745-2135
WEB SITE: www.hoborr.com
E-MAIL: form on Web site

Sandown Depot Museum 5

The museum is located in the restored Sandown railroad depot that was built in 1873. It contains a stationmaster's room with a working telegraph key and a waiting room with a pot-bellied stove. The museum also features two Flanger cars. It is open weekends May through October.

SITE LOCATION: 1 Depot Road, Sandown
PHONE: 603-887-6100
WEB SITE: www.sandown.us/historical_society/HistoricalHomePage.htm

Winnipesaukee Scenic Railroad 6

This scenic railroad operates along the shores of Lake Winnipesaukee. It runs from Meredith or Weirs Beach to Lakeport and offers one- or two-hour train rides and dinner trains. Special events include murder mysteries and fall foliage runs. Caboose rides and picnic lunches are available.

SITE LOCATION: 154 Main Street, Meredith
PHONE: 603-279-5253
WEB SITE: www.hoborr.com
E-MAIL: form on Web site

Conway Scenic Railroad ▪7

SITE LOCATION: 38 Norcross Circle, North Conway
PHONE: 800-232-5251 or 603-356-5251
WEB SITE: www.conwayscenic.com
E-MAIL: info@conwayscenic.com

Jim Wrinn

Here is a New England excursion train ride bursting with great scenery and Yankee character. The setting is in the Mount Washington Valley in the charming village of North Conway. With three different trips to choose from, this railroad offers a bounty of great journeys.

CHOICES: Two Valley Train excursions are offered: a 55-minute, 11-mile round trip to Conway and a longer 21-mile round trip to Bartlett. Passengers may choose from coach or lounge service. The Notch Train carries passengers from North Conway into the rugged Crawford Notch, as the first trains did more than 130 years ago. This train offers coach, first-class, and dome car seating. Some Valley Train departures include lunch or dinner options aboard the *Chocorua*, the railroad's elegant dining car.

WHEN TO GO: Valley Trains operate excursions April through January, and the Notch Train runs June through October. What can be better than a autumn train ride in New England? Special trains operate throughout the year. For a change of scenery, try riding a snow train in January.

GOOD TO KNOW: Stick to the right side of the Notch Train as it ascends Crawford Notch and crosses the Frankenstein Trestle and Willey Brook Bridge for excellent views of bluffs, ravines, and streams. The later in fall you travel, the fewer colors you'll see, but the better the vistas are from the train.

WORTH DOING: The surrounding Mount Washington Valley and White Mountain National Forest offer four seasons of recreational activities, attractions, and spectacular scenery.

DON'T MISS: Well, you can't miss the Victorian station in North Conway. Just take some time to appreciate this ornate structure that's been at work as a railroad depot since 1874.

GETTING THERE: The Conway Scenic Railroad is less than a three-hour drive from Boston. From Boston, take 1-95 to Route 16, which runs to North Conway.

DISCOUNT: Buy one full-price adult fare and receive a second fare at half price.

Mount Washington Cog Railway 8

SITE LOCATION: Base Road, Bretton Woods
PHONE: 800-922-8825 or 603-278-5404
WEB SITE: www.thecog.com
E-MAIL: info@thecog.com

Jim Wrinn

England may have invented the railroad, but the United States invented the cog railroad. The first such successful cog – a standard railroad with flanged wheels but with the addition of a gear engaging a cog down the center of the tracks – is credited to the Mount Washington Cog Railway in 1869, and it has been in operation since. The trip is to the top of 6,288-foot Mount Washington, infamous for its bad weather but famous for its great views.

CHOICES: Sit back and enjoy the views during the three-hour trip as a coal-fired steam engine takes you to the summit and back. On good days, you can see four states, Canada, and the Atlantic Ocean. The trains operate on a steep track that resembles a ladder plunked down on the mountainside. Because of the steepness, the locomotive boilers are tilted, and the passenger cars are as well so that passengers can ride upright.

WHEN TO GO: Excursion trains operate spring through fall, and reservations are recommended. In fall, the White Mountains are always spectacular. During summer, the trains run hourly, and in late fall, the trips are two hours long.

GOOD TO KNOW: The railway has introduced a new era of technology with the development of a biodiesel locomotive.

WORTH DOING: Explore the mountains. Mount Washington State Park is at the summit and contains hiking trails, an observatory, and the stone Tip Top House. It is surrounded by the White Mountain National Forest, which is filled with a variety of recreational activities.

DON'T MISS: View the railway's original cog engine, *Old Peppersass*, which is on display at the base station. The railway's museum is also located at the base.

GETTING THERE: The Cog Railway is a pleasant drive from Boston, Hartford, New York, or Montreal. It is 90 miles from Portland off Route 302. In Bretton Woods, follow Base Road for six miles to the railway.

White Mountain Central Railroad ▫9

SITE LOCATION: Route 3, Lincoln
PHONE: 603-745-8913
WEB SITE: www.clarkstradingpost.com
E-MAIL: info@clarkstradingpost.com

Priscilla Carton

The White Mountain Central Railroad is part of the popular family-owned Clark's Trading Post amusement park deep in New Hampshire's White Mountains. The railroad offers 30-minute excursions across the Pemigewasset River over a 1904 Howe-Truss covered bridge that was moved from the Barre & Chelsea Railroad in Vermont.

CHOICES: Once a center for the logging and paper industries, the region now caters to tourists. Five decades ago, the Clark family added a 1.25-mile railroad to their small amusement park and acquired an impressive collection of geared steam locomotives. The park includes a variety of museums, displays, and attractions. Admission includes the train ride as well as other activities.

WHEN TO GO: Operations are daily beginning in mid-June through the end of August and on weekends in early June, September, and October. The railroad also operates on Saturday nights during July and August. The best fall foliage usually occurs in early October, which is also the peak tourist season. Special excursions and displays occur on Railroad Days, which is scheduled on a September weekend.

GOOD TO KNOW: Lodging, including motels and B&Bs, and restaurants can be found in Lincoln and the surrounding communities. Rates will be the highest during fall, so reservations should be made far in advance for this season.

WORTH DOING: The White Mountain National Forest is worth visiting any time of year for camping, hiking, history, and scenic drives.

DON'T MISS: The star attractions of the park's locomotive collection are a wood-burning International Shoe two-truck Heisler and Beebe River Railroad two-truck Climax, joined by East Branch & Lincoln Baldwin 2-4-2, a Porter 0-4-0T, and a GE 65-ton diesel.

GETTING THERE: If driving on I-93, take Exit 33, and go south one mile on Route 3. In fall, driving along the Kangamangus Highway from Conway offers exceptional views.

NEW JERSEY

Cape May Seashore Lines ■

Take a ride on either of this railroad's two excursions, and you'll take a ride on the Reading, or over lines where the Reading used to operate, to the Jersey shore. There is a 30-mile round trip between Richland and Tuckahoe and a 22-mile round trip between Cape May Court House, Cold Spring Village, and Cape May City.

SITE LOCATION: 101 W. Pacific Avenue, Cape May
PHONE: 609-884-2675
WEB SITE: www.capemayseashorelines.org
E-MAIL: info@www.capemayseashorelines.org

Maywood Station Museum ❷

This station has been restored, inside and out, to preserve its Victorian style, including its original colors. The station museum features local railroad artifacts and displays. Also on display is a restored caboose that contains exhibits.

SITE LOCATION: 269 Maywood Avenue, Maywood
WEB SITE: www.maywoodstation.com
E-MAIL: info@maywoodstation.com

Black River & Western Railroad $\boxed{3}$

SITE LOCATION: 105 John Ringoes Road, Ringoes
PHONE: 908-782-6622
WEB SITE: www.brwrr.com
E-MAIL: psgrinfo@brwrr.com

Karl Zimmermann

The Black River & Western, which also hauls freight, operates hour-long passenger excursions over a short segment of the former Pennsylvania Railroad's Flemington Branch between Flemington and Ringoes.

CHOICES: Recent trains have been diesel-powered, but the railroad hopes for a return to service of American Locomotive 2-8-0 no. 60, which has done the honors for most years since 1963, when it arrived on the property. In addition to the standard excursions, there's a Great Train Robbery and special Easter and Halloween trains. The railroad also offers a Santa Express and Polar Express on three post-Thanksgiving weekends. June's Railroad Days features a variety of activities. You can board the trains for round trips from either station.

WHEN TO GO: The Black River & Western operates on weekends from May through October, and the fall foliage season is an ideal time to take this idyllic ride.

GOOD TO KNOW: Flemington is a mixture of quaint and commercial, with 60 percent of its buildings on the National Register of Historic Places. There are also plenty of shops and a handful of B&Bs.

WORTH DOING: Nordlandz, an extraordinary model railroad rich in spectacle, is located in Flemington. Don't expect prototypical authenticity, but with eight miles of track, dozens of trains moving at once, and 35-foot-tall model mountains, it's acres of often whimsical fun.

DON'T MISS: Just across the Delaware River in Pennsylvania is the New Hope & Ivyland Railroad, which makes it easy to ride two excursion trains in the same day. Almost as close is the Delaware River Railroad in Phillipsburg, New Jersey.

GETTING THERE: Flemington is roughly 35 miles from Philadelphia and 50 miles from New York City. Ringoes is about 15 miles farther from each city. Both Ringoes and Flemington are located just off Route 202. The Flemington station is on Stangl Road.

New Jersey

Delaware River Railroad

SITE LOCATION: 100 Elizabeth Street, Phillipsburg
PHONE: 877-872-4674
WEB SITE: www.nyswths.org
E-MAIL: ccotty@fastwww.com

Dave Crosby

Ride along the scenic Delaware River in western New Jersey from Phillipsburg to Carpentersville aboard the only steam train in the state. Although it resembles an early American locomotive, no. 142 was constructed in 1988 by the TangShan Locomotive Works in the People's Republic of China.

CHOICES: The Delaware River Railroad operates several themed trains in addition to the standard excursions along the Delaware River. Activities include Corn Maze and Mine Train specials, which are fun for the whole family as are the seasonal holiday rides, while the Warren County Wine Train offers more adult fare on its trip to two local wineries.

WHEN TO GO: Beginning in May, regular excursions operate on Saturdays and Sundays May through October. Autumn provides particularly breathtaking views of the changing leaves along the Delaware River.

GOOD TO KNOW: Engine no. 142 was purchased from the Valley Railroad in Essex, Conn., and was a replacement for the original locomotive, no. 141. On its way to the United States, the freighter carrying no. 141 capsized, and the locomotive sank to the bottom of the Indian Ocean.

WORTH DOING: Across the river, nearby Easton, Pa., features a historic downtown with activities the whole family can enjoy such as visiting the Crayola Museum or the National Canal Museum.

DON'T MISS: Having been served by five different railroads, Phillipsburg is rich in railroad history. Be sure to visit the nearby Phillipsburg Union Station, a museum containing artifacts, maps, and photos of New Jersey railroad history. A short distance away, the Phillipsburg Railroad Historians have a museum and a variety of railroad equipment on display.

GETTING THERE: Situated on the Delaware River, Phillipsburg is located along the New Jersey-Pennsylvania border. It is easily reached by automobile via Route 22 or I-78. The station is just off Main Street in Phillipsburg.

New Jersey Museum of Transportation ❺

SITE LOCATION: 4265 Route 524, Farmingdale
PHONE: 732-938-5524
WEB SITE: www.njmt.org

Jim Wrinn

The museum is home to many rare pieces of equipment, and it offers a short ride on a narrow gauge train on the grounds of Allaire State Park.

CHOICES: Besides looking at the equipment on display, you have the opportunity to tour the museum's shops and see the progress on the various restoration projects. The train travels through the scenic state park, which is home to the Manasquan River.

WHEN TO GO: The vintage locomotives run weekends April through November. In summer, diesels run daily. During the Railroader's Weekend Celebration in mid-September, all the equipment in running shape runs.

GOOD TO KNOW: One of the oldest all-volunteer railroad preservation groups, the museum began as the Pine Creek Railroad in 1952. The museum is the custodian of two 1850s steam locomotives submerged in 90 feet of water off the coast of New Jersey. How they got there is a mystery, and efforts have begun to recover the locomotives. The only other known engine of their kind is in the Smithsonian.

WORTH DOING: In the park, explore Allaire Village, a historic 19th century ironmaking town. The park also contains hiking and biking trails.

DON'T MISS: Look for the Ely-Thomas Lumber Company Shay locomotive. While not operable at present, it is one of the smallest Shays left in existence.

GETTING THERE: The museum is located in Allaire State Park, not far from the ocean. It is easily accessible from the Garden State Parkway or I-195 off Exit 31B. Signs show the way to the park.

Whippany Railway Museum ❻

New Jersey

SITE LOCATION: 1 Railroad Plaza, Whippany
PHONE: 973-887-8177
WEB SITE: www.whippanyrailwaymuseum.net
E-MAIL: wrym-web@comcast.net

Steve Hepler

The Whippany Railway Museum, which is housed in a restored 1904 freight house, displays a large selection of historic locomotives and rolling stock. Much of the collection focuses on New Jersey railroading.

CHOICES: The Whippany Railway Museum also operates several themed and special-event excursions throughout the year including caboose rides and Easter, pumpkin, and Santa Claus specials. The museum's collection features a 100-year-old Baldwin 2-8-0 steam locomotive, a CNJ observation car, a D&H caboose, a railbus, and several vintage diesels including an RS-1 and two GE 70-tonners. Among the structures on the grounds are a Morristown & Erie Railroad passenger station made of fieldstone and a wooden water tank. Interior exhibits are changed each year to highlight a different railroad.

WHEN TO GO: The Whippany Railway Museum is open Sundays April through October. Special excursions run on select dates throughout the year.

GOOD TO KNOW: The museum grounds are adjacent to the Morristown & Erie Railroad, an active freight hauler. The museum was originally founded as the Morris County Central Railroad Museum in 1967 to complement the Morris County Central's steam excursion line. Several pieces of former Morris County Central have been acquired by the museum.

WORTH DOING: The town of Whippany plays host to a number of outdoor recreational activities such as the Patriots Path hiking and biking trail.

DON'T MISS: View steam locomotive no. 4039, which is listed on the National Register of Historic Places. In service until 1980, the Alco 0-6-0 was built in 1942, became a U.S. Army base switcher, hauled freight on the Virginia Blue Ridge Railway, and pulled passenger excursions for the Morris County Central Railroad.

GETTING THERE: Whippany is in northeast New Jersey, about 20 miles from Newark. It easily reached via I-80, I-78, or I-287. The museum is located at the intersection of Routes 10 and 511 (Whippany Road) in Whippany.

158

NEW MEXICO

Belen Harvey House Museum ❶

Adjacent to the BNSF Division yard, the museum contains exhibits on Harvey Houses and the Santa Fe Railroad. Listed on the National Register of Historic Places, the Southwestern-style structure is one of state's few surviving Fred Harvey eating establishments. The museum is open Tuesday through Saturday.

SITE LOCATION: 104 N. First Street, Belen
PHONE: 505-861-0581
WEB SITE: www.belenharveyhouse.com
E-MAIL: museum@belenharveyhouse.com

Cumbres & Toltec Scenic Railroad ⏹

SITE LOCATION: 500 Terrace Avenue, Chama
PHONE: 888-286-2737 or 877-890-2737
WEB SITE: www.cumbrestoltec.com
E-MAIL: info@cumbrestoltec.com

Jim Wrinn

If you have ever craved going back in time to the 1920s to see what railroading was like, here's your chance. The Cumbres & Toltec operates 64 miles of track through the San Juan Mountains. Steam locomotives still labor up steep grades, cross 100-foot-tall trestles, and hug narrow shelves above yawning gorges. For more than 125 years, excursion passengers have ridden over Cumbres Pass, and the line crosses the border between Colorado and New Mexico 11 times.

CHOICES: The railroad offers a choice of excursions, and you can leave from either Chama or Antonito, Colo. From either station, there is a round trip to Osier, Colo., where a hot meal is provided. To see the scenic area in two different ways, you can ride the train one way and return by motor coach. The ride from Chama to Antonito shows you steam locomotives at work as the 2-8-2 Mikado type engines original to this line dig in and go upgrade for several miles. Ride an open-window coach or a first-class car, and as your train moves along, be sure and walk back to the open gondola car. It's a great view and a lot of fun.

WHEN TO GO: Excursion trains operate daily from the end of May until mid-October. During the summer, the Cinder Express runs weekly. The three-hour trip provides a fun and educational experience for children (and adults) that features Cinder Bear, surprises, and a picnic lunch.

GOOD TO KNOW: In both Antonito and Chama, you can sample authentic regional food and stay in historic B&Bs and interesting lodges.

WORTH DOING: The nearby Rio Grande National Forest contains the headwaters of the Rio Grande River, and it features the moonlike landscape of the Wheeler Geologic Area and a variety of other natural wonders.

DON'T MISS: Walk the Chama shop complex and yard and return to the 1920s. You'll see the coal tower, water tank, back shop, and all sorts of clutter that is natural to a railroad yard.

GETTING THERE: The railroad is located between Santa Fe and Colorado Springs. To reach Chama from Santa Fe, take Highway 285 to Highway 84. Highway 285 also takes you to Antonito.

Santa Fe Southern Railway

SITE LOCATION: 410 S. Guadalupe Street, Santa Fe
PHONE: 888-989-8600 or 505-989-8600
WEB SITE: www.sfsr.com
E-MAIL: depot@sfsr.com

Jim Wrinn

One of the most famous railroad names of all is the Atchison, Topeka & Santa Fe Railway, usually known simply as the Santa Fe. This railway offers the chance to ride through the desert from Santa Fe along a historic spur to the junction city of Lamy.

CHOICES: Even if it wasn't a beautiful trip through the desert, the Santa Fe Southern offers something special: a chance to ride a working freight train. The railroad's scenic Day Train is a four-hour round trip aboard a real working mixed train. Along with vintage coaches, the train will most likely pull boxcars between Santa Fe and Lamy. You have the choice of riding in coach or silver class. Silver-class cars are vintage AT&SF *Super Chief* cars.

WHEN TO GO: The excursion trains operate year-round. There are numerous special events scheduled throughout the year, especially around holidays, as well as barbecue dinners and evening runs.

GOOD TO KNOW: If you would like to see one of the last surviving Harvey Houses, you can visit La Fonda Hotel located in Santa Fe's historic plaza.

WORTH DOING: The Lamy depot, built in 1880, has been renovated to match the style of the depot in Santa Fe.

DON'T MISS: Santa Fe is well known for its Southwest culture and art galleries, which number more than 200. Be sure and see the Georgia O'Keefe Museum.

GETTING THERE: Santa Fe is 60 miles northeast of Albuquerque on I-25 and Highway 285. In Santa Fe, the station is on Guadalupe Street between Cerrillos Road and Agua Fria Street.

NEW YORK

Alco-Brooks Railroad Display ❶
Located at the Chautauqua County Fairgrounds, this display features an Alco-Brooks 0-6-0 locomotive built in 1916, a Delaware & Hudson wood-sided boxcar, a wooden New York Central caboose, and other railroad artifacts.

SITE LOCATION: 1089 Central Avenue, Dunkirk
PHONE: 716-366-3797
WEB SITE: www.wnyrails.org/cities/dunkirk/display.htm
E-MAIL: wnyrails@wnyrails.org

Catskill Mountain Railroad ❷
The railroad offers a 90-minute excursion along Esopus Creek in the beautiful Catskills. Along the 12-mile round trip, you'll view peaks such as Mount Tremper, Mount Pleasant, and Romer Mountain. The trip also includes a stop at the Empire State Railway museum in Phoenicia. Trains operate late May through October.

SITE LOCATION: Route 28, Mount Pleasant
PHONE: 845-688-7400
WEB SITE: www.catskillmtrailroad.com
E-MAIL: info@catskillmtrailroad.com

Central Square Station Museum ❸
The museum has various pieces of rail equipment on outdoor display including two 0-4-0 steam locomotives, a 1929 Brill car, a circus car, and a 25-ton diesel locomotive. Indoor exhibits are housed in an early 20th century depot. It is open Sundays May through October.

SITE LOCATION: 132 Railroad Street, Central Square
WEB SITE: www.cnynrhs.org/CentralSq.html
E-MAIL: cnynrhs@aol.com

Cooperstown & Charlotte Valley Railroad ❹

On a 16-mile round trip between Milford and Cooperstown, the railroad takes you through a variety of landscapes found in the Upper Susquehanna River Valley. You cross the river twice over two steel-truss bridges. In the restored 1869 Milford depot, you can view an array of rail exhibits and displays.

SITE LOCATION: 136 East Main Street, Milford
PHONE: 607-432-2429 or 607-286-7805
WEB SITE: www.lrhs.com
DISCOUNT: $1 off each ticket; excludes specials.

Delaware & Ulster Railroad ❺

This 100-minute round trip from Arkville to Roxbury takes you along the Delaware River and through the scenic Catskill Mountains. The railroad also offers a dinner train and special events. The Arkville depot features an exhibit on the area's rail history. Excursions take place late May through October.

SITE LOCATION: 43510 Route 28, Arkville
PHONE: 800-225-4132 or 845-586-3877
WEB SITE: www.durr.org

Empire State Railway Museum ❻

Through photos, films, and artifacts, the museum highlights the history of railroads that served the Catskills. The museum, located in a restored 1899 Ulster & Delaware Railroad station, is also restoring several railway cars and a 1910 2-8-0 locomotive. It is open weekends and holidays from Memorial Day through Columbus Day.

SITE LOCATION: 70 Lower High Street, Phoenicia
PHONE: 845-688-7501
WEB SITE: www.esrm.com

Hyde Park Railroad Station ❼

Built in 1914, the Hyde Park Railroad Station is listed on the National Register of Historic Places. You can tour the restored station, which was designed by the same architects who designed Grand Central Station, and view displays on the area's railroading history. It is open weekends during the summer and on holidays.

SITE LOCATION: 34 River Road, Hyde Park
PHONE: 845-229-2338
WEB SITE: www.hydeparkstation.com

Martisco Station Museum ❽

This restored 1870 New York Central station contains two floors of local railroad artifacts. On the first floor of this Victorian-style brick structure, you'll enter a replica of a small-town railroad station. Items are displayed outside as well. It is open Sunday afternoons May through October.

SITE LOCATION: Martisco Road, Marcellus
WEB SITE: www.cnynrhs.org/Martisco.html
E-MAIL: cnynrhs@aol.com

New York Museum of Transportation ❾

The museum exhibits various trolley cars, a steam locomotive, a caboose, and rail artifacts as well as highway and horse-drawn vehicles. It features trolley rides and a short track-car ride that takes you to the nearby Rochester & Genesee Valley Railroad Museum. The New York Museum of Transportation is open year-round.

SITE LOCATION: 6393 E. River Road, West Henrietta
PHONE: 585-533-1113
WEB SITE: www.nymtmuseum.org
E-MAIL: info@nymtmuseum.org

New York Transit Museum ❿

Housed in a 1936 subway station, the New York Transit Museum features restored subway cars and other exhibits related to urban transit. Exhibits highlight elevated rail lines and the construction of New York City's first subway line. The museum also offers special subway tours and events during the year.

SITE LOCATION: Boerum Place at Schermerhorn Street, Brooklyn
PHONE: 718-694-1600
WEB SITE: www.mta.info/mta/museum

North Creek Railway Depot Museum ⓫

Step into the North Creek Depot Museum and you'll relive a piece of presidential history. The depot was where Theodore Roosevelt learned he had become president at the death of President McKinley. The museum also tells the story of the Adirondack Railroad and the central Adirondack Mountains. The Upper Hudson River Railroad boards from the building's platform.

SITE LOCATION: 5 Railroad Place, North Creek
PHONE: 518-251-5842
WEB SITE: www.northcreekdepotmuseum.com
E-MAIL: director@northcreekdepotmuseum.com

Railroad Museum of Long Island [12]

The Railroad Museum of Long Island has two locations: Greenport and Riverhead. Greenport, situated in a Victorian-style LIRR freight station, exhibits photos and artifacts of Long Island rail history. It displays an 1898 snowplow and a 1927 wooden caboose. An operating tower and turntable are also on site. At Riverhead, the museum restores its rolling stock and displays several steam locomotives and various railcars. A miniature train ride also operates around the site. The Riverhead visitor center is located at 416 Griffing Avenue. At times, you can take the LIRR and tour both sites in one day.

SITE LOCATION: 440 Fourth Street, Greenport
PHONE: 631-477-0439 (Greenport) or 631-727-7920 (Riverhead)
WEB SITE: www.rmli.us
E-MAIL: info@rmli.us

Railroad Museum of the Niagara Frontier [13]

Housed in the restored Erie Railroad freight depot, which was built in 1922, the museum contains a collection of artifacts that recognizes the region's railroading heritage. Also on display are several industrial locomotives, an Erie caboose, and a New York Central caboose.

SITE LOCATION: 111 Oliver Street, North Tonawanda
PHONE: 716-694-9588
WEB SITE: www.railroadniagara.com
E-MAIL: rrmuseum@nfcnrhs.com

Rochester & Genesee Valley Railroad Museum [14]

The Rochester & Genesee Valley Railroad Museum is housed in a restored 1918 Erie Railroad train station. Inside, you'll see the original stationmaster's office and artifacts. You can also inspect various early diesel and steam locomotives, freight cars, and passenger cars. It is open Sundays from late May through October. Start your visit with a track-car ride from the nearby New York Museum of Transportation.

SITE LOCATION: 282 Rush-Scottsville Road, Rush
PHONE: 585-533-1431
WEB SITE: www.rgvrrm.org
E-MAIL: info@rgvrrm.org

Roscoe O&W Railway Museum ⓯

This museum complex features a station building, a restored Ontario & Western caboose, a Beaverkill trout car, and watchman shanties. The museum specializes in O&W memorabilia and artifacts but also contains other railroad and local historical items.

SITE LOCATION: 7 Railroad Avenue, Roscoe
PHONE: 607-498-4346
WEB SITE: www.nyow.org/museum.html
E-MAIL: wilsip@frontiernet.net

Salamanca Rail Museum ⓰

This Buffalo, Rochester & Pittsburgh depot has been fully restored right down to the telegraph key in the ticket office, and it includes a ladies retiring room and a baggage room. Artifacts and photos show the history of railroads in western New York and Pennsylvania. A boxcar, a crew camp car, and two cabooses are on display.

SITE LOCATION: 170 Main Street, Salamanca
PHONE: 716-945-3133
WEB SITE: mysite.verizon.net/bizxyrad/salamancarailmuseumassociation
E-MAIL: salarail@localnet.com

Trolley Museum of New York ⓱

The museum operates a trolley ride from Kingston to the banks of the Hudson River, where you can enjoy a picnic lunch. With a stop at the museum, you can learn about trolleys and see them being restored. The museum's collection dates back to 1897 with its Oslo, Norway, car that was built in Germany.

SITE LOCATION: 89 E. Strand Street, Kingston
PHONE: 845-331-3399
WEB SITE: www.tmny.org
E-MAIL: admin@tmny.org

Adirondack Scenic Railroad 🔲18

SITE LOCATION: 321 Main Street, Utica
PHONE: 800-819-2291 or 315-724-0700
WEB SITE: www.adirondackrr.com
E-MAIL: train@adirondackrr.com

Karl Zimmermann

The Adirondack Scenic Railroad currently operates excursions over two sections of line – 52 miles of the former New York Central's Adirondack Division from Utica to Thendara (plus an additional six miles on to Carter Station) and 10 miles between Lake Placid and Saranac Lake.

CHOICES: For serious riders, the railroad offers all-day excursions from Utica to Thendara Wednesdays through Sundays during summer and fall. There is time for visiting the resort town of Old Forge and taking a two-hour cruise on the Fulton Chain of Lakes. Shorter round trips (of 20 miles, either south to Otter Lake or north to Carter Station) are offered from Thendara. Similar trips operate between Saranac Lake and Lake Placid at the other end of the railroad. You can ride in coaches or in open-air cars to soak in the scenery.

WHEN TO GO: The brilliant foliage of fall makes that season perhaps the choicest time to ride. In late November through mid-December, the railroad offers Polar Express trains in emulation of the Chris Van Allsburg children's book.

GOOD TO KNOW: The Adirondack Scenic Railroad offers a complete smorgasbord of special trains and events throughout the year including wine-tasting, Halloween, and murder mystery trains.

WORTH DOING: Thendara (adjacent to Old Forge), Saranac Lake, and Lake Placid are all deep in the Adirondacks, replete with natural beauty. The region's history is interestingly presented at the Adirondack Museum in Blue Mountain Lake. The six-million-acre Adirondack Park offers 2,000 mikes of hiking trails and hundreds of miles of canoe routes.

DON'T MISS: The Adirondack Scenic Railroad shares Utica's grand 1914 Union Station with Amtrak, making it among the few excursion railroads with rail connections. Take time to look through this historic station. An easy walk away is the Hotel Utica, which predates the station by two years. Its restored lobby is also worth a look.

GETTING THERE: Served by multiple Amtrak trains each day, Utica also has excellent highway access, being located right on the New York State Thruway (I-90). The nearest major airport is in Syracuse, 56 miles away. Lake Placid is 30 miles from the Adirondack Northway (I-87). Adirondack Regional Airport is in Clear Lake, 15 miles away.

Arcade & Attica Railroad 19

SITE LOCATION: 278 Main Street, Arcade
PHONE: 585-492-3100 or 585-496-9877
WEB SITE: www.arcadeandatticarr.com
E-MAIL: form on Web site

Joe Cooper

When steam engine no. 18 blows its whistle, you get a real blast from the past. The Arcade & Attica Railroad offers the last remaining steam locomotive excursion in New York. This 90-minute scenic ride rolls through countryside that has changed little since the line was formed in the early 1880s.

CHOICES: On the 14-mile round trip, you can ride aboard heavyweight coaches that were built around 1915 or an open-air gondola observation car (just watch out for soot). The train may also be pulled by a General Electric 44-ton center cab diesel, either no. 111 or no. 112. No. 111 was originally purchased by the railroad in 1947. In the Arcade station, you can view historic photographs, artifacts, and operating model railroad layouts. A 1920s boxcar and caboose are also on display.

WHEN TO GO: Regular excursions run on weekends from Memorial Day through September. During July and August, additional rides take place on Wednesdays and Fridays, and there is a special extended schedule in October for viewing fall foliage. Murder mystery, Halloween, and Christmas trains also run during the season.

GOOD TO KNOW: Tourist steam excursions began in 1962 with the purchase of no. 18, a 1920 2-8-0 American Locomotive. The locomotive returned to service in 2008 after more than six years of restoration work.

WORTH DOING: A special Civil War reenactment takes place in August that includes a battle with Union and Confederate troops fighting on and off the train. A free shuttle bus takes you to a park where the troops are encamped, so you can see how soldiers and civilians lived in the 1860s.

DON'T MISS: On the 15-minute stopover at Curriers depot, watch the crew turn no. 18 around for the return trip to Arcade. You can even take pictures and talk to the crew. Then, for a unique experience, hop in the gondola, which is now in front of the engine, for the ride back.

GETTING THERE: Arcade is located about an hour's drive south of Buffalo. The museum is located three miles east of Route 16 on Main Street at Railroad Avenue.

Finger Lakes Scenic Railway [20]

SITE LOCATION: Railroad Place and Lewis Street, Geneva
PHONE: 315-781-1234 or 315-374-4994
WEB SITE: www.fingerlakesscenicrailway.com
E-MAIL: form on Web site

Karl Zimmermann

The Finger Lakes Railway runs freight trains and passenger excursions over 130 miles of track. The railroad offers a multitude of themed train rides, including the popular Blues-n-Brews trips. Family friendly outings focus on holidays such as Halloween and Christmas. Along the way, keep an eye out for historic passenger depots that exist along the tracks, however, in new capacities.

CHOICES: You definitely have choices. More than we could list. On some 60 days a year, the railroad operates excursions from no fewer than seven different boarding locations throughout the Finger Lakes region: Auburn, Camillus (near Syracuse), Canandaigua, Geneva, Seneca Falls, Victor, and Watkins Glen. To get close to nature, take the Montezuma Run. It crosses the north end of Lake Cayuga (the only place the railroad actually touches one of the Finger Lakes) and traverses the Montezuma National Wildlife Refuge. With luck, you'll see a majestic bald eagle.

WHEN TO GO: Excusions run April through December on most weekends and some weekdays. Each season in the scenic Finger Lakes area has its unique charms.

GOOD TO KNOW: Most of the line's locomotives sport New York Central's famous lightning-stripe paint scheme, and one wears Cornell red to honor the Lehigh Valley.

WORTH DOING: There are more than 70 wineries in the Finger Lakes region, and Cayuga, Seneca, Canandaigua, and Keuka Lakes all have wine trails to help visitors enjoy wine tastings and vineyard tours.

DON'T MISS: The railroad passes through Seneca Falls, which is the birthplace of the women's rights movement and full of historical interest. Its Heritage Area centers around classic Main Street architecture, and the town contains the Women's Rights National Historical Park and the National Women's Hall of Fame.

GETTING THERE: Located between Syracuse and Rochester, cities with major airports, the Finger Lakes Scenic Railway is easily accessible from the New York State Thruway (I-90).

Medina Railroad Museum ㉑

SITE LOCATION: 530 West Avenue, Medina
PHONE: 585-798-6106
WEB SITE: www.railroadmuseum.net
E-MAIL: office@railroadmuseum.net

Jim Wrinn

The area east of Buffalo provides a pleasant distraction with small towns, farms, and a relaxed existence. Here on a former New York Central main line is an opportunity to ride a streamlined passenger train behind a historic Alco Century diesel locomotive. The two-hour, 34-mile round trip parallels and then crosses the Erie Canal.

CHOICES: Housed in the old New York Central freight house, the museum exhibits a wide array of railroad displays. The freight house is huge – 301 feet long and 34 feet wide – and contains memorabilia, models, and artifacts. Enter the Union Station archway, and you'll see displays dedicated to the trains, such as the *Empire State Express* and *20th Century Limited*, and railroads, including the Pennsylvania Railroad, that helped develop the area.

WHEN TO GO: The museum is open year-round Tuesday through Sunday. Fall foliage trips during October and Santa trains during December are the most popular train rides. Excursion trains run on other special events during the year.

GOOD TO KNOW: Ask about the bridge at Lockport, which, according to legend, was built upside down so as to limit the size of barge traffic on the competing Erie Canal.

WORTH DOING: Take a one-of-a-kind ride in a mule-drawn packet boat on the Erie Canal.

DON'T MISS: In the museum, watch a large HO scale model railroad in action. The prototypical railroad layout measures 14 feet by 204 feet. Also, take a close look at the lobby, which is refinished as the freight depot office.

GETTING THERE: Medina is situated between Buffalo and Rochester, not far from Lake Ontario. From Buffalo, take I-90 east to Route 77. Continue north on Route 77/63 to downtown Medina. There, turn left onto North Avenue and then turn right onto West Avenue.

DISCOUNT: Receive $1 off each adult admission.

Upper Hudson River Railroad 22

SITE LOCATION: 3 Railroad Place, North Creek
PHONE: 518-251-5334
WEB SITE: www.uhrr.com
E-MAIL: form on Web site

Upper Hudson River Railroad

The Upper Hudson River Railroad operates over the former Delaware & Hudson Railway's Adirondack Branch from North Creek to Riverside Station in Riparius. The tracks follow the river here, where it is a scenic, rushing whitewater stream near its headwaters.

CHOICES: Round trips last more than two hours and include a layover at Riparius, where you can take in historical displays and a park with a bridge over the Hudson River. Some trains leave from North Creek and others from Riverside Station. When departing North Creek, sit on the left for views of the Hudson River. Recently, a new 40-mile stretch of line was opened, allowing occasional 40-milers from North Creek to Hadley. There is a variety of special trains and fun events during the season including barbecues at 1000 Acres Ranch.

WHEN TO GO: The Upper Hudson River Railroad operates from May through October, and the brilliant foliage makes autumn the season of choice for a visit.

GOOD TO KNOW: Trains are pulled by one of two Alco diesels – a road switcher built for the Delaware & Hudson or a yard switcher that Alco used at its own plant in Schenectady.

WORTH DOING: Nestled in the Adirondack Mountains, North Creek offers many opportunities for outdoor recreation, such as hiking, canoeing, or kayaking on the Hudson River. Just a few miles away, you can tour the historic Barton Garnet Mines and visit the Gore Mountain Ski Center.

DON'T MISS: Leave time to visit the North Creek Depot Museum, which contains exhibits about ski trains and President Theodore Roosevelt's famous train ride from North Creek. The depot is on the National Register of Historic Places.

GETTING THERE: North Creek is 18 miles from Exit 25 on the Adirondack Northway (I-87). Albany, the nearest city with a major airport, is 82 miles away.

DISCOUNT: Buy one ticket and get a second ticket free.

NORTH CAROLINA

Charlotte Trolley ①

Riding on Car 85 today is like going back to 1938. It is Charlotte's only original electric trolley car that remains in operation. Offering trolley service through the city's center on weekends, Charlotte Trolley also restores vintage electric streetcars, and its Powerhouse Museum highlights the use of streetcars in the South.

SITE LOCATION: 1507 Camden Road, Charlotte
PHONE: 704-375-0850
WEB SITE: www.charlottetrolley.org
E-MAIL: rtober@charlottetrolley.org

Wilmington Railroad Museum ②

The museum is housed in an 1880s railroad freight warehouse, where you can view an extensive artifact collection. Outside, you can inspect a 1910 Baldwin steam locomotive, a hobo display in a boxcar, and an Atlantic Coast Line caboose. The museum is open year-round.

SITE LOCATION: 505 Nutt Street, Wilmington
PHONE: 910-763-2634
WEB SITE: www.wilmingtonrailroadmuseum.org
E-MAIL: form on Web site

Great Smoky Mountains Railroad **3**

SITE LOCATION: 226 Everett Street, Bryson City
PHONE: 800-872-4681 or 828-586-8811
WEB SITE: www.gsmr.com
E-MAIL: info@gsmr.com

Jim Wrinn

Few mountain railroads in the southeastern United States traverse such splendid scenery as this line does. Created from a portion of Southern Railway's Murphy Branch, the GSMR hugs the Tuckaseegee and Nantahala Rivers, climbs a mountain at Red Marble Gap, and rolls out over a 700-foot-long trestle at Fontana Lake.

CHOICES: GSMR offers a variety of accommodations, from cabooses and open-air cars to traditional coaches and air-conditioned lounge cars. Excursions range from three-hour jaunts to all-day adventures.

WHEN TO GO: The railroad runs year-round. Spring and fall offer mild weather best suited to open cars and being able to see beyond the trees and into the forest. Summer can be humid, and the tremendous foliage of the Southeast can restrict the views.

GOOD TO KNOW: The railroad offers numerous special events throughout the year, including some ideal for kids (Thomas the Tank Engine and the Polar Express) and others for the enthusiast, such as the Railfest weekend each September.

WORTH DOING: Watch whitewater rafters in the Nantahala River. They'll put on a good show, while you stay dry. Also, take in the bluegrass and gospel show at the Bryson City depot before the train leaves. Sit in church pews and sample some mountain culture.

DON'T MISS: Try an adventurous combination package in which you ride the train from Bryson City into the Nantahala Gorge and then raft part of the way back.

GETTING THERE: The railroad is about three hours from Atlanta and one hour from Asheville. Major highways to the area include I-40, Route 19/23 and Route 441. Stations in both Bryson City and Dillsboro are downtown.

DISCOUNT: $3 off adult ticket, up to four; new reservations only, excludes special events.

New Hope Valley Railway ▪4

SITE LOCATION: 5121 Daisy Street, Bonsal
PHONE: 919-362-5416
WEB SITE: www.nhvry.org
E-MAIL: info@nhvry.org

Patrick Treadaway Jr.

Operating from the North Carolina Railroad Museum, the New Hope Valley Railway provides an hour-long trip through the scenic pine forests situated south of Raleigh and Durham in central North Carolina.

CHOICES: The railway offers both steam and diesel round trips between Bonsal and New Hill. You can ride in an open-air car, but try a ride in a real caboose. It doesn't get any better than that! The museum features an outdoor exhibit of railroad equipment as well as displays of local rail artifacts. It includes a variety of industrial and short line diesel locomotives.

WHEN TO GO: The railway operates on select days each month from May to December, with additional holiday trains scheduled in December. Go during a special event that includes music for a taste of regional entertainment. The museum is open Saturdays and Sundays.

GOOD TO KNOW: The railroad offers the chance to operate a diesel electric or 0-4-0T steam locomotive, which is an oil-burning switcher that began operation in 1941, by advance reservations.

WORTH DOING: The American Tobacco Trail runs near the railway. The trail is built over part of an old rail line that carried tobacco. You can hike, bike, and ride horses along the trail. Special events take place in the trail's New Hill parking lot.

DON'T MISS: Kids will especially enjoy the G scale garden railroad that operates on the grounds.

GETTING THERE: Located between Bonsal and New Hill, the railroad is a 30-minute drive from Raleigh along Route 1. Take Exit 89, turn right on New Hill Holleman Road, and then turn left onto old Route 1 for 2.5 miles. The museum is on the right on Daisy Street, and parking for the train rides is on the left on Bonsal Road.

North Carolina Transportation Museum ⑤

SITE LOCATION: 411 S. Salisbury Avenue, Spencer
PHONE: 877-628-6386 or 704-636-2889
WEB SITE: www.nctrans.org
E-MAIL: nctrans@nctrans.org

Jim Wrinn

The state's transportation museum is housed in shop buildings from Southern Railway's largest steam locomotive repair shop that date from before 1900 to 1924. But this is no static museum. Trains run most of the year on 2.5 miles of track, giving visitors the chance to experience a 20-minute train ride that covers most of the 57-acre site.

CHOICES: Among the giant structures you'll see are the nation's largest preserved roundhouse, the 37-stall Bob Julian Roundhouse, which houses railroad displays, a restoration shop, active locomotives, and rolling stock. You will also see the Back Shop, a 600-foot-long, 80-foot-tall building once used to overhaul steam locomotives that is under restoration as an exhibit hall. On some trains, you'll have the choice of riding in open-window or air-conditioned coaches or possibly a caboose.

WHEN TO GO: Any time of the year is enjoyable, but take plenty of water along if you go during the sweltering summer. Rail Days, the annual railroad festival when all the trains run, is usually held in spring, but it can be wet. Falls are long and mild. From November until April, winter hours are in effect.

GOOD TO KNOW: The visitor center served as a train depot in Barber. The building was cut into three sections and moved to the site in 1980. The Flue Shop, used to repair the flues (pipes) in steam locomotive boilers, houses a collection of antique automobiles.

WORTH DOING: There are plenty of pork barbecue places in the region if you want to sample real Piedmont food.

DON'T MISS: Take a five-minute ride on the turntable. The 100-foot-long lazy Susan is used to turn locomotives at the roundhouse, and it helps define the term "in the round." Ride in the locomotive cab for an extra fare. You'll get a unique view and a personalized tour. You might even get to blow the horn.

GETTING THERE: About an hour's drive from Charlotte or Winston-Salem, the museum is a few minutes off I-85. Take Exit 79 and then follow the brown signs to the museum in Spencer.

Tweetsie Railroad 6

SITE LOCATION: 300 Tweetsie Railroad Lane, Blowing Rock
PHONE: 800-526-5740 or 828-264-9061
WEB SITE: www.tweetsie.com
E-MAIL: info@tweetsie.com

Jim Wrinn

One of the original Wild West theme parks of the 1950s when TV cowboys were popular, Tweetsie has roots in one of the most famous Southeastern narrow gauge railroads, the East Tennessee & Western North Carolina. The three-mile train ride gives the historic, coal-fired engines a chance to work and show that they are still the real thing.

CHOICES: The train is pulled by steam locomotive no. 12. The native engine worked for the East Tennessee & Western North Carolina and is listed on the National Register of Historic Places. Ride in a coach close to the engine, so you can hear it work up grade and listen to the whistle echo about the mountains.

WHEN TO GO: The park is open May through October. From Memorial Day weekend through August, it is open daily. An annual railfan weekend is held in September, and a ghost train runs in October.

GOOD TO KNOW: The East Tennessee & Western North Carolina ran from Elizabeth City, Tenn., to Boone, N.C., for many years. Its whistle sounded a "tweet," and from that, locals nicknamed the railroad *Tweetsie*.

WORTH DOING: Visit the Blowing Rock and learn its legend. Hike or drive through the scenic Blue Ridge Mountains. At Grandfather Mountain, you can cross the Mile High Swinging Bridge, a 228-foot-long suspension bridge that spans an 80-foot chasm.

DON'T MISS: Bring the entire family along – there's lots to see and do for kids in the park. Admission to the railroad includes amusement rides, live shows, and other attractions.

GETTING THERE: The railroad is west of Winston-Salem in the Blue Ridge Mountains near the Tennessee border. It is located off Route 321 between Boone and Blowing Rock.

NORTH DAKOTA

Bonanzaville USA ❶

The museum features more than 40 historic buildings and 400,000 artifacts that depict life when bonanza homes dotted the Plains. Rail structures include a vintage Northern Pacific train depot, a water tower, and a train shed. The train shed displays an 1883 NP 4-4-0 steam locomotive, a caboose, and a 1930s Pullman car.

SITE LOCATION: 1351 Main Avenue W, West Fargo
PHONE: 701-282-2822
WEB SITE: www.bonanzaville.com
E-MAIL: info@bonanzaville.com

Fort Lincoln Trolley ❷

A restored trolley car takes you on a nine-mile excursion along the Heart River. The restored American Car streetcar, which was built in the 1890s, takes you from Mandan to Fort Abraham Lincoln State Park and back. The park features several reconstructed buildings that would have been found in the original fort.

SITE LOCATION: 2000 Third Street SE, Mandan
PHONE: 701-663-9018
WEB SITE: www.realnd.com/fortlincolntrolleyindex.htm

Old Soo Depot Transportation Museum ❸

This museum focuses on the transportation history of the American West and includes materials on trains, planes, and automobiles. Located in a completely restored 1912 Soo Line depot, it also offers an excellent location for train-watching. The museum is open Monday through Friday.

SITE LOCATION: 15 N. Main Street, Minot
PHONE: 701-852-2234
WEB SITE: www.ndtourism.com
E-MAIL: soodepot@srt.com

Railroad Museum of Minot ❹

The Railroad Museum of Minot contains artifacts relating to the Great Northern Railway and other railroads of the area. A Great Northern Railway caboose and a snowplow car are also on display. The museum is open on Saturdays.

SITE LOCATION: 19 First Street NE, Minot
PHONE: 701-852-7091
WEB SITE: www.railroadmuseumofminot.org
E-MAIL: tbolte@srt.com

OHIO

AC&J Scenic Line 1

The railway offers a one-hour round trip that takes you over the last remaining portion of the New York Central's Ashtabula-to-Pittsburgh passenger line. On the 12-mile excursion, you'll travel on 1920s passenger cars pulled by a first-generation diesel through scenic forests and farmland and cross two bridges. A variety of special events are scheduled throughout the year.

SITE LOCATION: 161 E. Jefferson Street, Jefferson
PHONE: 440-576-6346
WEB SITE: www.acjrscenic.net
E-MAIL: info@acjrscenic.net

Conneaut Railroad Museum 2

Located in a former New York Central depot, which was built in 1900, this museum displays railroad memorabilia, photos, and artifacts such as lanterns and timetables. Be sure to climb aboard and inspect the cab of Nickel Plate Berkshire no. 755 displayed outside.

SITE LOCATION: 363 Depot Street, Conneaut
PHONE: 440-599-7878

Hocking Valley Scenic Railway 3

The railway offers diesel-powered excursions between Nelsonville and Logan. Once part of the original Hocking Valley Railway's Athens Branch, the route is listed on the National Register of Historic Places. Regular excursions run on weekends during summer and include a stop at Robbins Crossing, a re-created pioneer village. Special trains also run throughout the year.

SITE LOCATION: 33 E. Canal Street, Nelsonville
PHONE: 800-967-7834 or 740-753-9531
WEB SITE: www.hockingvalleytrain.com
E-MAIL: larryblake@att.net

Jefferson Depot ❹

The Jefferson Depot is more than a depot. It is a small village. In addition to the restored 1872 Lake Shore & Michigan Southern Railroad station, the site features a 1918 caboose and several 19th century buildings including a one-room schoolhouse, a post office, and a church. From June through September, guided tours are offered on Sundays. The AC&J Scenic Line is right next door.

SITE LOCATION: 147 E. Jefferson Street, Jefferson
PHONE: 440-576-0496
WEB SITE: www.jeffersondepotvillage.org

Lebanon Mason Monroe Railroad ❺

The LM&M runs one-hour excursions through southwestern Ohio from spring through December. The railroad runs a variety of special events that include holiday trains, mystery trains, and Railroad Revealed events that allow you to talk to the engineer and tour the locomotive. You can ride in vintage coaches or an open-air gondola.

SITE LOCATION: 127 S. Mechanic Street, Lebanon
PHONE: 866-934-9464 or 513-933-8022
WEB SITE: www.lebanonrr.com
E-MAIL: info@lebanonrr.com

Lorain & West Virginia Railway ❻

Excursion rides take you on a 12-mile round trip over a restored portion of the L&WV. Trains run weekends August through October, with special service during Lorain County Fair week. Cab rides are available in the railway's E-8 locomotive.

SITE LOCATION: Route 18, Wellington
PHONE: 440-647-6660
WEB SITE: www.lakeshorerailway.org

Marion Union Station ❼

The station contains a museum, and a fully restored Erie Railroad tower is also on site. Located between two diamond crossovers, the station is a great place to watch trains from. More than 100 go by daily. The museum is open Monday through Friday.

SITE LOCATION: 532 W. Center Street, Marion
PHONE: 740-383-3768
WEB SITE: www.mariononline.com/agencies/MUSA.htm

Ohio Railway Museum 8

The museum's collection features more than 30 pieces and includes streetcars dating from the 1890s, interurban cars, passenger cars, steam locomotives, and a post office car. It also offers a one-mile demonstration ride on one of the streetcars or interurbans.

SITE LOCATION: 990 Proprietors Road, Worthington
PHONE: 614-885-7345
WEB SITE: www.ohiorailwaymuseum.net
E-MAIL: info@ohiorailwaymuseum.net

Orrville Railroad Heritage Society 9

The society offers excursions of various length, including trips to Pittsburgh, as well as fall foliage and holiday trains. The trips are run in conjunction with the Wheeling & Lake Erie Railway or the Ohio Central Railroad. Special events also take place at the Orrville depot.

SITE LOCATION: 145 Depot Street, Orrville
PHONE: 330-683-2426
WEB SITE: www.orrvillerailroad.com
E-MAIL: questions@orrvillerailroad.com

Toledo, Lake Erie & Western Railway 10

Board the *Bluebird* at a historic depot and take a 60-minute ride over the last remaining section of Nickel Plate Railroad. Along the way, you'll see an 1817 log cabin and other structures amid scenic views. Trains run Wednesdays and Thursdays during summer and on weekends in May, September, and October. Special events are also scheduled during the year.

SITE LOCATION: 49 N. Sixth Street, Waterville
PHONE: 866-638-7246 or 419-878-2177
WEB SITE: www.tlew.org
E-MAIL: info@tlew.org

Cuyahoga Valley Scenic Railroad 🔟

Ohio

SITE LOCATION: 1630 W. Mill Street, Peninsula
PHONE: 800-468-4070 or 330-657-2000
WEB SITE: www.cvsr.com
E-MAIL: cvsr@cvsr.com

Mark Perri

The Cuyahoga Valley Scenic Railroad operates over 47 miles of ex-B&O trackage through northeastern Ohio, from Independence (near Cleveland) through Peninsula and Akron to Canton. Much of the railroad is in the picturesque Cuyahoga Valley National Park, along the Cuyahoga River, and the route of the abandoned Ohio and Erie Canal.

CHOICES: The CVSR runs an extensive schedule of regular trains from various boarding stations. A dome car has been added to the railroad's fleet of first-class offerings. In addition, special events run February through November. They include wine trains, Young at Heart excursions, hobo trains, Thomas the Tank Engine, and one of tourist railroading's premier Polar Express trains.

WHEN TO GO: The summer months offer the most extensive schedule of regular trains. Mid-October offers extra trains for viewing the beautiful fall foliage. Trains are less crowded yet still offer spectacular scenery in April and September.

GOOD TO KNOW: The Cuyahoga Valley National Park also features the Towpath Trail, which was built along much of the Ohio and Erie Canal Towpath. It is excellent for hiking and biking, and CVSR trains usually include a baggage car if you want to bike one way and ride the train one way. Flag stops have been added to the regular schedule to accommodate bikers from the Towpath Trail.

WORTH DOING: Explore many of the restored historical buildings in the national park, including the Canal Visitor Center (accessible by train) that details the canal's history and includes an operating canal lock.

DON'T MISS: The east side of the train generally includes the best views of the Cuyahoga River, which essentially parallels the railroad, especially on the north end from Peninsula up to Independence. In addition, many photo opportunities abound, and the park has re-created the feel of the early 1900s by building many of the railroad's depots and shelters in a style modeled after the railroad's original structures.

GETTING THERE: By air, Cleveland is closest, but Akron-Canton is a convenient and often a more economical option. Amtrak's *Lakeshore Limited* and *Capitol Limited* stop in Cleveland. If driving, the Ohio Turnpike crosses the CVSR near Peninsula, and I-77 generally parallels the railroad from Cleveland to Canton.

Dennison Railroad Depot Museum ⑫

SITE LOCATION: 400 Center Street, Dennison
PHONE: 877-278-8020 or 740-922-6776
WEB SITE: www.dennisondepot.org
E-MAIL: depot@tusco.net

Mark Perri

This meticulously restored ex-Pennsylvania Railroad depot, built in 1873, houses a comprehensive collection of exhibits highlighting the depot's significance as a World War II serviceman's canteen. An extensive addition, comprised of five remodeled passenger cars, opened in March 2007.

CHOICES: Dennison Railroad Depot Museum offers both guided and self-guided tours. Take the time to explore the new addition, which includes a rare hospital car. A variety of interactive exhibits, many designed for children, allow visitors to climb in a caboose, sleep in a Pullman bunk, and send a message by telegraph. The museum also contains local history exhibits, houses a research library, and features a collection of railcars.

WHEN TO GO: The museum is open year-round but is closed on Mondays. It hosts several special events including an annual three-day Soldiers Homecoming Festival, complete with WWII reenactors, that celebrates the museum's wartime heritage.

GOOD TO KNOW: If you are hungry, a full-service restaurant, Trax Diner, is located in the depot and offers excellent lunches and dinners. Across the street, Dennison Yard, a local bar and grill, features a wonderful home-cooked Italian menu. There is also a picnic area on the museum's platform.

WORTH DOING: Dennison is close to Ohio's Amish Country in the east-central part of the state. The Pro Football Hall of Fame is 45 minutes north in Canton. If you would like to see a hand-carved locomotive, Warther Carvings Museum, 15 minutes away near Dover, features an extensive collection of carved railroad pieces in walnut, ebony, and ivory.

GETTING THERE: The nearest large cities having air service are Columbus, Akron, and Pittsburgh. By car, Dennison is easily reached from I-77 via Route 250 (from the north) or Route 36 (from the south). Once in Dennison, take Second Street past the tracks and then turn left on Center Street.

Ohio

Mad River & NKP Railroad Museum ⑬

SITE LOCATION: 253 Southwest Street, Bellevue
PHONE: 419-483-2222
WEB SITE: www.madrivermuseum.org
E-MAIL: madriver@onebellevue.com

Mark Perri

The Mad River & NKP Railroad Museum opened on our nation's bicentennial in 1976 as a lasting tribute to the transportation industry. The museum has a widely varied collection of railroad locomotives, coaches, freight cars, equipment, and structures. While the museum focuses on the Nickel Plate Road and its successors, many other unique pieces of equipment, such as CB&Q Silver Dome no. 4714 (the first dome car built in the United States) are presented.

CHOICES: The museum is comprised of static exhibits. However, many pieces, especially the passenger equipment, have interiors that are open for inspection. In addition, some equipment is outfitted with museum displays.

WHEN TO GO: Since the museum operates a seasonal schedule, summertime from Memorial Day to Labor Day is best. In addition, the museum is open on weekends in May, September, and October.

GOOD TO KNOW: Bellevue is a thriving, quaint rural Ohio town, with ample amenities for food and lodging, and many other options for tourists such as antique shops and flea markets. Henry Flagler, who built the Florida East Coast Railroad, once lived on the property where the museum is now located.

WORTH DOING: Bellevue is a 30-minute drive from Sandusky and the Cedar Point amusement park, which is known for its roller coasters and its steam-powered, narrow gauge railroad.

DON'T MISS: Many opportunities exist for watching and photographing trains from public property around town. It is a major hub for the Norfolk Southern and home of one of the largest classification yards in the eastern United States. Mainline tracks bisect the museum and also host regional Wheeling & Lake Erie Railway trains.

GETTING THERE: The nearest major airports are Toledo, Cleveland, and Detroit. Amtrak's *Lakeshore Limited* and *Capitol Limited* stop in Toledo. For those driving, Bellevue is 20 minutes from the Ohio Turnpike off Exit 110.

OKLAHOMA

Frisco Depot Museum ❶
Once a main hub for the Frisco, the depot in Hugo is now a museum. Listed on the National Register of Historic Places, the museum includes railroad artifacts and displays on local history. It also features a restored Harvey House restaurant.

SITE LOCATION: 309 N. B Street, Hugo
PHONE: 580-326-6630

Heritage Express Trolley ❷
This 25-minute trolley ride is the only rail-based trolley in operation in Oklahoma. It runs from Heritage Park to downtown. Heritage Park is also home of the Canadian County Historical Museum, which is based in a historical Rock Island train depot.

SITE LOCATION: 300 S. Grand Avenue, El Reno
PHONE: 888-535-7366
WEB SITE: www.elreno.org/tour/attractions.asp
E-MAIL: info@elreno.org

Oklahoma Railway Museum ❸
The Oklahoma Railway Museum possesses an interesting collection of equipment that includes a Santa Fe diner, a Porter 0-6-0, and a Santa Fe FP45 with a warbonnet paint scheme. It also operates a variety of train rides and special events. It is open Thursday through Saturday, with train rides taking place April to October.

SITE LOCATION: 3400 NE Grand Boulevard, Oklahoma City
PHONE: 405-424-8222
WEB SITE: www.oklahomarailwaymuseum.org
E-MAIL: drake@oklahomarailwaymuseum.org

Railroad Museum of Oklahoma ❹

Located in a former Santa Fe freight house, this museum houses a large collection of railroad artifacts and memorabilia. In the yard, you can climb aboard a 1925 steam locomotive, wander through cabooses from nine different railroads, and view an assortment of freight cars. The museum also sponsors two all-caboose excursions.

SITE LOCATION: 702 N. Washington Street, Enid
PHONE: 580-233-3051
WEB SITE: www.railroadmuseumofoklahoma.org
E-MAIL: information@railroadmuseumofoklahoma.org

Santa Fe Depot Museum ❺

This 1905 Santa Fe depot has been restored and now contains a collection of railroad photos and other local historical artifacts. On display are 1907 Baldwin steam locomotive Santa Fe no. 1951 a coal tender, and a caboose. The museum is open daily, and it features a convenient picnic area.

SITE LOCATION: 204 S. Santa Fe Street, Pauls Valley
PHONE: 405-238-2244
WEB SITE: www.paulsvalley.com/test/santa_fe.html

Waynoka History Museum ❻

The museum is housed in a restored 1910 Santa Fe depot and Harvey House, and one room remains as a Harvey Girl's bedroom. The museum contains displays on Fred Harvey and the Santa Fe Railroad as well as other subjects. It includes a section foreman's house, other historic buildings, and a diesel locomotive.

SITE LOCATION: 202 S. Cleveland, Waynoka
PHONE: 580-824-1886
WEB SITE: www.waynoka.org
E-MAIL: waynokahs@hotmail.com

Yukon's Best Railroad Museum ❼

Located in the hometown of Garth Brooks, the museum, made up of a Rock Island boxcar and a UP caboose, contains artifacts of the Rock Island and other railroads.

SITE LOCATION: Third Street and Main Street, Yukon
PHONE: 405-354-5079

Farmrail 🔟

SITE LOCATION: 1601 W. Gary Boulevard, Clinton
PHONE: 580-323-1234
WEB SITE: www.farmrail.com

Wes Carr

Farmrail's *Quartz Mountain Flyer* takes passengers through the scenic Wichita Mountains of southwestern Oklahoma. The two-hour narrated round trip on refurbished, air-conditioned coaches gives you a glimpse of the Wild West as it was 100 years ago.

CHOICES: Scheduled on select weekends from April through December, the passenger excursions run from Quartz Mountain to Lone Wolf and back. A limited number of one-way locomotive cab rides are available for an additional fee.

WHEN TO GO: The scenery is in bloom during the spring, and the fall colors can be spectacular. If you like it hot, plan a visit during the summer months. The grain rush is in full swing in late May and early June, which means the railroad is running unit trains to keep up with demand.

GOOD TO KNOW: Make a vacation of your trip by taking in Quartz Mountain Nature Park. The park offers numerous activities including rock climbing, fishing, and hiking. A 50-acre ATV riding area is located on the north shore of nearby Lake Altus-Lugert. The Quartz Mountain Lodge features rooms, cabins, and a 64-person bunkhouse, as well as RV hookups and primitive campsites.

WORTH DOING: For the transportation fan, head north to Elk City and see the National Route 66 Museum. The Oklahoma Route 66 Museum is located east of Elk City in Clinton.

DON'T MISS: Follow the railroad all the way down to the Red River into Texas, where it meets the BNSF Railway at Quanah.

GETTING THERE: Quartz Mountain is 100 miles southwest of Oklahoma City. The train departs from Quartz Mountain at the intersection of Routes 44 and 44A. Leaving Oklahoma City, travel west on I-40 to Clinton and then take Route 9 south to Lone Wolf. Travel west on Route 44, which parallels Farmrail's tracks, to the intersection with Route 44A.

OREGON

Canby Depot Museum ❶

The Canby Depot Museum is housed in what could be the oldest railroad station in Oregon, which has been around since at least 1873. The museum's displays provide a look at 19th century life of this historic community. It is open Thursday through Sunday March through December.

SITE LOCATION: 888 NE Fourth Avenue, Canby
PHONE: 503-266-6712
WEB SITE: www.canbyhistoricalsociety.org
E-MAIL: depotmuseum@canby.com

Crooked River Dinner Train ❷

Riding this three-hour, 38-mile round trip is murder – or robbery. As you travel through the Crooked River Valley on a Wild West dinner train, you can enjoy a murder mystery, train robbery, or other entertainment with your meal. Themed rides are offered year-round along with holiday trains and special events.

SITE LOCATION: 495 NE O'Neil Way, Redmond
PHONE: 541-447-4485
WEB SITE: www.crookedriverdinnertrain.com
E-MAIL: info@crookedriverdinnertrain.com

Eagle Cap Excursion Train 3

Explore the wilderness of northeast Oregon on the Eagle Cap Excursion Train. It operates over a 63-mile line that connects Wallowa, Elgin, Enterprise, and Joseph. Various trips are available, ranging from two-hour to five-hour round trips that travel through canyons and along the Grande Ronde and Wallowa Rivers.

SITE LOCATION: 209 E. First Street, Wallowa
PHONE: 800-323-7330 or 541-886-3200
WEB SITE: www.eaglecaptrain.com

Willamette Shore Trolley 4

You can ride an antique trolley along a scenic six-mile rail line between Lake Oswego and Portland. Traveling along the Willamette River, you'll go through parks, past mansions, over bridges, and through a tunnel. It is open mid-May through October. The trolley is operated by the Oregon Electric Railway Historical Society. The society also operates the Oregon Electric Railway Museum located in Brooks, which is 30 miles south of Lake Oswego. The museum's collection includes streetcars, interurbans, and several double-deck trams.

SITE LOCATION: 311 N. State Street, Lake Oswego
PHONE: 503-697-7436
WEB SITE: www.oregonelectricrailway.org
E-MAIL: webmaster@oregonelectricrailway.org

Mount Hood Railroad 🔢

Oregon

SITE LOCATION: 110 Railroad Avenue, Hood River
PHONE: 800-872-4661 or 541-386-3556
WEB SITE: www.mthoodrr.com
E-MAIL: form on Web site

Mount Hood Railroad

The Columbia River Gorge is filled with magnificent scenery, and the area around Mount Hood especially so because of its abundant orchards and vineyards. The Mount Hood Railroad offers a 44-mile round trip to Parkdale that features spectacular views of its namesake mountain. The train ends at a park, where passengers can relax and picnic before the return trip.

CHOICES: The four-hour excursion departs in the morning and follows the valley between the Columbia River and Mount Hood, providing views of Mount Adams as well. For half the journey, narration provides information about local history. Afternoon excursions also run on weekends. Brunch and dinner trains offer meals prepared onboard restored railcars.

WHEN TO GO: Excursion and dinner trains run April through December, and there are numerous special events scheduled throughout the year. The railroad operates five or six days a week, depending on the time of year.

GOOD TO KNOW: The railroad still carries a limited amount of freight, so don't be surprised if you see a boxcar somewhere along the line. Not far out of the Mount Hood depot, the train traverses a switchback, where it zigzags up the side of the mountain to gain elevation quickly. The rear of the train becomes the front for the rest of the trip into Parkdale.

WORTH DOING: There is much to do in the area. Sample apples and pears from orchards, visit a local winery, or watch wind surfers try to master the winds from the Columbia River Gorge. You can also take a drive on the Mount Hood Loop, which gives you a view of many scenic waterfalls.

DON'T MISS: On the excursion train, be sure to take in the open-air car *Lookout Mountain*, which offers you the chance to soak in the atmosphere of the ride.

GETTING THERE: The Mount Hood Railroad is located 60 miles east of Portland off I-84. In Hood River, take Exit 63 to reach the depot. If driving from the south, Highway 35 also goes to Hood River.

Oregon Coast Scenic Railroad 6

SITE LOCATION: Highway 101, Garibaldi
PHONE: 503-842-7972
WEB SITE: www.ocsr.net
E-MAIL: info@ocsr.net

Jim Wrinn

Experience the Pacific Ocean on a 10-mile, 90-minute excursion along the shores of Tillamook Bay. The train is pulled by a Heisler locomotive and runs between Garibaldi and Rockaway Beach. It operates weekends from Memorial Day through mid-September. A special fireworks train operates in July.

CHOICES: You can ride in a coach, or for an extra fee, in an authentic caboose or in the steam locomotive's cab. Wherever you are, find a seat on the left side of the train. It's on the ocean side, and the views are spectacular.

WHEN TO GO: The railroad operates from late May to early October. A July 4th fireworks train, dinner trains, and other special excursions also run during the year.

GOOD TO KNOW: The railroad has begun work on a major restoration shop and expansion of its operations. The $2.5 million restoration center will house several steam locomotives as well as rail and logging artifacts.

WORTH DOING: Oregon's dairy industry is based in Tillamook, and it produces some of the best cheese and ice cream in North America. Be sure to stop at the dairy cooperative outlet store in nearby Tillamook. In addition, the area sports an aviation museum housed in a World War II blimp hanger. You can also view numerous lighthouses along the Pacific shore.

DON'T MISS: There is a layover between each run that provides the opportunity explore, get a bite to eat, and just enjoy the day.

GETTING THERE: The railroad is located along the Oregon coast, 10 miles north of Tillamook, in Garibaldi just off Highway 101. From Portland, take Highway 26 west to Highway 6 at Banks and follow Highway 6 over the forested Coast Range Mountains to Tillamook. At Tillamook, take Highway 101 north to Garibaldi. In Garibaldi, turn left on Third Street to Lumberman's Park, where the train boards.

Sumpter Valley Railway 🔳

Oregon

SITE LOCATION: Highway 7, Sumpter
PHONE: 866-894-2268 or 541-894-2268
WEB SITE: www.svry.com
E-MAIL: svrydepotstaff@eoni.com

Jim Wrinn

A five-mile portion of one of the most charming narrow gauge lines of the Pacific Northwest has been re-created amid forests and the spoils of a former gold-mining dredge operation. It is a good approximation of a remote steam line in eastern Oregon, where snowcaps rise in the distance even in June.

CHOICES: The railway runs between McEwen and Sumpter. Both round-trip and one-way excursions are available at either station. The railroad runs two historic locomotives. No. 19, an oil-burning 2-8-2, or Mikado type, is indigenous to the railroad. The two-truck, geared Heisler is one of a handful of wood-burners running today.

WHEN TO GO: The railway is open on weekends and holidays from Memorial Day through September. A special fall foliage photography train runs in October.

GOOD TO KNOW: The Sumpter depot is a replica of the original depot. Located on the Elkhorn Scenic Byway, Sumpter is surrounded by the Elkhorn Mountains. The area is filled with history, and nearby Baker City boasts at least 60 restored buildings.

WORTH DOING: Near the Sumpter station, in the Sumpter Valley Dredge State Heritage Area, visit the historic gold dredge that churned up all the rocks the railroad runs through – it's as big as a house and a monster of a machine well worth touring.

DON'T MISS: The railroad offers an Engineer-for-a-Day program. Take the throttle, under supervision, and you'll have a unique experience as a steam locomotive engineer.

GETTING THERE: The railway is about 330 miles from Portland in northeast Oregon. From Portland, take I-84 to Baker City and then take Highway 7 south 22 miles to McEwen.

PENNSYLVANIA

Allegheny Portage Railroad ❶

This national historic site preserves the remains of the Allegeny Portage Railroad that operated from 1834 to 1854. You can explore the 900-foot Staple Bend Tunnel, the first railroad tunnel built in the United States, visit the engine house, or take a hike. For bikers, a 2.5-mile trail takes you to the Staple Bend Tunnel.

SITE LOCATION: 110 Federal Park Road, Gallitzin
PHONE: 814-886-6150
WEB SITE: www.nps.gov/alpo

Bellefonte Historical Railroad ❷

This railroad offers 60-mile trips over the Nittany & Bald Eagle Railroad to Lemont, Pleasant Gap, Tyrone, and Lock Haven. The Bellefonte Station, a restored former Pennsylvania Railroad structure built in 1888, houses historical photos and memorabilia of area railroading.

SITE LOCATION: 320 W. High Street, Bellefonte
PHONE: 814-355-1053
WEB SITE: www.bellefontetrain.com
E-MAIL: grupe@astro.psu.edu

Electric City Trolley Museum ❸

Located on the grounds of the Steamtown National Historic Site, the museum is housed in a restored mill building. In addition to displaying vintage regional trolleys, the museum features a unique under-the-skin look at a restored trolley and other interactive exhibits. Trolley excusions travel through a 4,747-foot interurban tunnel.

SITE LOCATION: 300 Cliff Street, Scranton
PHONE: 570-963-6590
WEB SITE: www.ectma.org
E-MAIL: webmaster@ectma.org

Fayette Central Railroad 4

The railroad operates weekend excursions from Uniontown to Dunbar or Fairchance with Budd Rail Diesel Car no. 9913 or behind a diesel locomotive. For a view of the Youghiogheny River, try the Dunbar excursion. The Fairchance run gives you a view of the mountains. On hot summer days, you can ride to Shady Grove and cool off in the pool.

SITE LOCATION: 39 N. Gallatin Avenue, Uniontown
PHONE: 877-321-3277
WEB SITE: www.fayettecentralrailroad.com

Franklin Institute Science Museum 5

The museum features the Train Factory, a permanent, interactive exhibit showcasing Baldwin locomotive no. 60,000. You'll explore past and present railroad technology as you journey through the exhibit and even take no. 60,000 for a test run. The museum is open year-round.

SITE LOCATION: 222 N. 20th Street, Philadelphia
PHONE: 215-448-1200
WEB SITE: www.fi.edu
E-MAIL: guestservices@fi.edu

Friends of the East Broad Top Museum 6

Located at the former southern operating terminus of the East Broad Top Railroad, the museum includes two historic buildings, an EBT station and a post office, both constructed around 1915. Exhibits illustrate the history of the railroad and the people who constructed, maintained, and operated it. The museum is open on weekends, June through mid-October.

SITE LOCATION: Main Street, Robertsdale
PHONE: 814-635-2388 or 412-441-7881
WEB SITE: www.febt.org/museum.html
E-MAIL: vckeller@comcast.net

Greenville Railroad Park and Museum 7

This railroad museum displays Union Railroad 0-10-2 no. 604. Built in 1936, it is largest, and only surviving, steam switch engine. Several other cars are also on display. The museum includes a reconstructed dispatcher's office and stationmaster's quarters. It is open weekends during April, May, September, and October. During summer months, the museum is open Tuesday through Sunday.

SITE LOCATION: 314 Main Street, Greenville
PHONE: 724-588-4009
WEB SITE: www.greenvilletrainmuseum.org
E-MAIL: greenvillerailroadpark@gmail.com

Kiski Junction Railroad 8

This freight-hauling railroad also hauls passengers. From June to October, it offers train rides along the scenic Kiski River to Bagdad and back. On Tuesdays and Fridays, the train may stop to service a steel mill, but on Saturdays, the rides are just for fun. You can ride aboard a caboose, coach, or open-air car.

SITE LOCATION: 130 Railroad Street, Schenley
PHONE: 724-295-5577
WEB SITE: www.kiskijunction.com
E-MAIL: info@kiskijunction.com

Museum of Erie GE History 9

The museum displays models, pictures, and memorabilia related to the production locomotives at the General Electric plant in Erie. The collection includes materials from 1906, when the plant was being planned, to the present. It is open most Saturdays during the year.

SITE LOCATION: 2901 E. Lake Road, Erie
PHONE: 814-875-2494
WEB SITE: www.goerie.com/erieyesterday/museum_of_erie_ge_history.html

Oil Creek & Titusville Railroad 10

Go with the flow on this railroad's two-hour train ride. As it rolls through Oil Creek State Park, you'll see where towns sprung up to follow the first oil boom and then disappeared when the oil did. The railroad operates the only working post office car in the country. Special excursions and biking and canoeing opportunities are offered.

SITE LOCATION: 409 S. Perry Street, Titusville
PHONE: 814 676 1733
WEB SITE: www.octrr.org
E-MAIL: ocandt@usachoice.net

Pennsylvania Trolley Museum 11

A visit to the museum includes a guided tour of the carbarn and unlimited four-mile trolley rides. In the carbarn, you can see some trolleys and restoration projects. For an added fee, you can tour the trolley display building that houses 30 additional trolleys.

SITE LOCATION: 1 Museum Road, Washington
PHONE: 724-228-9256
WEB SITE: www.pa-trolley.org
E-MAIL: ptm@pa-trolley.org

Pioneer Tunnel Coal Mine & Steam Train 12

Take a scenic ride along Mahanoy Mountain as you hear stories about mining, bootlegging, and the Centralia Mine fire. A 1927 narrow gauge 0-4-0 steam locomotive takes you around the mountain. You can also tour a real anthracite coal mine in open mine cars. It is open April through October.

SITE LOCATION: 19th Street and Oak Street, Ashland
PHONE: 570-875-3850 or 570-875-3301
WEB SITE: www.pioneertunnel.com

Portage Station Museum 13

The museum is located in a restored Pennsylvania Railroad train station, originally built in 1926. The stationmaster's office contains artifacts from the Pennsylvania Railroad, and on the second floor, there is a display of Alleghany Portage Railroad items. The building is listed on the National Register of Historic Places.

SITE LOCATION: 400 Lee Street, Portage
PHONE: 814-736-9223
WEB SITE: www.portagestationmuseum.org
E-MAIL: mlcgeo@verizon.net

Rockhill Trolley Museum 14

The museum offers a three-mile ride aboard a vintage electric trolley car past the site of the Rockhill Iron Furnace to Blacklog Narrows. You can tour the museum's collection, which includes an operating open trolley, high-speed interurban cars, and maintenance-of-way cars, and watch restoration projects in progress. It is open weekends June through October with special events in November and December.

SITE LOCATION: 430 Meadow Street, Rockhill Furnace
PHONE: 814-447-9576
WEB SITE: www.rockhilltrolley.org
E-MAIL: form on Web site

Stourbridge Line Rail Excursions 🔢

Offering views of the Lackawaxen River and the Pocono Mountains, this scenic round trip runs from Honesdale to Hawley, closely following the route of the Delaware & Hudson Canal. A restored BL2 diesel locomotive pulls vintage cars on a variety of themed excursions throughout the year.

SITE LOCATION: Torrey Lane, Honesdale
PHONE: 800-433-9008 or 570-253-1960
WEB SITE: www.waynecountycc.com
E-MAIL: train@waynecountycc.com

Tunnels Park & Museum 🔢

From the nearby Jackson Street Bridge, you get a great view of the twin tunnels, which are 3,605 feet long. The site also features a museum and a restored 1942 Pennsylvania Railroad caboose. The museum includes railroad artifacts and photos. It is open Tuesday through Sunday.

SITE LOCATION: 411 Convent Street, Gallitzin
PHONE: 814-886-8871
WEB SITE: www.gallitzin.info
E-MAIL: info@gallitzin.info

West Chester Railroad 🔢

The railroad offers special-events excursions during the year. The 16-mile round trip runs from West Chester to Glen Mills, following scenic Chester Creek. Events are scheduled around holidays, and excursions include train robberies, summer Sunday picnics, and fall foliage runs.

SITE LOCATION: 250 E. Market Street, West Chester
PHONE: 610-430-2233
WEB SITE: www.westchesterrr.net
E-MAIL: form on Web site

East Broad Top Railroad ⸢18⸣

SITE LOCATION: Route 994, Rockhill Furnace
PHONE: 814-447-3011
WEB SITE: www.ebtrr.com
E-MAIL: office@ebtrr.com

Jim Wrinn

The East Broad Top was the last common carrier narrow gauge railroad east of the Mississippi River. A National Historic Landmark, the EBT's line runs through a beautiful valley little changed since the line closed in 1956. The 4.5-mile excursion has been operating since the 1960s.

CHOICES: The railroad still uses one of six Baldwin Mikado steam locomotives and wooden coaches purchased second-hand in the 1920s over a line laid out in 1874. In addition to the wooden coaches, the train includes open cars, a caboose, and the wonderful observation car *Orbisonia*, which requires an extra fare. The Fall Spectacular, held in early October, is the railroad's biggest event. More than 20 trains run, all operational equipment is used, and guided tours of the shops and roundhouse are conducted. Take some time to wander around the nearby roundhouse, yard, and the sprawling shops complex where the railroad once built its own freight cars and maintained its fleet of locomotives.

WHEN TO GO: The EBT is open Saturdays and Sundays from the first weekend in June through the end of October. Three trips are scheduled each day.

GOOD TO KNOW: Several times a year, the all-volunteer Friends of the East Broad Top lead tours of the interior of the shops and roundhouse. The EBT superintendent's home located next to the station has been made into a B&B that features a railroad motif.

WORTH DOING: Be sure to visit the adjacent Rockhill Trolley Museum, whose trolley cars traverse the former Shade Gap Branch of the EBT. Other nearby attractions include Horseshoe Curve and the Railroaders Memorial Museum in Altoona, as well as Raystown Lake, a 29,000-acre recreational area.

DON'T MISS: Since the railroad parallels a highway, follow a train for photos across the fields or from an overhead bridge. Stick around after the day's runs are over on Saturday to watch the hostlers clean the fires and prepare the engine for its overnight rest.

GETTING THERE: The East Broad Top is off the beaten track in central Pennsylvania. The closest commercial airport is in Altoona, about 50 miles away. The drive from Harrisburg or Altoona on Route 22 parallels the former Pennsylvania Railroad main line, now operated by Norfolk Southern, with its heavy freight traffic.

Horseshoe Curve National Historic Landmark ⑲

SITE LOCATION: 1300 Ninth Avenue, Altoona
PHONE: 888-425-8666 or 814-946-0834
WEB SITE: www.railroadcity.com
E-MAIL: info@railroadcity.com

Robert McGonigal

Horseshoe Curve is an engineering marvel completed in 1854 as part of the Pennsylvania Railroad's main line over the Allegheny Mountains. By curving the track across the face of a mountain, builders were able to gain elevation without making the grade too steep for trains to climb. Today, the curve is as vital as ever, serving as a key link in the Norfolk Southern system, with more than 50 trains passing over its three tracks each day. A trackside park established in 1879 received major improvements in 1992, making it a premier train-watching spot.

CHOICES: Attractions at Horseshoe Curve consist of a visitor center at ground level and the trackside park, which is accessible by a 194-step walkway or by a funicular railway. First-timers will want to tour the visitor center, ride the funicular up to track level, and then take the stairway back down. The best show at the curve is the passage of a heavy westbound train, laboring up the grade with helper engines on the front and/or rear. Try to stay long enough to catch this spectacle.

WHEN TO GO: The visitor center and funicular are open daily April through October. In October, the fall colors can be brilliant. Freight traffic tends to build toward the end of each week, so there may be more trains to see on Thursday, Friday, and Saturday.

GOOD TO KNOW: The site is managed by the superb Altoona Railroaders Memorial Museum in downtown Altoona. Combined admission tickets are available.

WORTH DOING: Continue west on Kittanning Point Road to Gallitzin and visit the small park at the west portal of one of the tunnels the railroad uses to pierce the spine of the Alleghenies. Cresson, a little further west is also a good place to watch trains. Both towns have trackside, railfan-oriented lodging.

DON'T MISS: The longer you stay at Horseshoe Curve, the greater the chances of seeing two or even three trains rounding the curve, a thrilling occurrence.

GETTING THERE: Horseshoe Curve is located five miles west of Altoona. Altoona is on I-99, 33 miles north of I-70/76. Amtrak's New York-Philadelphia-Pittsburgh *Pennsylvanian* stops at Altoona daily.

Lake Shore Railway Museum ⑳

SITE LOCATION: 31 Wall Street, North East
PHONE: 814-725-1911
WEB SITE: www.velocity.net/~lsrhs
E-MAIL: lsrhs@velocity.net

Jim Wrinn

A restored 1899 New York Central passenger station, built by the Lake Shore & Michigan Southern, houses extensive rail displays. Displayed on the grounds are 24 pieces of rolling stock and an 1869 station. There are demonstrations of a Heisler fireless locomotive on select weekends.

CHOICES: The restored New York Central passenger station houses an extensive collection of displays, and rolling stock is also displayed outdoors. A passenger and freight station built in 1869 by the LS&MS also sits on the grounds. View fireless 0-6-0 no. 6, one of 29 such locomotives built between 1934 and 1941 by the Heisler Locomotive Works. Demonstrations of the locomotive occur on selected weekends.

WHEN TO GO: The museum building is open weekends from Memorial Day through Labor Day, while the grounds are open every day. The last full weekend of September is the town of North East's Wine Festival. The two weekends after Christmas are known as Christmas at the Station.

GOOD TO KNOW: The museum hosts occasional Dinner-in-the-Diner events.

WORTH DOING: Time your visit with the Cherry Festival in July or the Wine Festival in September. There are five wineries in or near North East. You can also drive along Lake Erie and stop at one of the local beaches.

DON'T MISS: CSX's Chicago-New York main line and Norfolk Southern's line to Buffalo run beside the museum. You can watch 60-80 trains each day from the platform, including Amtrak's *Lake Shore Limited* passenger train.

GETTING THERE: The museum is located about 15 miles east of Erie, Pa., near the New York state border. From Erie, take Route 20 to North East, where it becomes Main Street. Turn right on Clinton, right on Mill Street, and then left on Wall.

DISCOUNT: $1 off each adult ticket, up to four adults.

Lehigh Gorge Scenic Railway 21

SITE LOCATION: 2 Susquehanna Street, Jim Thorpe
PHONE: 570-325-8485
WEB SITE: www.lgsry.com
E-MAIL: info@lgsry.com

Scott Snell

This 16-mile round trip into the Lehigh Gorge is among the most beautiful in Pennsylvania, a state blessed with numerous great tourist railroads and museums because of its abundant railroad development. Trains run on the tracks of the Reading & Northern regional railroad, paralleling a state bike path into an isolated, narrow chasm.

CHOICES: The one-hour excursion follows the winding Lehigh River, curve after curve, and crosses it in several places, until it reaches Old Penn Haven. Leaving from the renovated, distinct Central Railroad of New Jersey depot, the diesel-powered trains consist of vintage 1920s open-air coaches.

WHEN TO GO: The railway operates on Saturdays and Sundays mid-May through mid-December. The mountains present a new look for each season, but fall offers beautiful foliage and an extended schedule in October.

GOOD TO KNOW: In 1953, the towns of Mauch Chunk and East Mauch Chunk merged into one town with the name of Jim Thorpe when that famous athlete was buried there. Looking for a place that would help develop a memorial for her husband, who had no previous ties to the area, Thorpe's widow found assistance from the two towns.

WORTH DOING: Explore the town of Jim Thorpe, a charming village of shops, stores, and B&Bs, many featuring Victorian architecture. The town was once known as the Switzerland of America for its steep hillsides, narrow streets, and terraced gardens.

DON'T MISS: Ride the train one day and then get an outfitter to set you up with a bicycle and a shuttle to White Haven and ride back down the gorge the next day for a different perspective.

GETTING THERE: Located in the heart of the Poconos, Jim Thorpe is approximately 90 miles from Philadelphia. From there, take I-476 to Exit 74. Then take Route 209 south into Jim Thorpe, where it becomes Susquehanna Street, and follow it to the railway.

Middletown & Hummelstown Railroad [22]

SITE LOCATION: 136 Brown Street, Middletown
PHONE: 717-944-4435
WEB SITE: www.mhrailroad.com
E-MAIL: traingal@mhrailroad.com

Jim Wrinn

If you're looking for that relaxed train ride in central Pennsylvania, here's your ride. The M&H provides a trip along the Swatara Creek, past the ruins of a canal, and ends with a dramatic bridge crossing the creek and a stop at another tourist attraction, Indian Echo Caves. A nice package in an 11-mile round trip.

CHOICES: The M&H offers plenty of different trips, from scenic outings to murder mystery barbecues. You have a choice of departure locations, as trains operate from both the 1891 freight station in Middletown and the Indian Echo Caverns Platform. However, the special event trains operate only out of Middletown. Aboard the train's Delaware, Lackawanna & Western coaches, you'll hear informative narration about the area and be prepared to sing some railroading songs. You can even reserve a hobo sack lunch, complete with bandana and pole.

WHEN TO GO: Excursions begin Memorial Day weekend and end in October. There are numerous special events during the year.

GOOD TO KNOW: Formerly part of the Reading Railroad, the M&H is also provides freight service. At the Middletown yard, the railroad displays a collection of rolling stock.

WORTH DOING: This close to Hershey, how could you go wrong with a Sunday Sundae trip that includes a stop at the Cone-A-Cabana. And in Hershey, you can hop on more than 60 rides, including roller coasters and water rides, at Hersheypark amusement park.

DON'T MISS: The railroad offers a combination ticket with Indian Echo Caves for an interesting rail-cavern outing.

GETTING THERE: Middletown is situated between Harrisburg and Hershey, both 10 miles away, and 100 miles from Philadelphia. From Philadelphia, take I-76 to Route 283. Exit at Middletown and from Main Street, turn left on Pine Street and then left on Brown Street to get to the station.

DISCOUNT: Buy one adult ticket and get one child's ticket free.

New Hope & Ivyland Railroad 23

SITE LOCATION: 32 W. Bridge Street, New Hope
PHONE: 215-862-2332
WEB SITE: www.newhoperailroad.com
E-MAIL: info@newhoperailroad.com

Jim Wrinn

The New Hope & Ivyland Railroad provides a scenic, 45 minute trip through the rolling hills and valleys of Bucks County, leaving from the quaint resort village of New Hope on the Delaware River.

CHOICES: There are lots of trains to ride, from scenic excursions to dinner trains, as well as story-time rides for children. You can board regular excursion trains at either New Hope or Lahaska. The 1920s vintage passenger coaches are pulled by a steam engine, including Old Number 40, a 1925 Baldwin-type 2-8-0, or a diesel locomotive.

WHEN TO GO: The New Hope & Ivyland operates year-round. From January through March, excursions run on Saturdays and Sundays. In April, May, and November, Friday runs are added to the weekend schedule. And beginning Memorial Day weekend, excursions operate daily through the end of October. Special trains operate throughout the year, and December is filled with holiday trains. The annual railfan weekend in September, when all of the trains run, is a great time to visit.

GOOD TO KNOW: The line follows the ex-New Hope Branch of the Reading Railroad, and way back in 1914, the silent movie series *Perils of Pauline* was filmed along these same tracks. The restored Victorian station at New Hope has been in operation since 1891. An original "witch's hat" station, it once housed the railroad's telegraph operator.

WORTH DOING: History buffs can visit Valley Forge National Historical Park, which is about 40 miles from New Hope.

DON'T MISS: You can get off at either station and take a later train back to the originating station. At Lahaska, you can enjoy a family picnic, and in New Hope, you can take a mule-drawn boat ride in the Delaware Division of the Pennsylvania Canal or stroll along the Delaware River.

GETTING THERE: New Hope is 45 miles northeast of Philadelphia. From Philadelphia, take the Pennsylvania Turnpike east to the Willow Grove exit. Then take Route 611 to Route 202. Turn north on Route 202 and go 10 miles to Route 179, which leads you into New Hope. In town, take a left onto Bridge Street to the station. Lahaska is five miles southwest of New Hope, and the station is on Street Road one mile east of Route 202.

Pioneer Lines Scenic Railway 24

SITE LOCATION: 106 N. Washington Street, Gettysburg
PHONE: 717-334-6932
WEB SITE: www.gettysburgrail.com
E-MAIL: info@gettysburgrail.com

Jim Wrinn

Abraham Lincoln rode a train to Gettysburg to deliver his famous Civil War address. Today, Gettysburg visitors can take a train ride into history, passing through a portion of the battlefield and within sight of monuments marking the first day of the battle. From there, depending on the length of your excursion, it's a delightful trip through the Pennsylvania countryside.

CHOICES: The railroad's scenic train offers a 75-minute tour, with the conductor providing historic narration on the 16-mile round trip. Dinner and murder mystery trains are three-hour, 36-mile trips. The railroad offers the option of riding in the engine cab with the engineer for a fantastic view of the railroad.

WHEN TO GO: The railroad's excursions begin in April and run through November. Fall is among the most pleasant seasons to ride the train and visit Pennsylvania, and the railroad offers added runs in October. Special theme trains operate throughout the year.

GOOD TO KNOW: The railroad uses a pair of streamlined F units from the 1950s that provide a striking silhouette for the train.

WORTH DOING: After riding the train, visit Gettysburg National Military Park, which recently built a new visitor center. The battlefield remains much as it did in the 1860s. You can take a self-guided tour while listening to an audio tape, tour the park by bus, or sign up with a licensed battlefield guide.

DON'T MISS: For a chilling experience, take the eerie Ghost Train that rolls past the battlefield to the haunted engine house as you hear haunted tales of the area.

GETTING THERE: Gettysburg is in south-central Pennsylvania, just across the border with Maryland and about 60 miles from Baltimore. The railroad is a few blocks north of the downtown square in Gettysburg.

Railroad Museum of Pennsylvania ㉕

SITE LOCATION: 300 Gap Road, Strasburg
PHONE: 717-687-8628
WEB SITE: www.rrmuseumpa.org
E-MAIL: info@rrmuseumpa.org

Robert McGonigal

The Railroad Museum of Pennsylvania boasts one of the top rolling stock collections in the United States. The highlight is a dozen steam locomotives preserved by the Pennsylvania Railroad in the 1950s; very few PRR engines exist elsewhere. The collection also includes about 100 other locomotives and cars from the PRR and other railroads serving the state, many displayed in a 100,000-square-foot exhibition hall.

CHOICES: Go up, down, and out: an elevated walkway gives a fine view of the Rolling Stock Hall, a pit between the rails allows inspection of the underside of one of the locomotives, and tours of the rolling stock yard are sometimes available. Be sure to see PRR 4-4-2 no. 7002, a beautiful example of a high-wheeled passenger speedster from the early 20th century; PRR GG1 no. 4935, one of the best-preserved of the most famous class of electric locomotives; and PRR E7 no. 5901, the only surviving example of General Motors' top-selling passenger diesel.

WHEN TO GO: The museum is open every day except for certain major holidays and most Mondays November through March. A variety of special events are scheduled throughout the year.

GOOD TO KNOW: Lancaster County is in the heart of Pennsylvania Dutch country and home to Amish communities. On a drive through the county's scenic farmlands, you can experience Amish culture.

WORTH DOING: Spend part of the day at the museum and then take a ride on a steam train on the Strasburg Rail Road, located right across the road.

DON'T MISS: If you would like to see trains on a smaller scale, the National Toy Train Museum is also located in Strasburg.

GETTING THERE: The museum is on Route 741 (Gap Road) one mile east of Strasburg, which is about 15 minutes from Lancaster, one hour from Harrisburg or Reading, and 90 minutes from Philadelphia. Most folks take Route 30 to Route 896 south to Route 741.

DISCOUNT: $1 off regular adult admission.

Railroaders Memorial Museum 26

SITE LOCATION: 1300 Ninth Avenue, Altoona
PHONE: 888-425-8666 or 814-946-0834
WEB SITE: www.railroadcity.com
E-MAIL: info@railroadcity.com

Railroaders Memorial Museum

Of all the places in the United States deserving a first-rate railroad museum, Altoona is certainly at the top of the list. The museum here is among the best when it comes to providing an interactive experience and telling the story of this shop town that in the 1920s employed more than 15,000 Pennsylvania Railroad workers. Today, Altoona is still a shop city for Norfolk Southern, and the museum tells the story of how it became so important and the people who made it so.

CHOICES: Be sure to step into the bar exhibit and hear all about the lives of railroaders as they sit and sip a cold one. Also look at the exhibit on the PPR's testing and research lab. Some of their efforts were astounding.

WHEN TO GO: The museum is open daily May through October and Friday through Monday in November and December.

GOOD TO KNOW: The museum is housed in the Pennsylvania Railroad's former master mechanic's building, which was built in 1882.

WORTH DOING: The Allegheny Portage Railroad National Historic Site and Staple Bend Tunnel are both within 25 miles of Altoona.

DON'T MISS: Take a day and spend half of it in the museum and the other half watching trains at Horseshoe Curve. Combined admission tickets are available.

GETTING THERE: Altoona is about 95 miles east of Pittsburgh. From Pittsburgh, take Route 22 to I-99 north. Take Exit 33, 17th Street, and a right turn on Ninth Avenue takes you to the museum.

Steamtown National Historic Site ㉗

SITE LOCATION: Cliff Avenue, Scranton
PHONE: 888-693-9391 or 570-340-5200
WEB SITE: www.nps.gov/stea

Jim Wrinn

The former Delaware Lackawanna & Western railroad shop complex is home to one of the East's most complete railroad history exhibits. Housed in several buildings on the site of the Lackawanna's roundhouse, Steamtown provides a shrine to steam-era railroading in the northeastern United States. It also offers both short and long train rides. The real treat is a walk through the active portion of the roundhouse, where steam locomotives are still maintained.

CHOICES: The site includes both a steam history museum as well as a technology museum. The orientation movie, hands-on exhibits about workers as well as hardware, and equipment displays are excellent. Demonstrations of the turntable and shop tours are also conducted. For a brief visit, you can walk through the exhibits and take the *Scranton Limited*, a half-hour ride on vintage commuter coaches. But if you have time, schedule your visit when you can spend a day with the exhibits and then ride an excursion train to Moscow, a two-hour trip that includes a climb up the Poconos, or through the countryside to Tobyhanna. This is one of the few places where a large, mainline steam locomotive can operate at track speed on a mountain railroad.

WHEN TO GO: Steamtown is open year-round. Summer can be sultry, but spring and fall are pleasant. Winter sees less activity. Steamtown's trains run seasonally on select days. The *Scranton Limited* usually runs May through November, and the longer excursions from Memorial Day weekend through October.

GOOD TO KNOW: The Union Pacific Big Boy, one of 25 of its type built in the early 1940s, is one of the largest steam locomotives ever built. Operated in Wyoming and Utah, this is the only one of its type on exhibit in the eastern United States. It is so big, you could hold a dinner party in the firebox.

WORTH DOING: Nearby, you can view the Scranton Iron Furnaces or tour a coal mine.

DON'T MISS: The 45-minute shop tour, offered regularly, provides a good behind-the-scenes look at heavy-duty restoration work underway on several locomotives.

GETTING THERE: From I-81, take Exit 185. Stay in the left lanes to downtown Scranton and turn left at first traffic light. Follow Lackawanna Avenue to Cliff Avenue, where the park entrance is located.

Strasburg Rail Road 28

SITE LOCATION: 301 Gap Road, Strasburg
PHONE: 717-687-7522
WEB SITE: www.strasburgrailroad.com
E-MAIL: srrtrain@strasburgrailroad.com

Strasburg Rail Road

Founded in 1832, the Strasburg Rail Road is the oldest railroad company in the nation. It might have died if not for the efforts of local railfans who resurrected it as a tourist line in 1959. The nine-mile, 45-minute round trip from Strasburg to Paradise through Amish farmland aboard authentic 19th century wooden coaches recalls travel before automobiles. Trains are nearly always powered by one of the Strasburg's four operable steam locomotives.

CHOICES: Several different types of accommodations are available on most trains, including coach, open-air, deluxe lounge, and first-class parlor. Lunch, dinner, and wine-and-cheese trains are offered as well. Get off the train at Groffs Grove for a picnic or just to watch the action, which in the busy season includes a meet between two trains every half hour. Tours of the shop and engine house are available.

WHEN TO GO: Steam trains run every day nearly all year. In summer, two trains run simultaneously. A rare, wooden self-propelled doodlebug from a long-abandoned Lancaster County short line runs several days in March and in November. Strasburg's Thomas the Tank Engine events draw immense crowds.

GOOD TO KNOW: Located in the heart of Pennsylvania Dutch country, and a drive through the area gives you an opportunity to explore scenic farmlands with covered bridges and experience Amish culture.

WORTH DOING: There are no turning facilities on the Strasburg, so locomotives pull trains tender-first east out of the Strasburg station and pilot-first west. Sit on the right-hand side of the train out of Strasburg for the best view of the engine changing ends at Paradise.

DON'T MISS: Drive out to a country grade crossing to watch trains. At Cherry Hill Road, westbound trains work hard up a 1.5 percent grade. At Black Horse Road, an 18th century cemetery beside the track provides a fine vantage point for westbounds. Also, visit the Railroad Museum of Pennsylvania's world-class collection, right across the road.

GETTING THERE: For a scenic ride, approach Strasburg on Route 741 from either the east or west – just watch out for Amish buggies! The railroad is on Route 741 (Gap Road) one mile east of Strasburg.

DISCOUNT: 10% off one non-sale item in the gift shop.

Tioga Central Railroad 🔟29

SITE LOCATION: Route 287, Wellsboro
PHONE: 570-724-0990
WEB SITE: www.tiogacentral.com
E-MAIL: form on Web site

Tioga Central Railroad

Here's a short railroad that still carries freight on its 34-mile route but also knows how to have some fun. The ride takes you along Crooked Creek, through forests, and to Hammond Lake, a large reservoir. It's a good trip at a brisk pace behind rare Alco diesels.

CHOICES: The Tioga Central, in addition to operating its regular, 24-mile, 90-minute excursions, offers several special trains during summer, including a Friday night ice cream train and a 40-mile, Saturday sunset outing along Lake Hammond to the New York state line. Ride the train's open-air car and keep a lookout for wildlife such as osprey, blue herons, deer, and even bald eagles.

WHEN TO GO: The railroad offers regular excursions on Saturdays and Sundays from Memorial Day weekend through October. In fall, to take advantage of the spectacular foliage, special weekday excursions operate.

GOOD TO KNOW: The railroad owes its good views of Lake Hammond, which it parallels for much of its journey, to a dam project that almost resulted in the railroad's abandonment. Fortunately, the railroad was relocated to the side of the reservoir.

WORTH DOING: Explore the nearby Pine Creek Gorge however you like. You can take a hike, ride a bike, or raft a river. Called the Grand Canyon of Pennsylvania, the 1,000-foot-deep gorge winds its way through acres of scenic landscape. Various parks provide breathtaking views of the canyon from hiking trails. You can also bike the Pine Creek Trail, a former rail line, through the canyon. Rafting is best in spring.

DON'T MISS: At the station, take a look at the railroad's oldest piece of rolling stock. Now an office, Car 54 was originally a double-ended, open-platform paymaster car built in 1894 for the Grand Trunk Western.

GETTING THERE: Wellsboro is in north-central Pennsylvania, 50 miles north of Williamsport. Trains leave from Wellsboro Junction, which is about three miles north of Wellsboro on Route 287.

Wanamaker, Kempton & Southern Railroad ③⓪

SITE LOCATION: 42 Community Center Drive, Kempton
PHONE: 610-756-6469
WEB SITE: www.kemptontrain.com
E-MAIL: info@kemptontrain.com

Jim Wrinn

The Wanamaker, Kempton & Southern, while short on mileage, is long on atmosphere. The WK&S has been successful for more than 40 years by striving to preserve the feeling of a Reading Railroad branch line, operating authentically painted and lettered equipment.

CHOICES: Both steam and diesel locomotives are used on the 40-minute trips, with several departures each day. There are Easter Bunny, Harvest Moon, Halloween, and Santa specials scheduled throughout the season. Once each year, the WK&S hosts a Kids Fun Weekend that includes train rides, extra activities, and free ice cream for all train riders.

WHEN TO GO: The WK&S operates weekends May through October. Passing prosperous farms and crossing Ontelaunee Creek, the excursion takes you through beautiful scenery at any time of the year. The fall colors in late September and early October on the surrounding mountains can be breathtaking.

GOOD TO KNOW: The WK&S is much less formal than some tourist railroads, and it features a picnic grove that is accessible only by train.

WORTH DOING: Ride the left side of the train as you leave Kempton for the best views of Ontelaunee Creek and the surrounding mountains. Be sure to leave the train at Wanamaker while the engine runs around the train for the return trip to Kempton.

DON'T MISS: A visit to the WK&S can easily be combined with a trip to Steamtown, where the Railroad Museum of Pennsylvania is located, or to Strasburg and the Strasburg Rail Road.

GETTING THERE: The WK&S is located in eastern Pennsylvania, five miles north of I-78 just off Route 737 in Kempton. In Kempton, follow the signs to the station, which is located at the north end of town.

RHODE ISLAND

Newport Dinner Train ▮

Aboard the Newport Dinner Train, you can enjoy lunch or dinner in elegantly restored 1940s Budd dining cars. The 22-mile round trip takes you along scenic Narragansett Bay. The menu offers several entree choices including the train's specialty, baby back ribs. The Islander Touring Train offers 90-minute scenic train excursions aboard self-propelled commuter cars. Special packages are offered that include boat cruises of Newport Harbor.

SITE LOCATION: 19 America's Cup Avenue, Newport
PHONE: 800-398-7427 or 401-841-8700
WEB SITE: www.newportdinnertrain.com
E-MAIL: info@newportdinnertrain.com

SOUTH CAROLINA

Railroad Historical Center ❶

A walk-through display of rolling stock includes a Mikado type steam engine, a dining car, a sleeper car, a caboose, and other cars. It is operated in partnership with The Museum in Greenwood, located four blocks north, which features a wide range of historical exhibits and educational programs. The Railroad Historical Center is open Saturdays April through October.

SITE LOCATION: 908 S. Main Street, Greenwood
PHONE: 864-229-7093
WEB SITE: www.themuseum-greenwood.org/train.shtml
E-MAIL: themuseum@greenwood.net

South Carolina Railroad Museum ❷

SITE LOCATION: 110 Industrial Park Road, Winnsboro
PHONE: 803-635-4242 or 803-635-9893
WEB SITE: www.scrm.org
E-MAIL: info@scrm.org

South Carolina Railroad Museum

A slice of Southeastern shortline history awaits visitors to the South Carolina Railroad Museum. Located on the former Rockton & Rion Railway, a granite quarry short line, this museum brings the experience of a casual Southeastern short line to life through a 10-mile, one-hour ride, interesting exhibits, and rolling stock displays.

CHOICES: The museum operates the Rockton, Rion & Western Railroad on a five-mile stretch of the former Rockton & Rion Railway line. The line runs west past antebellum plantation remains and through pine forests to Rion. Its collection showcases South Carolina's railroad heritage and includes exhibits of track tools, artifacts, and photographs. Rolling stock features passenger cars, freight cars, cabooses, and other equipment from the Lancaster and Chester, Norfolk Southern, CSX, and other railroads.

WHEN TO GO: The museum is open on the first and third Saturdays June through October, with regular train rides scheduled on those days. It also hosts a variety of special events throughout the year.

GOOD TO KNOW: The railroad's 100-ton General Motors diesel saw action during the Korean War. Late in the year, children can mail letters to Santa from a 1927 Railway Post Office car.

WORTH DOING: Wet a line in one of the state's top fishing lakes. Lake Wateree has more than 13,700 acres and contains bream, catfish, crappie, and bass. Dammed in 1919, it is also one of the oldest manmade lakes in the state.

DON'T MISS: Check out the two steam locomotives in the collection: 4-6-0 no. 44 from the Hampton & Branchville and no. 712, one of only five existing Atlantic Coast Line steam locomotives and a veteran of the Rockton & Rion.

GETTING THERE: About 30 miles from Columbia, Winnsboro is between Columbia and Rock Hill, just off I-77. Take Exit 34 and follow Route 34 about five miles and turn left at the steam locomotive that marks the museum's entrance.

SOUTH DAKOTA

Prairie Village ❶

Prairie Village is a collection of restored buildings, rail equipment, and farm machinery that preserves the past. Rail structures include several historical depots, a roundhouse, and a turntable. On Sundays, you can take a two-mile train ride around the village. Several steam and diesel locomotives, various cabooses, and a unique chapel car are featured. Railroad Days takes place in June.

SITE LOCATION: Highway 34, Madison
PHONE: 800-693-3644 or 605-256-3644
WEB SITE: www.prairievillage.org
E-MAIL: info@prairievillage.org

Black Hills Central Railroad ▣

SITE LOCATION: 222 Railroad Avenue, Hill City
PHONE: 605-574-2222
WEB SITE: www.1880train.com
E-MAIL: office@1880train.com

J m Wrinn

This railroad gives you a chance to ride on a real mountain railroad with its steep grades, mines, and scenic hills. Situated close to Mount Rushmore, the Black Hills Central, also known as the 1880s Train, carries riders between Keystone and Hill City.

CHOICES: The two-hour, 20-mile round trip is a beautiful journey through the historic, rugged landscape of the Black Hills. You can ride in a coach or pile into the drover's car, believed to be one of only two left from the Chicago & North Western Railroad and the only one in use. Cattlemen lived in these cars while following their herds, which were loaded onto stock cars, to market.

WHEN TO GO: With a few exceptions, trains operate several times daily between May and October, departing from both Keystone and Hill City. Some last-train departures from Keystone are one-way trips only.

GOOD TO KNOW: Keystone is rich in tourist offerings including restaurants, shows, and shops. Hill City has amenities but without the tourist hubbub. Engine no. 7, its tender, and the drover's car were used in TNT's 2005 miniseries *Into the West*.

WORTH DOING: Ride on steam locomotive no. 110, the nation's only operating Mallet locomotive. What makes this engine special is that it has two sets of cylinders and drivers, and the exhaust steam from the back set of cylinders moves the front set of drivers. It is like having two smaller engines under one boiler. The locomotive is impressive as it tackles grades as steep as 5 percent for almost a mile but never breaks a sweat.

DON'T MISS: The Black Hills area is filled with must-see activities, including a trip to Mount Rushmore. You can experience the rugged beauty of the Badlands, see bison in Custer State Park, and visit the Wild West town of Deadwood.

GETTING THERE: Whether traveling east or west, I-90 gets you to the train. To reach Keystone from Rapid City, take Highway 16 to Highway 244. To reach Hill City from Deadwood, take Highway 385.

TENNESSEE

Casey Jones Railroad Museum ❶

Although Casey Jones has been dead for more than 100 years, his legend lives on. His former home has been turned into a railroad museum located in Casey Jones Village. The museum includes artifacts related to Casey Jones as well as Jackson's railroad history. The museum is expanding with an addition that re-creates an 1890s train station. You can also step into a replica of no. 382, Casey's engine.

SITE LOCATION: 30 Casey Jones Lane, Jackson
PHONE: 731-668-1222
WEB SITE: www.caseyjones.com
E-MAIL: caseyjonestn@yahoo.com

Cookeville Depot Museum ❷

The railroad museum is housed in a Tennessee Central Railway depot. Built in 1909, the building is listed on the National Register of Historic Places. Inside, there are changing displays of railway artifacts and photos highlighting local railroad history. A renovated caboose contains additional exhibits, and a Tennessee Central locomotive, tender, and caboose are on display. It is open year-round Tuesday through Saturday.

SITE LOCATION: 116 W. Broad Street, Cookeville
PHONE: 931-528-8570
WEB SITE: www.cookeville-tn.org/ls
E-MAIL: depot@cookeville-tn.com

Cowan Railroad Museum ❸

Photos, relics, and memorabilia from the age of steam are located in a restored, century-old depot. Outdoor displays include a GE 44-ton diesel switcher, a 1920 Porter locomotive, a flatcar, and a caboose. Nearby is the Franklin-Pearson House, which was built in 1850 as a boarding house for workers constructing the Cumberland Mountain Tunnel. Trainspotting opportunities also exist.

SITE LOCATION: 108 Front Street, Cowan
PHONE: 931-967-3078 or 931-968-9877
WEB SITE: www.visitcowan.com

Little River Railroad Museum ❹

The museum holds a number of tools, artifacts, and photographs dedicated to the Little River Railroad and the lumber company it served. It displays a restored 1909 Shay locomotive, several pieces of rolling stock, logging equipment, and a water tower. It is open April through October.

SITE LOCATION: 7747 E. Lamar Alexander Parkway, Townsend
PHONE: 865-428-0099
WEB SITE: www.littleriverrailroad.org
E-MAIL: president@littleriverrailroad.org

Nashville, Chattanooga & St. Louis Depot and Railroad Museum ❺

The museum houses a collection of artifacts, photographs, and memorabilia associated with railroad and local history. The grounds feature a dining car and two cabooses. Built in 1907, the depot is listed on the National Register of Historic Places. It is open year-round Monday through Saturday.

SITE LOCATION: 582 S. Royal Street, Jackson
PHONE: 731-425-8223
WEB SITE: www.cityofjackson.net/departments/recpark/newrecpark/depot.html
E-MAIL: thedepot@cityofjackson.net

Southern Appalachia Railway Museum ⑥

SITE LOCATION: Highway 58, Oak Ridge
PHONE: 865-241-2140
WEB SITE: www.techscribes.com/sarm

Southern Appalachia Railway Museum

For many years, the government did not acknowledge the existence of the huge nuclear research lab at Oak Ridge or the railroad that served it. Now that the lab is closed, the railroad to "Secret City" is now a tourist attraction, giving visitors some insight into this unusual bit of railroading as well as a nice ride through the east Tennessee hills.

CHOICES: Pulled by 1950s Alco diesels, the 14-mile, 60-minute round trip takes you through the former secret atomic facility. Once outside the Secret City, the train enters the countryside, where it crosses Poplar Creek and passes Watts Bar Lake before returning. Several two-hour dinner trains and theme trains are scheduled during the year.

WHEN TO GO: Excursions run several Saturdays a month from April to September. Special runs occur in February, November, and December, and fall foliage runs happen in October.

GOOD TO KNOW: Non-U.S. citizens must show a passport and visa before riding the train. When the train leaves, it passes through an enclosure used to check railcars for hobos, and it still provides a way to screen the train from unwanted spies. The boarding station is a former guardhouse.

WORTH DOING: To learn more about the secrets of atomic power, you can visit the American Museum of Science & Energy in Oak Ridge or take a self-guided auto tour of some Manhattan Project sites in the area.

DON'T MISS: Arrive 30 minutes early and you may be able to get a caboose seat when they are available.

GETTING THERE: Oak Ridge is about 30 miles west of Knoxville, and the Heritage Center is situated between Oak Ridge and I-40 on Route 58. To get there from Knoxville, take I-40 west to Exit 356. Turn right and travel north on Route 58 approximately five miles to the Heritage Center. Turn left into the main entrance and take the first left inside the plant.

Tennessee Central Railway Museum ❼

SITE LOCATION: 220 Willow Street, Nashville
PHONE: 615-244-9001
WEB SITE: www.tcry.org

Jim Wrinn

The museum offers day trips on a streamlined passenger train through scenic middle Tennessee over the tracks of the Nashville & Eastern Railroad to various destinations.

CHOICES: The museum operates a variety of excursions throughout the year. Most depart from Nashville and travel to Watertown or Cookeville, but some also depart from the Cookeville depot. A typical excursion will carry about 400 passengers. You can ride coach, first-class, or dome seating. First-class offers reclining seats and large windows. With dome seating, you get a spacious ride with a panoramic view. The museum displays a representative selection of cars.

WHEN TO GO: The museum is open on Tuesdays, Thursdays, and Saturdays year-round. Excursions run throughout the year. The majority of the longer, 180-mile round-trip excursions to Cookeville take place in the fall when the foliage is most brilliant.

GOOD TO KNOW: The museum is housed in the former Tennessee Central Railway's master mechanic's office, and it includes a large collection of Tennessee Central Railway artifacts.

WORTH DOING: If available, try riding on the Seaboard Air Line Railway sun-lounge car. With its curved oversize windows, the *Hollywood Beach* is a unique car that occasionally is seen in an excursion train consist. Be sure and photograph the museum's E and F units, which are 1950s streamliners.

DON'T MISS: There is much to see and do in Nashville. You can tour numerous mansions and historic buildings including the Hermitage, the home of Andrew Jackson, and Ryman Auditorium, the former home of the Grand Ole Opry. Make sure to sample some of the city's famous music and barbecue.

GETTING THERE: The museum is located near downtown Nashville on Willow Street one block north of Hermitage Avenue.

Tennessee Valley Railroad 8

SITE LOCATION: 4119 Cromwell Road, Chattanooga
PHONE: 423-894-8028
WEB SITE: www.tvrail.com
E-MAIL: form on Web site

Jim Wrinn

If you were to take a major steam railroad from the 1920s, shrink it and preserve it, you'd have the Tennessee Valley Railroad. It offers a steam-powered train ride that leaves from a magnificent station, crosses trestles over streams and another active railroad line, and passes through a tunnel before it reaches the terminal at the opposite end of the run.

CHOICES: The railroad offers a variety of excursions. You can take the *Missionary Ridge Local* on a six-mile round trip between Grand Junction and East Chattanooga, traveling through a unique horseshoe tunnel as you do. On the *Chickamauga Turn*, a six-hour ride takes you to Chickamauga and back. Departing out of Etowah, the railroad, with the Tennessee Overhill Association, also offers a trip through the Hiwassee River Gorge that rides to the top of the Great Hiwassee Loop. The railroad's Dixie Land excursions feature various special trains.

WHEN TO GO: Excursions run March through December, with specials scheduled throughout the year. Anytime the steam train is running is a good time to go. Take a day to explore the railroad's equipment and then take a day-long ride on the same weekend.

GOOD TO KNOW: If you want an all-railroad experience, stay at the Chattanooga Choo Choo, a Holiday Inn in the former terminal station. You can eat at the station complex in one of several venues, including a real railroad dining car, and sleep on a train car.

WORTH DOING: In Chattanooga, activities include visiting the Tennessee Aquarium and taking a riverboat cruise on the Tennessee River. History buffs can explore both the Lookout Mountain and Chickamauga battlefields.

DON'T MISS: Be sure and walk into the shop at East Chattanooga, where volunteers and professionals restore railroad equipment dating back to 1903. East Chattanooga features one of the few complete wheel shops in the country, and on any given visit, there's no telling what set of wheels from what engine is there for repairs.

GETTING THERE: The railroad is in the northeast section of Chattanooga. To get there, take Route 153 to Exit 3. At the end of the exit ramp, turn left over Route 153 and turn right onto Cromwell Road.

Three Rivers Rambler 9

SITE LOCATION: Volunteer Landing on Neyland Drive, Knoxville
PHONE: 865-524-9411
WEB SITE: www.threeriversrambler.com
E-MAIL: form on Web site

Jim Wrinn

There are few perfect chances to ride a steam train in a beautiful part of the Appalachians, leaving from one of the more pleasant areas of a small city like Knoxville. But the *Three Rivers Rambler* offers just such an outing. From its departure point on the Tennessee River, it makes its way into the country to its namesake point: the confluence of the Holston and French Broad Rivers that creates the mighty Tennessee. The train bridges this point on a magnificent trestle that puts an exclamation point on the trip.

CHOICES: On the 90-minute round trip, you'll have the choice of riding in an air-conditioned coach, an open-air car, or a caboose. The vintage cars are pulled by a restored 1925 Baldwin steam engine. No. 203 is decked out in historical attire as Washington & Lincolnton for the Georgia short line it first worked.

WHEN TO GO: Excursions operate on Saturdays during summer and fall. Special trains, including the Circus Express, also run. You can't beat autumn, especially for the colors, but on Saturdays featuring University of Tennessee home football games, you may be swamped with orange-clad fans and find the train being used for railgate parties.

GOOD TO KNOW: The railroad has begun restoration of steam engine no. 154, which has been on display for 55 years in Chilhowee Park.

WORTH DOING: The departure point on the Tennessee River is adjacent to the university in an area with several good restaurants (try Calhoun's cheesy spinach dip – it's delicious!). Sports fans could try and catch a University of Tennessee football or basketball game or visit the Women's Basketball Hall of Fame.

DON'T MISS: Along the way, feel free to ask the conductor or volunteer staff questions about the train or local history.

GETTING THERE: From I-40, take Exit 386B to Neyland Drive and turn left. Drive two miles to the parking lot on your left and look for signs. After parking, cross under Neyland Drive and proceed left down the riverwalk to the train at Volunteer Landing.

TEXAS

Galveston Railroad Museum ❶

The museum displays three steam locomotives, including a vintage Houston and Texas Central 4-6-0, and three diesels as well as numerous passenger and freight cars. It also features a collection of railroad china. The museum closed to repair damage caused by Hurricane Ike in 2008. Please check its Web site to see if it has reopened and for scheduling information.

SITE LOCATION: 25th Street at the Strand, Galveston
PHONE: 409-765-5700
WEB SITE: www.galvestonrrmuseum.com
E-MAIL: galvrrmuseum@sbcglobal.net

History Center ❷

The History Center features indoor and outdoor interpretive exhibits. Permanent displays include a 1920 Baldwin 4-6-0 from Texas Southeastern Railroad, a log car, a caboose, and two motor cars. Its research center is open to the public.

SITE LOCATION: 102 N. Temple Drive, Diboll
PHONE: 936-829-3543
WEB SITE: www.thehistorycenteronline.com
E-MAIL: info@thehistorycenteronline.com

Houston Railroad Museum ❸

The museum features a unique collection of locomotives, freight cars, and passenger cars with a Texas flavor. At the museum, you can tour a *Texas Special* coach and a *Texas Eagle* sleeping car, view artifacts, and even blow a diesel's whistle. It is open Saturdays April to November.

SITE LOCATION: 7390 Mesa Road, Houston
PHONE: 713-631-6612
WEB SITE: www.houstonrrmuseum.org
E-MAIL: info@houstonrrmuseum.org

McKinney Avenue Trolley ⁴

McKinney Avenue Trolley operates a fleet of vintage streetcars, built between 1909 and 1945. You can hop on and off a trolley and explore the city's Uptown area. Trolley rides are free, so you can hop all you want. Trolleys run daily, every 25 minutes on weekends and every 15 minutes on weekdays. Look for an extension soon down Olive Street.

SITE LOCATION: McKinney Avenue, Dallas
PHONE: 214-855-0006
WEB SITE: www.mata.org
E-MAIL: ask_mata@yahoo.com

New Braunfels Railroad Museum ⁵

Housed in the restored 1907 International & Great Northern depot, the museum displays a 0-6-0 Porter oil-fired steam locomotive, a Missouri Pacific caboose, and numerous railroad artifacts. It is open Thursday through Monday.

SITE LOCATION: 302 W. San Antonio Street, New Braunfels
PHONE: 830-627-2447
WEB SITE: www.newbraunfelsrailroadmuseum.org
E-MAIL: info@newbraunfelsrailroadmuseum.org

Railroad & Heritage Museum ⁶

Housed in a 1910 Gulf, Colorado & Santa Fe depot, the museum features early Santa Fe and Missouri-Kansas-Texas station equipment, including a working telegraph. Outdoor exhibits feature a variety of cars, a steam locomotive, and a diesel engine. The museum is open Tuesday through Saturday.

SITE LOCATION: 315 W. Avenue B, Temple
PHONE: 254-298-5172
WEB SITE: www.rrhm.org

Railroad and Transportation Museum of El Paso ❼

A restored 1857 4-4-0 locomotive and other railroad exhibits are on display in the Transit Terminal of Union Plaza. One exhibit covers urban transit from the mule car through streamlined Art Deco streetcars. It is open daily.

SITE LOCATION: 400 W. San Antonio Avenue, El Paso
PHONE: 915-422-3420
WEB SITE: www.elpasorails.org
E-MAIL: form on Web site

Railway Museum of San Angelo ❽

Located in the historic Kansas City, Mexico and Orient depot, which was completed in 1910, the museum highlights local railroad history. Static displays include two diesel locomotives, a boxcar, and a caboose. It is open on Saturdays.

SITE LOCATION: 703 S. Chadbourne, San Angelo
PHONE: 325-486-2140
WEB SITE: www.railwaymuseumsanangelo.homestead.com
E-MAIL: form on Web site

Rosenberg Railroad Museum ❾

The museum features Tower 17, the last manned interlocking tower in Texas, which was moved to the site. Inside the fully restored tower, you can work the interlocking machine. Other exhibits include signaling, station agent, and telegraph artifacts. The museum is also restoring an 1879 business car.

SITE LOCATION: 1921 Avenue F, Rosenberg
PHONE: 281-633-2846
WEB SITE: www.rosenbergrrmuseum.org

Texas & Pacific Railway Museum ➓

The museum is housed in a historic Texas & Pacific depot that was built in 1912. It contains artifacts and photos dating from the 1870s and a replica of an agent's office. For a panoramic view of the area, go to the depot's upper level and look out from the balcony. A Union Pacific caboose is also on the grounds. The Texas & Pacific Railway Museum is open Tuesdays through Saturdays.

SITE LOCATION: 800 N. Washington Avenue, Marshall
PHONE: 800-513-9495 or 903-938-9495
WEB SITE: www.marshalldepot.org
E-MAIL: info@marshalldepot.org

Texas Transportation Museum ⓫

The museum displays a variety of railroad structures and equipment. It features a Southern Pacific depot built in 1913 that was moved from Converse. The two-room building contains memorabilia from the SP and two other railroads that served San Antonio. The museum also operates a short train ride. On display are two steam locomotives, two diesel engines, and a variety of rolling stock.

SITE LOCATION: 11731 Wetmore Road, San Antonio
PHONE: 210-490-3554
WEB SITE: www.txtransportationmuseum.org
E-MAIL: ttm1964@sbcglobal.net

Wichita Falls Railroad Museum ⓬

The museum's collection includes a Fort Worth & Denver steam locomotive, a Missouri-Kansas-Texas switch engine, a 1913 Pullman all-steel sleeper, troop sleepers, cabooses, and other cars. Artifacts center on the railroads that served Wichita Falls, especially the Missouri Kansas-Texas Railway. The museum is open year-round Tuesday through Saturday.

SITE LOCATION: 500 Ninth Street, Wichita Falls
PHONE: 940-723-2661
WEB SITE: www.wfrrm.com

Austin Steam Train 🔳

SITE LOCATION: 401 E. Whitestone Boulevard, Cedar Park
PHONE: 512-477-8468
WEB SITE: www.austinsteamtrain.org
E-MAIL: info@austinsteamtrain.org

J. Parker Lamb

This tourist line was formed in 1989 to provide weekend service over a portion of a 167-mile route purchased from Southern Pacific. The train operates out of Cedar Park and rolls through the Texas hills – and history.

CHOICES: The railroads's operating hub is in Cedar Park, 19 miles from downtown Austin. The *Hill Country Flyer* makes a 70-mile round trip between Cedar Park and Burnet, and the trip includes a leisurely layover. On the 46-mile round trip aboard the *Bertram Flyer*, you'll leave Cedar Park, cross the South San Gabriel River, and arrive in Bertram. Rolling stock consists of six vintage Pennsylvania P70 coaches, along with three first-class parlor cars of AT&SF, NKP, and MP heritage. You have a choice of riding coach, excursion, or first-class.

WHEN TO GO: Many visitors choose to ride during the spring and fall or enjoy special runs such as the North Pole Flyer. Each June, the railroad hosts a day-long Railfair at its Burnet terminal. This event, featuring 24-mile round trips to Bertram, also incorporates large numbers of hobby and book vendors, plus numerous outdoor activities for families.

GOOD TO KNOW: The Austin Steam Train should once again be powered by steam as the restoration of SP Mikado no. 786 nears completion. Trains are also pulled by an Alco RSD-15 in a black widow paint scheme.

WORTH DOING: Both Cedar Park and Burnet have numerous lodging and dining options for visitors, while Austin is famous for its museums, entertainment, and scenic drives.

DON'T MISS: Twilight Flyers, which feature nighttime entertainment, run periodically. Some incorporate storytellers for children while others feature adult-oriented murder mysteries.

GETTING THERE: Cedar Park can be reached from the north by leaving I-35 at Round Rock and using Highway 45 westward, while visitors arriving from the south will travel northward though Austin on I-35 and connect directly with Highway 183. Cedar Park is also served by Capital MetroRail, a commuter route from downtown Austin.

Grapevine Vintage Railroad 14

SITE LOCATION: 709 S. Main Street, Grapevine
PHONE: 817-410-3123
WEB SITE: www.gvrr.com
E-MAIL: twayne@ci.grapevine.tx.us

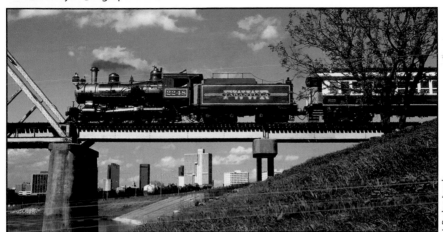

J. Parker Lamb

With its home base at the restored 1888 Cotton Belt depot in downtown Grapevine, the GV Railroad operates over 21 miles of ex-Cotton Belt trackage into the famous Fort Worth Stockyards Mall. It also includes a six-mile branch line (ex-Frisco) running southward from the mall across the Trinity River into the western part of the city. Grapevine operates the only 19th century steam locomotive in Texas, an 1896 Cooke 4-6-0 used for decades by the Southern Pacific in fire service on Donner Pass.

CHOICES: For maximum mileage, passengers can board at Grapevine, travel to the Fort Worth Stockyards, and then ride the Trinity River turn that passes through Trinity Park and the Fort Worth Zoo along a segment of the famous Chisholm Trail. It connects with the return train to Grapevine. The two-hour layover allows ample time to explore the mall's many offerings. Trains carry four 1925-era day coaches (19th century décor) plus a pair of open-air excursion coaches.

WHEN TO GO: Four-day operation (Thursday through Sunday) is offered between Memorial Day and Labor Day. Frequency is reduced to three days (Friday to Sunday) during the rest of the season. There is no service January to mid-February. Steam power is generally used on Saturdays.

GOOD TO KNOW: Grapevine features numerous lodging and dining opportunities as well as proximity to the Ballpark at Arlington (Texas Rangers) and Six Flags Over Texas. The Fort Worth Stockyards complex includes the Texas Cowboy Hall of Fame and weekend rodeo shows. Just north of the city is Grapevine Lake, a mecca for water sports.

WORTH DOING: True to its name, Grapevine is home to numerous wineries with regular tours and a special Grapefest celebration in September.

DON'T MISS: The line offers numerous trips that include entertainment such as mock gun fights and train robberies, visits to historical frontier forts, and children's activities such as Easter Bunny runs and North Pole trains with a storytelling Santa.

GETTING THERE: The city of Grapevine is adjacent to the northwest corner of the DFW Airport, midway between the two hubs of the Metroplex. Three major highways (114, 121, and 360) intersect at Grapevine, with I-30 being only a few miles south of the airport.

Museum of the American Railroad ⑮

SITE LOCATION: 1105 Washington Street, Dallas
PHONE: 214-428-0101
WEB SITE: www.dallasrailwaymuseum.com
E-MAIL: info@dallasrailwaymuseum.com

Museum of the American Railroad

Founded in 1963, the museum features more than 30 pieces of vintage equipment. It is located in downtown Dallas at Fair Park, home of the annual Texas State Fair. The museum contains an eclectic mix of all types of locomotives from both the United States and Canada. It features one of the nation's largest collections of pre-World War II heavyweight passenger equipment. It also has variety of lightweight passenger cars, freight cars, and cabooses.

CHOICES: At few other locations can you find two of UP's largest locomotives, a Big Boy and a Centennial DD40AX, along with a Pennsylvania GG1. Other engines range in size from a Frisco 4-8-4 down to a diminutive 0-6-0 from the Dallas Union Terminal. The display also includes two historic structures from Dallas' rail history, the city's first depot and a Santa Fe interlocker, along with a 1941 Ford truck used by the Railway Express Agency.

WHEN TO GO: The museum is open Wednesday through Sunday throughout the year and closed on all national holidays. A special August event is a Whistle Fair that employs the museum's steam calliope and its many steam engine whistles. During the two-week state fair, held in mid-October, the museum is open daily, but with the event's vast crowds, access to the rail site is more difficult.

GOOD TO KNOW: The museum's collection rests on a half-dozen parallel tracks that offers close inspection, inside and out, of the equipment. Along with the museum's new name (formerly Age of Steam), the museum plans to build a larger facility.

WORTH DOING: Dallas' Fair Park is home to other museums and performance venues including the African American Museum, Museum of Nature and Science, Dallas Aquarium, and Texas Music Center. The 225-acre site is a registered National Historic Landmark and includes a large collection of Art Deco buildings.

DON'T MISS: Rail enthusiasts may also wish to visit Dallas Union Terminal, which is served by Amtrak, Dallas Area Rapid Transit, and Trinity River Express (commuter rail to Fort Worth). Vintage streetcars also ply the nearby McKinney Avenue Trolley lines.

GETTING THERE: Downtown Dallas is easily accessible by 10 major highways (including I-30, I-35, and I-45) plus two airports.

Texas State Railroad 16

SITE LOCATION: Highway 84 and Park Road 76, Rusk
PHONE: 888-987-2461 or 903-683-2561
WEB SITE: www.texasstaterr.com
E-MAIL: info@texasstaterr.com.

Jonethan Gerland

Established in 1881 and operating excursions since 1972, the Texas Sate Railroad offers a relaxing, enjoyable ride through the piney woods region of east Texas at a leisurely pace between the towns of Rusk and Palestine. Steam and diesel locomotives with local history pull the trains through tall stands of timber in the I. D. Fairchild National Forest, giving riders a glimpse into the railroad's origin of hauling agricultural and timber products.

CHOICES: The Texas State Railroad offers visitors several options for trips on the 25-mile ride. You can ride in either open-air cars or in climate-controlled coaches (recommended during the summer months). Round trips are available from either depot, and there is a 90-minute layover for lunch at the opposite destination. Box lunches are available for regular excursions but must be ordered during ticket reservation. Alternating each month, the steam and diesel locomotives swap the trains they pull.

WHEN TO GO: Trains currently operate year-round, mostly on weekends, but the schedule varies in frequency during non-summer months. Autumn and winter are usually mild, so open-air seating is very enjoyable. However, east Texas weather changes rapidly, so have a jacket or coat handy. The railroad also offers special holiday trips and events.

GOOD TO KNOW: Of the two towns, Palestine is larger and offers more accommodations and services. Rusk is headquarters for the railroad and offers several small hotels and B&Bs. Additional lodging and amenities are located in nearby Jacksonville. Full-service camping and picnic sites are available adjacent to each depot.

WORTH DOING: Several times a year, various historical and military reenactments are incorporated into the train rides.

DON'T MISS: Check to see if shop tours are available in Rusk and for tours of Texas & Pacific 2-10-4 no. 610 housed in the shop at Palestine. Both depots are Victorian-styled stations and contain historical exhibits.

GETTING THERE: Major airlines to Dallas or Houston provide the closest air transportation. From there, a leisurely three-hour drive is required to reach the two east Texas towns.

DISCOUNT: $3 off adult ticket, up to four; new reservations only, excludes special events.

UTAH

Ogden Union Station ➊
Built in 1924, Ogden Union Station now houses a variety of museums and galleries, including the Utah State Railroad Museum and Eccles Rail Center. The museum contains artifacts of Utah railroading, and the rail center displays a UP Northern 4-8-4 locomotive and other historic pieces of equipment. Other museums in the station focus on history, firearms, gems, classic cars, and the arts.

SITE LOCATION: 2501 Wall Avenue, Ogden
PHONE: 801-393-9886
WEB SITE: www.theunionstation.org
E-MAIL: keri29@theunionstation.org

Western Mining and Railroad Museum ➋
Museum exhibits feature the Denver & Rio Grande Western and other railways. Located in the old Helper Hotel, which was completed in 1914, the museum contains four floors of artifacts. The third floor contains a railroad office and two rooms of railroading artifacts. A 100-year-old caboose is also on display. Other exhibits focus on the mining industry and its workers. A simulated coal mine is featured. It is open year-round.

SITE LOCATION: 296 S. Main Street, Helper
PHONE: 435-472-3009
WEB SITE: www.wmrrm.org
E-MAIL: helpermuseum@helpercity.net

Golden Spike National Historic Site ❸

SITE LOCATION: Golden Spike Drive, Promontory
PHONE: 435-471-2209
WEB SITE: www.nps.gov/gosp
E-MAIL: form on Web site

Jim Wrinn

The construction of the transcontinental railroad is one of the pivotal events in the nation's history. Completed May 10, 1869, at this remote spot northwest of Ogden, the National Park Service does justice to the event by running replica locomotives and conducting reenactments.

CHOICES: Reenactments of the Last Spike Ceremony, complete with dignitaries in period dress, take place on Saturdays and holidays May through Labor Day. The two steam locomotive replicas, the coal-burning Union Pacific's no. 119 and the wood-burning Central Pacific *Jupiter*, are accurate reproductions and fully functional. The visitor center offers informative films and exhibits.

WHEN TO GO: Except for Thanksgiving, Christmas, and New Year's Day, the visitor center is open. Between May and Labor Day, the steam locomotives are on display and operate demonstrations daily. During winter, when the locomotives are being maintained, rangers conduct engine house tours on Saturdays and Sundays.

GOOD TO KNOW: The correct name for the location of Golden Spike National Historic Site is Promontory Summit, not Promontory Point, which is 35 miles to the south. The summit is the highest point of Promontory Pass. For some reason, the wrong location was reported in some records in 1869 and perpetuated throughout history.

WORTH DOING: To the west, a dirt road leads to one of the original grades. Take your vehicle and put it on the grade pointed east. It's a one-lane, one-way road that goes back to the visitor center. Driving at 20 mph, you'll get a good sense of what it was like to ride an early 4-4-0 steam engine down these very tracks. At one point, you'll pass a spot where 14 miles of track were laid in one day during 1869, a record that has never been broken.

DON'T MISS: Drive through Brigham City and view the interesting Box Elder Tabernacle, and stop at the restored early 20th century train depot.

GETTING THERE: Golden Spike National Historic Site is in northern Utah, 32 miles west of Brigham City. From Brigham City, take Highway 83 to the entrance, which is Golden Spike Drive. The area is still very rugged and sparsely populated. Food and fuel are available in Brigham City.

Heber Valley Railroad 4

SITE LOCATION: 450 S. 600 W, Heber
PHONE: 435-654-5601
WEB SITE: www.hebervalleyrr.org
E-MAIL: reservations@hebervalleyrr.org

Jim Wrinn

This railroad offers a scenic ride beside Deer Creek Reservoir and down Provo Canyon in unspoiled country with the Wasatch Mountains as a backdrop over a line that began operating in 1899.

CHOICES: Heber Valley offers two regular excursions in the shadow of 12,000-foot Mount Timpanogos aboard vintage coaches. The *Provo Canyon Limited* is a three-hour round trip that runs to Vivian Park and back. Along the way, you'll hear about the history of the area. The 90-minute *Soldier Hollow Express* goes to Deer Creek Reservoir and returns. Summer excursion packages combine river rafting or bike riding with a train ride. In winter, you can train to a 1,000-foot hill and tube down. Numerous special events take place throughout the year, from sunset barbecues to fiddlers 'n' fireworks.

WHEN TO GO: The railroad operates year-round. Each season has something special to offer, but summer is especially beautiful in Utah.

GOOD TO KNOW: The railroad helped to move spectators and athletes to and from venues during the 2002 Olympics. With repairs underway to the railroad's steam locomotives, most trains will operate under diesel power, but steam will operate on a limited basis.

WORTH DOING: Take a scenic drive along the Provo Canyon Scenic Byway (Highway 189) that runs between Heber Valley and Provo. A short side trip on the Alpine Scenic Loop (Highway 92) takes you past Robert Redford's Sundance Resort.

DON'T MISS: If you can, ride the caboose. It's the first steel caboose that belonged to the Union Pacific. The railroad also offers cab rides for a fee.

GETTING THERE: The railroad is located between Salt Lake City and Provo. From Salt Lake City, take I-80 east to Exit 148 and then follow Highway 40 into Heber. Turn right on W. 300 S and then left on S. 600 W to the station.

DISCOUNT: $5 off each adult ticket; daytime excursions only.

VERMONT

Green Mountain Railroad ▮

The railroad offers three distinct scenic excursions. Leaving Bellows Falls, the *Green Mountain Flyer* crosses two covered bridges on its way to Chester Depot. The *White River Valley Flyer* travels from White River Junction along the Connecticut River to Norwich and the Montshire Museum of Science. On the *Champlain Valley Flyer*, you'll see the state's two highest mountains as well as Lake Champlain.

SITE LOCATION: 54 Depot Street, Bellows Falls
PHONE: 800-707-3530 or 802-463-3069
WEB SITE: www.rails-vt.com
E-MAIL: railtour@vermontrailway.com
DISCOUNT: $1 off each adult ticket, up to four adults; excludes specials.

New England Institute and Transportation Museum ❷

The centerpiece of the museum's railroad exhibit is the renovated Boston & Maine no. 494. The museum also celebrates the railroad with its annual Glory Days of the Railroad festival. Other exhibits are dedicated to aviation and river commerce. It has winter and summer hours.

SITE LOCATION: 100 Railroad Row, White River Junction
PHONE: 802-291-9838
WEB SITE: www.newenglandtransportationmuseum.org
E-MAIL: info@netransportation.org

Shelburne Museum ❸

Outside the museum, you'll see the 1890 Shelburne passenger station, locomotive no. 220, which pulled the trains of four presidents, and an 1890 private luxury car. Other historic buildings, a steamship, and fine and folk art are also on display.

SITE LOCATION: Route 7, Shelburne
PHONE: 802-985-3346
WEB SITE: www.shelburnemuseum.org
E-MAIL: info@shelburnemuseum.org

VIRGINIA

Eastern Shore Railway Museum ❶

The museum is housed in a restored 1906 Pennsylvania Railroad passenger station. On the siding are two cabooses, a baggage car, a Pullman sleeper, a Budd dining car, and a touring car. The museum also includes an 1890s maintenance-of-way tool shed, a crossing guard shanty, and various railroad artifacts. It is open year-round.

SITE LOCATION: 18468 Dunne Avenue, Parksley
PHONE: 757-665-7245
WEB SITE: www.parksley.com/seeus.shtml

Old Dominion Railway Museum ❷

The Old Dominion Railway Museum tells the story of Virginia's railroading heritage through artifacts, videos, displays, and an HO layout. Located near the birthplace of Virginia railroad operations, it is open Saturdays and Sundays year-round.

SITE LOCATION: 102 Hull Street, Richmond
PHONE: 804-233-6237
WEB SITE: www.odcnrhs.org

Suffolk Seaboard Station Railroad Museum ❸

The restored 1885 Seaboard Airline passenger station features permanent and seasonal displays of railroad memorabilia and a caboose built for the Nickel Plate Line. It is open Wednesday through Sunday.

SITE LOCATION: 326 N. Main Street, Suffolk
PHONE: 757-923-4750
WEB SITE: www.suffolktrainstation.org
E-MAIL: info@suffolktrainstation.org

O. Winston Link Museum ❹

SITE LOCATION: 101 Shenandoah Avenue NE, Roanoke
PHONE: 540-982-5465
WEB SITE: www.linkmuseum.org
E-MAIL: programs@linkmuseum.org

O. Winston Link Vuseum

Only two photographers in the United States have their own museums. One belongs to noted landscape photographer Ansel Adams. The other is O. Winston Link. A commercial photographer, Link was fascinated with steam locomotives and made a pilgrimage to record the last of these on the Norfolk & Western in the late 1950s.

CHOICES: The museum is housed in the former Norfolk & Western passenger station in downtown Roanoke. The station was the departure point for many of the trains Link photographed, making it an excellent departure point for a world of Link's photography. More than 300 of Link's photographs are on display. The museum includes interactive exhibits, Link's photography equipment, and his railroad sound recordings. Be sure to watch the documentary film on Link's life. It's an excellent look at the man and his work through his voice and those of many others.

WHEN TO GO: The museum is open daily except for Easter, Thanksgiving, Christmas, and New Year's Day. Fall and spring in the Blue Ridge Mountains are magnificent.

GOOD TO KNOW: Famous for his nighttime scenes that record the passing railroad as well as slices of rural life, Link took many photos of the region in the late '50s and early '60s. For years, Link's work languished, but in the 1980s, his career rebounded as the art world discovered his genius of capturing steam at night in (mostly) black and white.

WORTH DOING: The Hotel Roanoke, directly behind the museum, is a former railroad hotel and a great place to spend the night. Spend some time on the front lawn and watch the coal trains lumber by as they have for more than 120 years.

DON'T MISS: The former station is a Virginia Historic Landmark and is listed on the National Register of Historic Places. It is one of several renovated railroad buildings in the area. Another is the Virginia Museum of Transportation, which is a short walk away. The two museums offer a combined admission.

GETTING THERE: Roanoke is about 190 miles west of Richmond and near West Virginia and North Carolina. To reach the museum from I-81, take I-581 south and exit at Williamson Road and turn right on Shenandoah Avenue.

Virginia Museum of Transportation ❺

SITE LOCATION: 303 Norfolk Avenue SW, Roanoke
PHONE: 540-342-5670
WEB SITE: www.vmt.org
E-MAIL: info@vmt.org

Jim Wrinn

Roanoke was once synonymous with the best steam locomotives in the land. The Norfolk & Western built many of them right here, just a few blocks away. While the museum's scope is the broad subject of transportation, its heart is in railroading.

CHOICES: The museum is housed in a historic rail setting, the city's old N&W freight station. Through exhibits and rolling stock displays, you'll learn a lot about how people got around in the Old Dominion State. It displays steam and diesel locomotives, antique automobiles, trucks, and even a post office bus. The museum also includes several ongoing exhibits dedicated to railroading and a model railroad.

WHEN TO GO: The museum is open daily, except for various holidays, throughout the year.

GOOD TO KNOW: The museum also contains a research library that includes books, photographs, periodicals, blueprints, maps, and timetables.

WORTH DOING: Take a stroll along the rail walk that connects the museum with the O. Winston Link Museum and Hotel Roanoke. The walk parallels the Norfolk Southern's mainline track.

DON'T MISS: Climb into the crew cab of the streamlined Norfolk & Western 4-8-4 Class J. Built in 1950, no. 611 is the last of its kind, one of 13 that pulled the railroad's named trains. Capable of sprinting faster than 100 mph, or climbing the mountains of West Virginia, these locomotives were considered to be among the best in the nation. You can stand in the cab and see the gauges, handles, and levers that made it all happen. Next door to no. 611 is no. 1218, a Class A. Built in 1943, this articulated locomotive features two sets of drivers and cylinders.

GETTING THERE: Situated in the Blue Ridge Mountains, Roanoke is served by a regional airport and several major highways. The museum is located downtown on Norfolk Avenue between Second and Fifth Streets.

WASHINGTON

Dayton Historical Depot ❶

Built in 1881, this is the oldest surviving railroad station in Washington. The stylish Stick/Eastlake building is now a museum of local history. It includes artifacts from the Union Pacific and the Oregon Railroad and Navigation Company, and a UP caboose is also on display. It is open year-round.

SITE LOCATION: 222 E. Commercial Street, Dayton
PHONE: 509-382-2026
WEB SITE: www.daytonhistoricdepot.org
E-MAIL: depot1881@bmi.net

Lake Whatcom Railway ❷

This 90-minute train ride takes you from the shores of Lake Whatcom into the wooded countryside and back. The vintage coaches and diesel were all used on the Northern Pacific. A 100-year-old steam engine and wooden Great Northern freight cars are also on site. For a good workout, you can try your hand at riding a handcar. Excursions run during summer and for special events.

SITE LOCATION: NP Road, Wickersham
PHONE: 360-595-2218
WEB SITE: www.lakewhatcomrailway.com

Northern Pacific Railway Museum ❸

The 1911 Northern Pacific railroad depot in Toppenish now serves as a museum to that railroad. The site's freight house has been converted to an engine house, where several steam locomotives are being restored. The museum offers several special events during the year. It is open Tuesday through Sunday May through October.

SITE LOCATION: 10 S. Asotin Avenue, Toppenish
PHONE: 509-865-1911
WEB SITE: www.nprymuseum.org

Pioneer Village and Museum ❹

The village features 20 historical structures dating back to the late 1800s. Railroad displays include a caboose, a dining car, and a section house that contains artifacts. The museum is open March through December.

SITE LOCATION: 600 Cotlets Way, Cashmere
PHONE: 509-782-3230
WEB SITE: www.cashmeremuseum.org

Washington State Railroads Historical Society Museum ❺

The museum features artifacts and photos of the railroads involved in the state. Outdoors, it displays a variety of locomotives, passenger cars, freight cars, and cabooses. It is open on Saturdays.

SITE LOCATION: 122 N. Tacoma Avenue, Pasco
PHONE: 800-465-5430 or 509-543-4159
WEB SITE: www.wsrhs.org
E-MAIL: email@wsrhs.org

Chehalis-Centralia Railroad 6

SITE LOCATION: 1101 Sylvenus Street, Chehalis
PHONE: 360-748-9593
WEB SITE: www.steamtrainride.com
E-MAIL: info@steamtrainride.com

Jim Wrinn

In the shadow of Mount Saint Helens, this relaxing train ride takes you into the forests of western Washington. You'll ride behind a steam locomotive that saw many years of service logging these very forests.

CHOICES: The railroad offers two different excursions. The 12-mile Milburn run takes you through forests and countryside. A longer 18-mile round trip to Ruth extends the ride by following the Chehalis River. The railroad's dinner train follows the Ruth route and serves a four-course meal in a refurbished 1920s dining car.

WHEN TO GO: Summer steam train rides begin Memorial Day weekend and operate Saturdays and Sundays through September. Dinner trains, murder mystery trains, and special events are scheduled throughout the year.

GOOD TO KNOW: Trains travel over trackage that was once part of the Milwaukee Road, and a restored Milwaukee Road depot serves as the boarding point.

WORTH DOING: Take time to visit Mount Saint Helens National Volcanic Monument and view the dramatic changes the area has undergone since the 1980 eruption. The 110,000-acre site contains hiking trails, several visitor centers, and an observatory.

DON'T MISS: On summer Saturdays, the railroad usually makes an early 12-mile run to Milburn and then follows up with an 18-mile run to Ruth later in the afternoon. You can catch the early run, take pictures with Mount Saint Helens as a background, and return on the later trip.

GETTING THERE: The railroad is about a 90-minute drive from either Portland or Seattle. From I-5, take Exit 77 (Main Street) into Chehalis. Turn left on Riverside Drive and then left again on Sylvenus Street. Nearby Centralia is also served by Amtrak.

DISCOUNT: $1 off each adult ticket, up to four adults; valid on regular runs only.

Chelatchie Prairie Railroad

SITE LOCATION: 207 N. Railroad Avenue, Yacolt
PHONE: 360-686-3559
WEB SITE: www.bycx.com
E-MAIL: tickets@bycx.com

Jim Wrinn

The train runs on a remote former logging railroad line in western Washington from Yacolt to Lucia. The 5-mile route includes a 330-foot-long tunnel, a trestle over the Lewis River, and a half-hour layover at Moulton Falls.

CHOICES: On the layover in Moulton Falls Park, you can have a picnic and take in two waterfalls and a tall arched bridge.

WHEN TO GO: The railroad operates February through December. It runs on various weekends and offers train robbery and fall color excursions as well as other specials throughout the year, including those for Mother's Day, Father's Day, Halloween, and Christmas.

GOOD TO KNOW: The railroad had shut down after the last lumber mill closed and it was sold. Volunteers brought it back to life in 2001.

WORTH DOING: A half hour may not be enough time to see Moulton Falls Park. The park contains a hiking trail and volcanic rock formations. It also connects to Lucia Falls Park and the Bells Mountain Trail. Mount Saint Helens is about an hour's drive north of Yacolt.

DON'T MISS: Take a good look at engine 16, which is a rare 2-8-2 tank engine. For excellent photos of the train, first take one trip and then photograph the train on the portions of the ride that parallel the tracks into Yacolt.

GETTING THERE: The railroad is located an hour's drive from Vancouver, Wash., and Portland. From I-5, take Exit 16 through Fargher Lake or Exit 9 through Battle Ground to Yacolt. In Yacolt, the station is on Railroad Avenue at Yacolt Road.

Mount Rainier Scenic Railroad ⑧

SITE LOCATION: 49 Mineral Creek Road, Mineral
PHONE: 888-783-2611 or 360-492-5588
WEB SITE: www.mrsr.com

Jim Wrinn

Here's a chance to experience a real Pacific Northwest logging railroad at work. The locomotives, the setting, and the route all have the feel of a working railroad.

CHOICES: A pure steam experience, a 2-8-2T logging engine usually pulls the passenger coaches through the foothills of Mount Rainier on a two-hour round trip. You'll ride out to a tall trestle near Morton and return. The railroad offers all three major types of geared logging locomotives as possible power: a Shay, a Climax, and a Heisler.

WHEN TO GO: The railroad operates weekends from Memorial Day weekend through September. October is filled with special events including autumn foliage trains, pumpkin runs, and ghost trains. The Snowball Express runs in November and December. A winter photo outing with multiple locomotives is perfect for anyone who really likes trains.

GOOD TO KNOW: Flooding in 2006 washed out the approaches to the Nisqually River bridge and caused the railroad to alter its route as repairs are made. Trains now depart from the railroad's restoration facility in Mineral, but the railroad hopes to restore service at its Elbe station for the 2010 season. The Elbe depot remains open for ticket purchasing.

WORTH DOING: Ride one trip and photograph another one, especially if you can get Mount Rainier to peek out from behind the clouds.

DON'T MISS: Mount Rainier National Park offers scenic drives and hikes around the 14,410-foot active volcano. Some areas remain closed due to damage from the flooding. However, the park has opened a new visitor center and still remains an enjoyable recreational destination.

GETTING THERE: Mineral is located in western Washington near Mount Rainier National Park, approximately 75 miles south of Seattle and 125 miles north of Portland. A 10-minute drive from Elbe, Mineral is off Highway 7. In Mineral, turn on Front Street to reach the boarding area.

Northwest Railway Museum ❾

SITE LOCATION: 38625 SE King Street, Snoqualmie
PHONE: 425-888-3030
WEB SITE: www.trainmuseum.org
E-MAIL: info@trainumseum.org

Northwest Railway Museum

The museum is home to more than 70 pieces of rolling stock, the bulk of it from the Pacific Northwest. The museum also includes a collection of dining car china, tools, signs, and lanterns. It offers a short train ride from either Snoqualmie or North Bend.

CHOICES: The museum is headquartered at Snoqualmie depot, a restored 1890 Queen Anne-style building that is on the National Register of Historic Places. It features exhibits inside the depot and outdoor displays of restored steam locomotives, passenger cars, freight cars, and maintenance equipment. It offers 10-mile round trips to Snoqualmie Falls in restored heavyweight coaches pulled by first-generation diesel locomotives.

WHEN TO GO: The museum is open daily year-round except for Thanksgiving, Christmas, and New Year's Day. It offers train rides on weekends April through October, with special events scheduled during the year. Railroad Days takes place the beginning of August.

GOOD TO KNOW: The museum has restored a unique logging caboose. Built by White River Lumber Company in 1945, the caboose is just 24 feet long. Because of wartime shortages of raw materials, the caboose was made of wood and recycled parts.

WORTH DOING: View Snoqualmie Falls, one of the state's most popular attractions. The waterfall cascades down 270 feet, which is 100 feet more than Niagara Falls. You can see the falls from an observation platform inside Snoqualmie Falls park.

DON'T MISS: Check out the nine steam locomotives in the collection, including the unusual Mallet engines that were used for logging – they're basically two locomotives under one boiler.

GETTING THERE: The museum is 30 miles east of Seattle on I-90. From I-90 east, take Exit 25. Heading north, follow Snoqualmie Ridge Parkway for approximately four miles to Highway 202. Turn right on Highway 202 and proceed a half-mile to the Snoqualmie depot on your right. To get to the North Bend depot, take Exit 31 off I-90. Follow Bendigo Street into North Bend and turn right on North Bend Way.

WEST VIRGINIA

Huntington Railroad Museum ❶

This outdoor museum, located in Ritter Park, displays a Chesapeake & Ohio Mallet locomotive, a Porter 0-4-0, a C&O caboose made in Huntington, and other pieces of equipment. The museum is open Sundays from Memorial Day through September. Run by the Collis P. Huntington Railroad Historical Society, the group also operates New River Train excursions during October to view autumn foliage. The train travels over the former C&O main line from Huntington to Hinton through the New River Gorge for a scenic all-day trip.

SITE LOCATION: Memorial Boulevard and 14th Street W, Huntington
PHONE: 304-523-0364
WEB SITE: www.newrivertrain.com

Cass Scenic Railroad State Park 2

SITE LOCATION: Highway 66, Cass
PHONE: 800-225-5982 or 304-456-4300
WEB SITE: www.cassrailroad.com
E-MAIL: cassrailroad@wvdnr.gov

Jim Wrinn

The Cass Scenic Railroad is as close as you'll ever come to experiencing a mountain logging railroad – because it once was one. Leaving from the mill town of Cass along the beautiful Greenbriar River, trains climb steep grades out of the Leatherbark Creek area, negotiate two switchbacks, and hug hillsides to gain elevation. It was all about getting to the timber 100 years ago. Today, it's all about getting above it all. And Cass does that.

CHOICES: Got only a little time? Ride a 90-minute trip to Whitaker station and back for a taste. Got plenty of time? Sink your teeth into a half-day trip to Bald Knob and back. At an intermediate point, trains pause for servicing, and you can inspect a re-created railroad logging camp. Continuing on, trains powered by unusual geared steam locomotives work their way to Bald Knob, which, at 4,880 feet, is the second highest point in West Virginia. The view there is spectacular, and the trains climb an 11 percent grade. There is also an excursion to Spruce. The railroad schedules special events during the season and runs a Fiddles and Vittles Train with dinner and bluegrass music.

WHEN TO GO: The railroad runs Memorial Day through October, with heavy passenger counts during the colorful autumn.

GOOD TO KNOW: In spring, the railroad's support organization, the Mountain State Railroad & Logging Historical Association, holds a railfan weekend when all the Shay geared locomotives run. This event covers tracks not normally used by Cass trains.

WORTH DOING: Stay in one of the restored mill workers' houses. Most of the two-story cottages sleep eight, are furnished, and come with a fully equipped kitchen. Several motels are nearby, but the cottages add to the mill atmosphere.

DON'T MISS: Walk up to the shop where the Shay and Heisler locomotives are maintained. It's a great opportunity to see the engines and meet the crews. Be sure and check out Western Maryland no. 6, the last Shay built, and at 162 tons, the largest one left.

GETTING THERE: Cass Scenic Railroad is located in eastern West Virginia, and I-64 is the closest major road. From there, narrow, winding two-lane roads are the rule, so take plenty of time and watch for deer. Route 66 connects to Route 219 at Slatyfork.

DISCOUNT: $2 off standard fare Monday through Thursday, up to four fares.

Durbin & Greenbrier Valley Railroad 🔳

SITE LOCATION: Main Street, Durbin
PHONE: 877-686-7245
WEB SITE: mountainrail.meer.net
E-MAIL: ticketinfo@mountainrail.com

Jim Wrinn

The Durbin & Greenbrier Valley Railroad operates three separate and distinct railways over 135 miles of scenic railroad through the Mountain State. The *Cheat Mountain Salamander* offers a ride on a replica Edwards railcar, the *Durbin Rocket* operates a 1910 Climax locomotive, and the *New Tygart Flyer* is a diesel-powered train that pulls coaches and first-class cars through the wilderness.

CHOICES: This railroad is all about choices. The *Salamander* provides rides of various lengths including a nine-hour round trip that features a stop at the High Falls of the Cheat, an impressive waterfall that puts an exclamation point on the journey. The *Rocket* is a peaceful ride behind a Climax geared steam locomotive, believed to be one of only three in operation in the United States, along the unspoiled Greenbrier River. The *Flyer* provides a dramatic trip through a curved tunnel, across a deep canyon, and over a rushing river.

WHEN TO GO: The trains operate May through October, with some November trips as well.

GOOD TO KNOW: The *Flyer* boards in Elkins or Belington. The *Rocket* takes off from the restored C&O Railway depot in Durbin, and the *Salamander* departs from Elkins or Cheat Bridge.

WORTH DOING: You can spend the night at a remote location aboard the *Durbin Rocket*'s Castaway Caboose, a restored Wabash caboose. The railroad's location is close to the Cass Scenic Railroad, enabling you to visit four great railroads in one impressive mountain setting.

DON'T MISS: The *Mountain Explorer* dinner train combines fine dining with a scenic rail journey through the mountains.

GETTING THERE: Route 250 connects the railroad's locations. Durbin is 35 miles south of Elkins at the base of Cheat Mountain, and the *Rocket* leaves from the station on Main Street. Cheat Bridge is seven miles north of Durbin and 30 miles south of Elkins. The *Salamander*'s station is on Red Run Road. The *Flyer*'s station in Elkins is located at 12th Street and Davis Avenue, and the Belington station is a half-block west of Route 250 in town.

DISCOUNT: $1 off each adult ticket.

Potomac Eagle Scenic Railroad 4

SITE LOCATION: Route 28 N, Romney

PHONE: 304-424-0736

WEB SITE: www.potomaceagle.info

J. Alex Lang

Here's a three-hour train ride for the birdwatchers among us. After all, who doesn't enjoy the sight of a bald eagle floating on the currents. The *Potomac Eagle* goes in search of bald eagles down the remote South Branch of the Potomac just inside West Virginia.

CHOICES: All trains depart from the Wappocomo station, just north of Romney. The 40-mile excursion travels along the South Branch of the Potomac River and through the six-mile Trough, a narrow mountain valley where eagles are often seen. You can ride coach, or better yet, ride in a first-class car, where you get lunch as part of the package. Historic narration adds extra insight into the journey. General Motors locomotives provide power for the trains.

WHEN TO GO: Trains run mid-May through the beginning of November. Departures are on Saturdays with a few Sundays sprinkled in. Autumn makes an especially great time to visit this railroad, and it offers trips almost daily during October. A special photo weekend is perfect for train lovers.

GOOD TO KNOW: The railroad says eagles are spotted on 90 percent of its trains. As it enters the most remote and steepest portion of the South Branch valley, the train pauses, so you can find a seat in the open gondola for the best views.

WORTH DOING: Possibly the oldest town in West Virginia, and said to have changed hands 56 times during the Civil War, Romney includes historic homes and buildings.

DON'T MISS: The railroad offers occasional 70-mile, all-day trips down the length of the railroad.

GETTING THERE: Romney is in the northeast corner of the state. It is about 25 miles from Cumberland, Md. Route 28 takes you to the station, which is 1.5 miles north of Romney.

DISCOUNT: $1 off each adult ticket, up to four adults.

WISCONSIN

Brodhead Historical Society Depot Museum ❶

This restored Chicago, Milwaukee & St. Paul depot, built in 1881, houses a permanent railroad display with rotating historical displays. Milwaukee Road switch engine no. 781 and caboose no. 1900 stand alongside the depot. It is open on Wednesdays, Saturdays, and Sundays May through September.

SITE LOCATION: 1108 First Center Avenue, Brodhead
PHONE: 608-897-4150
WEB SITE: www.madison.com/communities/brodheadhs

Colfax Railroad Museum ❷

This museum includes a large collection of railroad memorabilia and an outdoor display of locomotives and rolling stock that features a Soo Line GP30 diesel engine, a wooden Soo caboose, a heavyweight coach, and other pieces of rolling stock. It is open May through September.

SITE LOCATION: 500 E. Railroad Avenue, Colfax
PHONE: 715-962-2076
WEB SITE: colfaxrrmuseum.org
E-MAIL: form on Web site

Historical Village ❸

The village features a restored C&NW depot and several other historical structures, including an octagon house. Built in 1923, the depot is authentically furnished and contains railroad artifacts. It also displays a 1941 diesel engine, a Soo caboose, and a C&NW caboose. The museum is open during summer.

SITE LOCATION: 900 Montgomery Street, New London
PHONE: 920-982-8557 or 920-982-5186
WEB SITE: www.historicalvillage.org

Railroad Memories Museum ❹

This museum contains 12 rooms filled with railroad memories. Artifacts include lanterns, track equipment, photos, and other items. Housed in a former C&NW depot, it is located next to the Wisconsin Great Northern Railroad. The museum is open Memorial Day through Labor Day, and guided tours are available.

SITE LOCATION: 424 Front Street, Spooner
PHONE: 715-635-3325 or 715-635-2752
WEB SITE: www.railroadmemoriesmuseum.org
E-MAIL: info@railroadmemoriesmuseum.org

Camp Five 5

SITE LOCATION: 5480 Connor Farm Road, Laona
PHONE: 715-674-3414
WEB SITE: www.camp5museum.org
E-MAIL: info@lumberjacksteamtrain.com

Jim Wrinn

Camp Five offers a steam train powered by a vintage 2-6-2 type logging locomotive. It takes you to the site of a timber company's 1914 farm camp, where you can tour a logging museum.

CHOICES: After boarding at an 1880s Soo Line depot, you ride the steam train 2.5 miles to the museum. You can sit in a passenger coach or ride in one of the cupola cabooses. At Laona, you can climb a set of steps to inspect the engine's cab.

WHEN TO GO: Camp Five has a short season. It is open Monday through Saturday mid-June through mid-August. It is also open several days in fall.

GOOD TO KNOW: The railroad crosses the Rat River on a bridge. Lumber men who worked this river, floating giant rafts of logs together, became known as river rats. At the farm camp, the lumber company raised meat, produce, and horses to supply other camps as they set up in the forest.

WORTH DOING: Forest County is filled with lakes and covered by the Nicolet National Forest, so there are plenty of opportunities for fishing, hiking, and other recreational activities.

DON'T MISS: There is plenty to do at Camp Five. You can view exhibits on forestry, examine logging equipment, visit a nature center, or take an ecology walking tour.

GETTING THERE: Camp Five is off Highway 8 west of Laona, about two hours north of Green Bay. From Green Bay, take Highway 141 north to Highway 64. Follow Highway 64 west to Highway 32. Continue on Highway 32 and turn left on Highway 8 past Laona to Connor Farm Road.

DISCOUNT: $2 off each adult ticket.

East Troy Electric Railroad ⑥

SITE LOCATION: 2002 Church Street, East Troy
PHONE: 262-642-3263
WEB SITE: www.easttroyrr.org
E-MAIL: info@easttroyrr.org

Jim Wrinn

Interurban railroads once plied much of the Midwest, moving passengers easily from farm to city and vice versa. Today, a sprig of that heritage remains at the East Troy Electric Railroad, where electric trains run through the countryside.

CHOICES: On an 10-mile round trip, the railroad offers a variety of cars to ride, depending on the day, that include trolleys, electric freight motors pulling a caboose, and electrically powered traditional coaches from the famous South Shore line. Trains depart from both East Troy and Mukwonago. The railroad also offers dinner trains that run to Phantom Lake and back. After viewing the exhibits in the depot, walk two blocks to the shops and look at the equipment being restored.

WHEN TO GO: Regular weekend excursions run mid-May through October. From mid-June through August, trains also operate on Wednesdays, Thursdays, and Fridays. There are many special events during the year including Railroad Days and Fall Fun Days.

GOOD TO KNOW: Sheboygan car no. 26 is a 1908 interurban built by the Cincinnati Car Company for Sheboygan Light, Power and Railway. These cars ran in daily service for 30 years connecting the towns of Sheboygan, Kohler, Sheboygan Falls, Plymouth, Crystal Lake, and Elkhart Lake. No 26 later became a summer cottage until it was restored.

WORTH DOING: Regular excursions operate from East Troy to the Elegant Farmer near Mukwonago. What's an Elegant Farmer? It makes a great destination as the Farmer provides a deli, greenhouse, and market all in one. Be sure and try the award-winning baked apple pie in a bag.

DON'T MISS: Be sure to explore the substation in East Troy, which is the heart of the operating gear for the electric railroad.

GETTING THERE: East Troy is located in southeastern Wisconsin, about 35 miles from Milwaukee and 15 miles from Lake Geneva. From Milwaukee, take I-43 south to Exit 38. Take Highway 20 to Main Street. Follow Main Street to Church Street and turn right to the museum.

Mid-Continent Railway Museum ❼

SITE LOCATION: E8948 Diamond Hill Road, North Freedom
PHONE: 800-930-1385 or 608-522-4261
WEB SITE: www.midcontinent.org
E-MAIL: inquiries@midcontinent.org

Mid-Continent Railway Museum

One of the best museums for the preservation of wooden railroad cars, Mid-Continent features a large collection of rolling stock, much of it kept indoors, and numerous exhibits. The museum also offers a train ride. It's all aimed at re-creating the experience of a branch or short line between 1885 and 1915.

CHOICES: Leaving from a restored 1894 C&NW depot, the seven-mile, 50-minute ride takes you through the rolling countryside. You can ride the coaches, but you can also get a ticket for the locomotive cab or the caboose.

WHEN TO GO: The railway operates from mid-May into September and also includes a variety of special events.

GOOD TO KNOW: More than 100 pieces of equipment are on display. One is an office car of Great Northern Railway founder James J. Hill's son that included space for hauling an automobile. Structures include a water tower, a crossing shanty, a section shed, a crossing tower, and a freight house.

WORTH DOING: Explore Devil's Lake State Park near Baraboo. This large park features 500-foot cliffs, hiking trails, and kayaking.

DON'T MISS: Make sure you go into the coach shed to see some of the finest wood craftsmanship around when it comes to railroad cars and also check out the engine house, where craftsmen are restoring a steam locomotive for operation.

GETTING THERE: The scenic route from Madison is along Highway 12 going north. Turn left on Highway 36 and then left again on Highway PF to North Freedom. In North Freedom, follow Walnut Street west to the museum.

DISCOUNT: Buy one coach ticket and get one of equal or lesser value free.

National Railroad Museum ⑧

SITE LOCATION: 2285 S. Broadway Street, Green Bay
PHONE: 920-437-7623
WEB SITE: www.nationalrrmuseum.org
E-MAIL: staff@nationalrrmuseum.org

Jim Wrinn

Begun in 1956 by a group wishing to preserve a steam locomotive, the museum has grown to encompass more than 70 pieces of rolling stock, a seasonal train ride, and an unmatched collection of drumheads, the illuminated signs seen on the rear of many passenger trains.

CHOICES: Explore the museum on your own and then take a train ride. During the 25-minute train ride, the conductor provides information about railroad history and museum exhibits. Highlights include a Union Pacific Big Boy, a 1950s Aerotrain, and a Pennsylvania Railroad GG1 electric locomotive. The command train for General Dwight D. Eisenhower is also located at the museum in the company of a British Railways Pacific locomotive named for the World War II general. Group tours are also available.

WHEN TO GO: The museum is open daily year-round, except for several holidays. Train rides operate May through October, and numerous special events are scheduled during the year.

GOOD TO KNOW: The museum contains 40 drumheads from a variety of famous trains including the *20th Century Limited*, *Super Chief*, and *Empire Builder*.

WORTH DOING: Take the kids to Bay Beach Amusement Park for some old-fashioned fun on classic midway rides. Football fans can visit the Green Bay Packers Hall of Fame and tour historic Lambeau Field.

DON'T MISS: Climb to the top of the 85-foot-tall observation tower for a bird's-eye view of the museum.

GETTING THERE: Green Bay is two hours north of Milwaukee. From Milwaukee, take I-43 to Exit 180. Take Highway 172 west and exit at Ashland Avenue. Bear right on Pilgrim Way and then turn left on Broadway Street.

Osceola & St. Croix Valley Railway 9

SITE LOCATION: 114 Depot Road, Osceola
PHONE: 715-755-3570
WEB SITE: www.trainride.org
E-MAIL: admin@mtmuseum.org

Steve Glischinski

The Osceola & St. Croix Valley Railway offers rides through the scenic St. Croix River Valley along the Wisconsin-Minnesota border. Operated by the Minnesota Transportation Museum, the trains are diesel powered. A former Rock Island GP7 repainted in Soo Line's classic maroon and gold colors and a Burlington Northern SD9 6234, repainted in fresh BN green paint, pull the trains.

CHOICES: Two routes leave from Osceola. One heads west 10 miles to Marine on St. Croix, Minn. This highly recommended trip follows the beautiful St. Croix Valley for its entire length. The other trip goes east to Dresser, Wis., a former Soo Line junction town that still has its original wooden depot. The railway also offers special trips that include brunch trains, dinner trains, fireworks trains, and fall color trains. Another option is a guided tour through Minnesota's William O'Brien State Park with the train as your transportation.

WHEN TO GO: There's nothing like a crisp, blue-sky autumn day in the open-window coaches rolling through the St. Croix Valley. The first weeks of October offer the chance to view the fall colors before the long northern winter begins. For the best views of the St. Croix River, May is the time to ride before the leaves obstruct the river.

GOOD TO KNOW: Osceola is a small town of around 2,000. There are several good local hotels, restaurants, and B&Bs, but those who desire all the amenities may wish to drive south to the larger communities of Stillwater, Minn., or Hudson, Wis.

WORTH DOING: Take the train to Marine and ride over the Cedar Bend swing bridge across the St. Croix River. While the bridge doesn't swing open any more, it's a classic steel structure complete with "tell tales" on each end to warn brakemen of close clearances.

DON'T MISS: Watch ex-Northern Pacific Railway post office-baggage-coach combine no. 1102 pick up the mail on the fly from a mail crane at Osceola's restored depot, one of the few places where this once common occurrence can be seen.

GETTING THERE: Osceola is about an hour's drive from Minneapolis. For a scenic drive, follow Highway 95 along the east bank of the St. Croix from Stillwater north to Osceola. Once in Osceola, you'll come to Highway 35. Turn right and proceed under the railroad bridge and immediately turn right again onto Depot Road.

DISCOUNT: $3 off each adult ticket, up to four adults.

Wisconsin Great Northern Railroad ⑩

SITE LOCATION: 426 N. Front Street, Spooner
PHONE: 715-635-3200
WEB SITE: www.spoonertrainride.com
E-MAIL: office@spoonertrainride.com

Steve Glischinski

The Wisconsin Great Northern Railroad offers special train rides and casual dining excursions in the North Woods along the picturesque Namekagon River. The 30-mile round trip between Spooner and Springbrook takes you over former Chicago & North Western track.

CHOICES: In addition to regular excursions, the Wisconsin Great Northern offers dinner trains on weekends as well as special events throughout the year, including trains for fall colors, Halloween, and even breakfast or pizza with Santa in December. The railroad runs trains on just about every holiday.

WHEN TO GO: Regular excursions run Saturdays in May and June; Tuesday through Saturday during late June, July, and August; and weekends in September. For children, a great time to visit is in October, when the railroad runs the Great Pumpkin Train on weekends to a pumpkin patch near Trego, Wis. There, the kids can take a hay ride, enjoy a bonfire, roast marshmallows, and pick out a pumpkin. Reservations are a must since the train sells out.

GOOD TO KNOW: Unique among tourist railroads, the Wisconsin Great Northern offers the Great Wedding Train, the only true wedding train in the nation. It features the custom-built replica chapel car *Everlasting*, and the railroad offers all-inclusive wedding packages.

WORTH DOING: Adjacent to the railroad's ticket office is the former Chicago & North Western depot, which also houses Railroad Memories Museum. The museum contains a large collection of lanterns, track equipment, photos, and other railroad memorabilia.

DON'T MISS: Ride in the cab of an F7 diesel. The railroad offers cab rides on most of its dinner and special occasion trains, usually selling half-trip fares. Take the trip on the return to Spooner since the train backs up leaving Spooner for Springbrook.

GETTING THERE: The Wisconsin Great Northern is about 90 minutes from Eau Claire and two hours from Minneapolis and St. Paul. After you enter Spooner on Highway 70, turn left onto Front Street. Travel four blocks north on Front Street and then look for signs to the depot.

WYOMING

Cheyenne Depot Museum ❶

Cheyenne's historic depot stands as a monument to a railroading history in the area. Built in 1886, the Union Pacific depot is now a museum that showcases the history of this beautifully restored building as well as the railroad and the city. The museum also may run a summer train excursion.

SITE LOCATION: 121 W. 15th Street, Cheyenne
PHONE: 307-632-3905
WEB SITE: www.cheyennedepotmuseum.org
E-MAIL: info@cheyennedepotmuseum.org

Douglas Railroad Interpretive Center ❷

The Douglas Railroad Interpretive Center is housed in a restored 1886 passenger depot belonging to the Fremont, Elkhorn & Missouri Valley Railroad. It displays a 1940 Chicago, Burlington & Quincy steam locomotive and seven railcars. The building is listed on the National Register of Historic Places, and the cars, in various stages of restoration, are available for tours.

SITE LOCATION: 121 Brownfield Road, Douglas
PHONE: 877-937-4996 or 307-358-2950
WEB SITE: www.jackalope.org
E-MAIL: chamber@jackalope.org

Union Pacific Roundhouse ❸

This complex includes a 28-bay roundhouse, a working turntable, and a renovated machine shop. Each year, Roundhouse Restoration, the group restoring the facility, holds a weekend festival in the roundhouse and gives yard tours. It is open other times during the year as well. Nearby Depot Square includes a restored 1900 depot and other historic buildings.

SITE LOCATION: 1440 Main Street, Evanston
PHONE: 307-783-6320

Union Pacific Railroad ▪4

SITE LOCATION: UP Steam Shop, Cheyenne
PHONE: 307-778-3214
WEB SITE: www.uprr.com/aboutup/excurs/index.shtml

Jim Wrinn

This Class I mainline railroad maintains the only steam locomotive never retired, no. 844, a 4-8-4 built in 1944. Rebuilt between 1999 and 2004, it is used on occasional excursions and display tours.

CHOICES: Home for the locomotive is a nonpublic shop in Cheyenne, where the Union Pacific also maintains steam engine 4-6-6-4 no. 3985, believed to be the largest steam locomotive operating today. Departures occur from the UP rail yards as well as from the Cheyenne Depot Museum.

WHEN TO GO: Schedules and routes vary from year to year. One annual outing is the Denver Post Frontier Days excursion train that runs from Denver to Cheyenne for the big rodeo event.

GOOD TO KNOW: The Union Pacific provides a GPS trace system for its steam train at www.uprr.com/aboutup/excurs/trace.cfm.

WORTH DOING: In July, you can take part in Frontier Days, a 10-day rodeo event that celebrates the West and features entertainment and other activities.

DON'T MISS: Visit the Cheyenne Depot Museum in the restored UP depot. Two historic engines are displayed in Cheyenne parks: a Big Boy engine in Holliday Park and the state's oldest steam locomotive, no. 1242, in Lions Park.

GETTING THERE: Cheyenne is in southeast Wyoming, about 90 minutes from Denver on I-25.

ALBERTA

Alberta Railway Museum ❶
The museum's collection of railway equipment and buildings focuses on the Canadian National Railway and the Northern Alberta Railway. It includes more than 50 locomotives and cars, three stations, and a water tank. The museum is open weekends during the summer. You can take a guided tour and ride a speeder. On select holiday weekends, passenger excursions run.

SITE LOCATION: 24215 34th Street, Edmonton
PHONE: 780-472-6229
WEB SITE: www.railwaymuseum.ab.ca
E-MAIL: form on Web site

Edmonton Radial Railway ❷
The Edmonton Radial Railway operates streetcars in Fort Edmonton Park and in Old Strathcona. Once you are admitted to the park, the one-mile streetcar rides are free. In Old Strathcona, the trolley crosses High Level Bridge over the North Saskatchewan River.

SITE LOCATION: 700 143rd Street, Edmonton
PHONE: 780-437-7721
WEB SITE: www.edmonton-radial-railway.ab.ca
E-MAIL: info@edmonton-radial-railway.ab.ca

Fort Edmonton Park ❸
Nestled in Edmonton's river valley, Fort Edmonton Park is a living history museum that represents four historical periods between 1840 and 1920. It contains more than 75 buildings. A 1919 steam train takes you through the park, and caboose rides are available. A streetcar also travels along the historic streets.

SITE LOCATION: Fox Drive and Whitemud Drive, Edmonton
PHONE: 780-496-8787
WEB SITE: www.fortedmontonpark.ca
E-MAIL: attractions@edmonton.ca

Alberta Prairie Railway Excursions 🔲

SITE LOCATION: 4611 47th Avenue, Stettler
PHONE: 800-282-3994 or 403-742-2811
WEB SITE: www.absteamtrain.com
E-MAIL: info@absteamtrain.com

Jim Wrinn

A trip aboard the Alberta Prairie conjures up visions of what a central Alberta wheat line must have been like 100 years ago. Traveling from the well-developed community of Stettler, it passes through forests and fields before reaching Big Valley, where the ruins of a roundhouse and a well-kept depot remain.

CHOICES: The railroad offers an extensive schedule, including numerous specials such as murder mystery, Christmas, dinner theater, family, and teddy bear trains. The most popular excursion is the A Train, which includes a full-course buffet meal and an occasional train robbery. The winter fine-dining trains provide a five-course meal and entertainment. The trains are pulled by a steam engine, either Baldwin 2-8-0 no. 41 or Montreal 4-8-2 no. 6060, or General Motors diesel no. 1259.

WHEN TO GO: Summer excursions begin in May and continue until mid-October each year. Dinner trains are offered November through April.

GOOD TO KNOW: The railway was once part of a vast grain railroad network belonging to the Canadian Northern. Be sure to chat with the train crew. Many of the veteran railroaders on this line have great stories. And if you get the right conductor, he might just sing you a song or recite a poem for you en route.

WORTH DOING: For steam fans, there is a no-frills special aboard one of the steam trains without any of the extras.

DON'T MISS: For an added prairie experience, the railway offers a two- or three-day package that includes a train ride and a 20-mile covered wagon trip along historic rail rights-of-way.

GETTING THERE: Stettler is about three hours northeast of Calgary on Highway 12.

Canadian Pacific Railway Steam Train 5

SITE LOCATION: 401 Ninth Avenue SW, Calgary
PHONE: 403-837-0113
WEB SITE: www.cpr.ca
E-MAIL: form on Web site

John Godfrey

Based in Calgary, the CPR hosts Canada's only mainline, railway-operated steam train. Trips have operated across the CPR and Soo system from Delson, Quebec, to Vancouver and from Chicago to Portal, N.D. Often, passenger trips run in conjunction with a charity or special event, such as the Holiday Train that runs through parts of Canada and the United States during November and December.

CHOICES: The *Empress* steamed back into service in 2001 as a roving ambassador for the CPR. Built by Montreal Locomotive Works in 1930, it is the only surviving H1b Hudson. After a complete rebuild, the *Empress* was restored to original specifications with external details from the 1940s and '50s. It pulls passengers in former intercity coaches that feature reclining seats.

WHEN TO GO: Trips are not regularly scheduled so check the CPR Web site often. Look for trip announcements under the Steam Train link of the General Public section on the Web site.

GOOD TO KNOW: Make reservations early as seating capacity on the excursions is limited. While most departure and arrival locations are accessible via some form of public transportation, not all one-way trips include return transportation to the point of origin.

WORTH DOING: Many runs are made west of Calgary through the mountains, giving the engine a good workout.

DON'T MISS: Runs through Crowsnest Pass, which straddles the Alberta-British Columbia border, offer a good mix of engine noise and scenic highlights.

GETTING THERE: Departure and arrival locations vary by trip.

Heritage Park Historical Village ❻

SITE LOCATION: 1900 Heritage Drive SW, Calgary
PHONE: 403-268-8500
WEB SITE: www.heritagepark.ca
E-MAIL: info@heritagepark.ab.ca

Alberta

John Godfrey

Discover what life was like in the Canadian West between 1864 and 1914 by visiting this 66-acre re-created village framed by the Rockies. More than 150 exhibits, including many buildings transplanted from Calgary and other locations throughout Alberta, bring the past to the present.

CHOICES: The park includes a roundhouse and turntable along with more than 20 locomotives and cars. A train ride is an excellent way to see the park. You have a variety of admission options to choose from, depending on your available time and level of interest. Make a day of your visit and wander from building to building, paying particular attention to the transplanted railway stations, rolling stock, and re-created carbarn. If it's too hot, take a cruise on the water aboard the replica sternwheeler SS *Moyie*. Park expansion may cause temporary relocation or closing of some exhibits.

WHEN TO GO: Heritage Park is open daily from the third weekend in May to Labour Day, and then only on weekends until Canadian Thanksgiving. Avoiding the crowds found throughout the city during Stampede in early July would probably make for a more leisurely visit.

GOOD TO KNOW: A short streetcar line connects the outer parking area to the main entrance. It's well worth it to park out there, view ex-CPR 2-10-4 no. 5931 and S-2 no. 7019, and then ride over to the gate in a replica Calgary or Winnipeg trolley. Many photographic opportunities are available around the park's railway loop.

WORTH DOING: Calgary's 10-day annual Stampede, which can draw more than one million people, is the world's largest rodeo. The event also features chuck wagon racing, agricultural exhibits, entertainment, and a parade.

DON'T MISS: During Railway Days, held toward the end of June, the park celebrates Canadian railways and rolls out much of its collection. Steam doubleheaders often operate for this event, and ex-CP Car 76, present at the driving of the last spike on the CPR in Craigellachie in 1885, is usually rolled out.

GETTING THERE: Heritage Park is approximately a 20-minute drive southwest from downtown Calgary. A shuttle service operates during park hours from the Heritage light rail stop. Calgary is serviced by scheduled bus and air service.

Royal Canadian Pacific 🔢

SITE LOCATION: 201 Ninth Avenue SW, Calgary
PHONE: 877-665-3044 or 403-508-1400
WEB SITE: www.royalcanadianpacific.com
E-MAIL: info@royalcanadianpacific.com

Alberta

J. David Ingles

The Royal Canadian Pacific, an arm of the passenger department of Canadian Pacific Railway, offers periodically scheduled all-inclusive luxury-train ride packages on CPR's route through the spectacularly scenic Canadian Rockies. The operation is often called Canada's *Orient Express*. Restored vintage diesel locomotives haul a consist of about eight cars – all vintage, heavyweight CPR sleeping, observation, and dining cars with lavishly restored interiors. Cuisine in the dining room equals the finest on the continent.

CHOICES: The RCP's signature six-day, five-night Royal Canadian Rockies Experience tour circles from Calgary to the west into British Columbia, traversing some Alberta prairie lines and then two mountain summits, Crowsnest Pass and Kicking Horse Pass, at the Continental Divide. It travels through the railway's famous twin Spiral Tunnels and follows the headwaters of the Columbia River. Other themed experiences include golf, fly-fishing, and culinary excursions.

WHEN TO GO: The Canadian Rockies and the prairies have unpredictable weather with temperatures that can fall or rise quickly. The mountains offer spectacular scenery during every season.

GOOD TO KNOW: Calgary, Canada's largest city between Toronto and Vancouver, is a cosmopolitan city that still retains its western flavor and offers many cultural and entertainment opportunities. Calgary's C-Train light-rail system, with three routes radiating from downtown, is an efficient and fun way to see much of the city.

WORTH DOING: While in Calgary, you can visit the Glenbow Museum, Calgary Zoo, Calgary Tower, Canada Olympic Park, and Fort Calgary.

DON'T MISS: Along the way, watch for the fascinating rock walls and waterfalls of Yoho National Park and enjoy the views from an open-air vestibule as the train climbs through Kicking Horse Pass.

GETTING THERE: Calgary is served by many major airlines and the *Rocky Mountaineer* tourist train from Vancouver.

Skeena  8

SITE LOCATION: 607 Connaught Drive, Jasper
PHONE: 888-842-7245
WEB SITE: www.viarail.ca

John Godfrey

The *Skeena*, operated by VIA Rail Canada between Jasper and Prince Rupert, British Columbia, is one of the scenic highlights of any trip to western Canada. Work-horse F40s haul this vest-pocket, largely stainless-steel domeliner over what was originally the Grand Trunk Pacific, making an overnight stop in both directions in Prince George. The 725-mile trip takes you from the Rocky Mountains in Jasper National Park to the Pacific coast.

CHOICES: Travelers can opt for one of three onboard accommodation classes when departing from either Jasper or Prince Rupert. Budget-minded vacationers can relax in the leg-rest seats found in comfort (coach) class. Those with a voracious appetite for scenery may want to spend a little more for totem class (glass-roofed, low-level coach). Those with even deeper pockets and a desire to experience vintage deluxe travel will enjoy totem deluxe class (day space in Park series dome observation car).

WHEN TO GO: The *Skeena* operates Wednesday, Friday, and Sunday year-round, with extra trips often added in both directions during the high-tourist summer weeks. The shorter days and deep snows of winter give way to a plethora of spring flowers in May. Long, hot summer days morph into colorful, cool fall days by October.

GOOD TO KNOW: Jasper is a typical tourist town, with a variety of hotels and services catering to the traveler who likes pampering as well as serving those who enjoy being more in touch with nature. Prince Rupert has a broad choice of accommodations. When arriving in Prince George, you may want to take a taxi, even though accommodations are a few blocks away as the area around the VIA station may be considered rough.

WORTH DOING: Splurging for space in the Park observation car will provide all the scenic views available to those in the totem car ahead, with the added bonuses of forward visibility and a place to escape the rays of the hot summer sun.

DON'T MISS: Just west of Jasper, Mount Robson, the highest peak in the Canadian Provinces, is visible from the train for only a few cloudless days a year. You may also see moose, bear, elk, wolves, seals, and eagles along the way.

GETTING THERE: VIA Rail operates the Vancouver-Toronto Canadian three days a week through Jasper in each direction. Jasper is also served by bus from Edmonton and other points. Scheduled air service operates from Prince Rupert.

BRITISH COLUMBIA

Downtown Historic Railway ◼1

This railway takes you on a ride between Science World Station and Granville Island Station in Downtown Vancouver. Restored interurban cars 1207 and 1231 are two of the last B.C. Electric cars in existence. The railway runs weekends and holidays Victoria Day weekend through Canadian Thanksgiving. It is near the SkyTrain's Main Street station. The streetcars are operated in conjunction with Transit Museum Society volunteers.

SITE LOCATION: Quebec Street and Terminal Avenue, Vancouver
PHONE: 604-871-6935
WEB SITE: www.city.vancouver.bc.ca/engsvcs/transport/railway
E-MAIL: jonas.moon@vancouver.ca

Fort Steele Steam Railway ◼2

Fort Steele Heritage Town is a restored 1890s pioneer town complete with railway. The railway is located outside the historic park, so you ride the rails separately or as part of an all-inclusive ticket. A Montreal Locomotive Works 2-6-2 prairie-type locomotive takes you around a 2.5-mile loop. Along the way, you'll learn about local railroad history.

SITE LOCATION: 9851 Highway 93/95, Fort Steele
PHONE: 250-417-6000
WEB SITE: www.fortsteele.bc.ca
E-MAIL: info@fortsteele.bc.ca

Kwinitsa Railway Station Museum ◼3

Now located in Prince Rupert's waterfront park, this restored station house is an excellent example of the small stations once found along Canada's northern railway line. Photographs, videos, and detailed restorations depict the life of station agents and linemen who worked for the Grand Trunk Railway at the turn of the 20th century. It is open daily June through August.

SITE LOCATION: Bill Murray Way and First Avenue, Prince Rupert
PHONE: 250-624-3207
WEB SITE: www.museumofnorthernbc.com
E-MAIL: mnbc@citytel.net

Malahat 4

VIA's *Malahat* runs across scenic Vancouver Island. The excursion runs between Victoria, at the southern tip of the island, and Courtenay, at the northern end. Beside seeing the island's beautiful countryside, with a comfort-class (economy) ticket, you can get off at other stops along the way and experience Duncan's totem poles, Nanaimo's harbor, and Courtenay's downtown.

SITE LOCATION: 450 Pandora Avenue, Victoria
PHONE: 888-842-7245
WEB SITE: www.viarail.ca/malahat

Prince George Railway & Forestry Museum 5

The museum displays historic railway and forestry exhibits in a park-like setting. The extensive rail collection dates to 1899 and includes two stations and a turntable. It also contains both steam and diesel locomotives and more than 40 pieces of rolling stock.

SITE LOCATION: 850 River Road, Prince George
PHONE: 250-563-7351
WEB SITE: www.pgrfm.bc.ca
E-MAIL: trains@pgrfm.bc.ca

Revelstoke Railway Museum 6

This railway museum focuses on the history of the Canadian Pacific Railway in western Canada. You can take a walk through Official Car no. 4 and view other CP cars, locomotives, and artifacts. The museum also operates a small facility at Craigellachie, 28 miles west of Revelstoke, where the last spike of the Canadian Pacific Railway was driven. The museum is open year-round.

SITE LOCATION: 719 Track Street W, Revelstoke
PHONE: 877-837-6060 or 250-837-6060
WEB SITE: www.railwaymuseum.com
E-MAIL: railway@telus.net

Alberni Pacific Railway 7

SITE LOCATION: Kingsway Avenue and Argyle Street, Port Alberni
PHONE: 250-723-1376
WEB SITE: www.alberniheritage.com
E-MAIL: info@alberniheritage.com

Alberni Pacific Railway

The Alberni Pacific offers passengers a chance to visit the former McLean Paper Mill, six miles east of Port Alberni over the former Canadian Pacific Railway Port Alberni Subdivision. The mill is a National Historic Site that now commemorates the history of logging and milling in British Columbia.

CHOICES: Trains to the mill are pulled by a 1929 Baldwin 2-8-2T, and passengers ride in converted former Canadian National transfer cabooses, three of which are open and two are covered. Trips leave from a restored 1912 CPR station. Cab rides are also available.

WHEN TO GO: Runs are made over this scenic trackage twice daily from Thursday to Monday between the end of June and September. Special events occur throughout the year.

GOOD TO KNOW: The McLean Mill is the only steam-operated sawmill in Canada. This historic site and the railway are part of the Alberni Valley Heritage Network that celebrates the area's history and culture. Also included are the Alberni Valley Museum and Maritime Discovery Centre.

WORTH DOING: Visit Port Alberni's quaint harbor, which offers a mix of restaurants, galleries, tours, and shops. The Western Vancouver Island Industrial Heritage Society also operates a train ride along the waterfront.

DON'T MISS: Include a stop at the Chase & Warren Estate Winery, either as part of your train trip or separately. The Alberni Pacific Railway makes daily stops at the winery, offering wine connoisseurs the opportunity to sample the wares of the small Vancouver Island winery.

GETTING THERE: Bus service is available from Vancouver Island to Port Alberni. Scheduled air service is available from Victoria to the south. Ferry service operates between the mainland and various points on Vancouver Island including Port Alberni.

Canadian Museum of Rail Travel ⑧

SITE LOCATION: 57 Van Horne Street S, Cranbrook
PHONE: 250-489-3918
WEB SITE: www.trainsdeluxe.com
E-MAIL: mail@trainsdeluxe.com

John Godfrey

The Canadian Museum of Rail Travel is a magnet for anyone interested in Canadian passenger rail travel as it once was. It is home to the only surviving train set of equipment from the 1929 *Trans-Canada Limited* as well as the beautifully reconstructed Royal Alexandra Hall.

CHOICES: Visitors can elect to examine the collection at their own pace or join an informative tour that examines the interiors of various cars of the *Soo-Spokane Train Deluxe* as well as business cars and cars of state. The museum's collection contains equipment from the consists of the *Pacific Express* and the *Chinook*. It also includes historic structures.

WHEN TO GO: The museum is open to the public daily from mid-April to Canadian Thanksgiving in October. During the remainder of the year, it is open Tuesday through Saturday.

GOOD TO KNOW: Cranbrook is a full-service mountain city. It is a major gateway to the Canadian Rockies, which are 15 miles away. With a wide range of accommodations and eateries, something will likely be suitable to most tastes.

WORTH DOING: Tour the exquisitely recreated Royal Alexandra Hall from the Canadian Pacific Railway's Royal Alexandra Hotel that once stood near that road's Winnipeg Station. The hall was the grand café of the hotel and features Edwardian architectural style.

DON'T MISS: Take the museum's guided tour. Guides not only explain the history of the equipment, but they bring to life the detailed work of the restoration process. The museum continues to add cars to its tours.

GETTING THERE: Air service to Cranbrook is available. Greyhound also operates daily scheduled service to the city. Many Royal Canadian Pacific trains spend the night right outside the facility's trackside entrance and include the museum on their itinerary.

Kamloops Heritage Railway 9

SITE LOCATION: 6-510 Lorne Street, Kamloops
PHONE: 250-374-2141
WEB SITE: www.kamrail.com
E-MAIL: info@kamrail.com

John Godfrey

This steam-powered tourist line's regular excursion is a seven-mile round trip on the Canadian National's Okanagan Subdivision that features mountain vistas, lakeside scenery, and an occasional train robbery.

CHOICES: On the *Spirit of Kamloops'* 70-minute excursion, you can ride in an a restored 1930s air-conditioned coach or in an open-air car to take in the sounds of the railway's former CN 2-8-0 and the sights of mountain and lakeside scenery. The train departs from a restored 1927 CN station and crosses the South Thompson River on a 1927 steel trestle bridge. The railway also runs ghost trains, a dinner train, and other specials. All-day, 115-mile excursions may also run several times a year.

WHEN TO GO: The *Spirit of Kamloops* operates Friday to Monday during July and August and on a limited schedule during June and September. Illuminated with hundreds of lights, the *Spirit of Christmas* is a one-hour special, complete with candy canes, hot chocolate, and caroling.

GOOD TO KNOW: Kamloops is a regional center that has a wide range of accommodations to choose from, as well as all the services one would expect in a small-sized city, including city bus service. The former courthouse, where train robber Bill Miner was tried and convicted, is now a popular hostel.

WORTH DOING: Bring your camera as the *Spirit of Kamloops* stops on the trestle bridge to allow passengers to photograph the scenic vistas.

DON'T MISS: On the *Spirit of Kamloops*, masked riders reenact the famous 1906 train robbery by the Bill Miner gang. Following the robbery, listen to Bill Miner's ghost tell his story.

GETTING THERE: Scheduled air service is located at Kelowna, two hours to the south of Kamloops. Daily bus service operates in the city, and VIA Rail Canada's *Canadian* calls at Kamloops Junction three times a week in each direction.

Kettle Valley Steam Railway 🔟

SITE LOCATION: 18404 Bathville Road, Summerland
PHONE: 877-494-8424 or 250-494-8422
WEB SITE: www.kettlevalleyrail.org
E-MAIL: kvr@telus.net

John Godfrey

The Kettle Valley Steam Railway operates over a preserved portion of the famed Kettle Valley Railway between Faulder and the Trout Creek trestle. Between May and October, passengers can enjoy the view across Okanagan Lake and the surrounding hills from a steam-powered train traveling over the remaining portion of the CPR's famed southern route through British Columbia.

CHOICES: The KVR offers conventional excursions over its 10-mile right-of-way. The two-hour trip winds through Prairie Valley and its scenic vistas. Former BC 2-8-0 no. 3716 has returned to service on the KVR, on an extended loan from the provincial government. You can ride in two 1950s passenger coaches or several open-air cars. Special events are scheduled throughout the year and include a trick-or-treat train, a Christmas train, and a train robbery.

WHEN TO GO: The KVR operates from late May through Canadian Thanksgiving in October on a varied schedule. Spring and fall excursions run Saturday through Monday. In summer, Thursday and Friday excursions are added.

GOOD TO KNOW: Summerland is situated in the Okanagan Valley amid lush orchards and vineyards, and the valley is home to more than 50 wineries.

WORTH DOING: Take a side trip into nearby Penticton and tour the former CP ship SS *Sicamous*. This steel-hulled sternwheeler was built in 1914 as a multipurpose vessel that provided first-class passenger service as well as delivering cargo and daily mail.

DON'T MISS: The Trout Creek trestle, at the current turnaround point south of Summerland, sits 238 feet above the canyon floor and provides spectacular views.

GETTING THERE: Air service is scheduled into and out of Kelowna, less than an hour's drive to the east. The Prairie Valley Station is located off Highway 97.

Rocky Mountaineer Vacations ⑪

SITE LOCATION: 1755 Cottrell Street, Vancouver
PHONE: 877-460-3200 or 604-606-7200
WEB SITE: www.rockymountaineer.com
E-MAIL: reservations@rockymountaineer.com

John Godfrey

What many consider to be Canada's premier rail tour company offers a variety of rail outings. In addition to its signature Vancouver to Jasper route, there are trips from Vancouver to Banff or Calgary, from North Vancouver to Whistler, and from Whistler to Jasper.

CHOICES: The *Rocky Mountaineer* offers two-day trips over three routes: Kicking Horse, Yellowhead, and Fraser Discovery. Kicking Horse takes you over the Rockies from Vancouver to either Banff or Calgary in Alberta. On the Yellowhead route, you travel through the Rockies to Jasper, Alberta. The Fraser Discovery Route follows the Fraser River from Whistler to Jasper. The *Whistler Mountaineer* is a three-hour journey between Vancouver and Whistler, British Columbia, following the Sea to Sky corridor, which provides scenic views of waterfalls, forests, and mountains. All routes offer a choice between GoldLeaf or RedLeaf service. GoldLeaf service features bi-level dome coaches with full-length windows, and RedLeaf service includes reclining seats, extended legroom, and at-seat food service.

WHEN TO GO: Although trains operate on select dates on some routes during the off-season, aim for the longer days of the year if possible. While passengers are accommodated in hotels during overnight stops, the longer days of the year provide more hours during which to view the spectacular scenery.

GOOD TO KNOW: The Jasper and Banff/Calgary trains are combined between Vancouver and Kamloops. Trains operating on the former British Columbia Railway north of greater Vancouver arrive and depart from the vicinity of the former BCR station in North Vancouver. You can also begin your trip in Jasper, Banff, or Calgary.

WORTH DOING: Go for the gold. You may as well take advantage of the fancy digs and pampering with GoldLeaf service. It is a cruise train, after all.

DON'T MISS: Scenic highlights include Fraser Canyon and Thompson Canyon on the Yellowhead run, the spiral tunnels on the Kicking Horse route, and Cheakamus Canyon on the *Whistler Mountaineer*.

GETTING THERE: Air service is available to Vancouver and Calgary. Scheduled motor coach service connects Jasper, Banff, and Whistler to the outside world. VIA Rail Canada provides service to Jasper and Vancouver.

West Coast Railway Heritage Park ⑫

SITE LOCATION: 39645 Government Road, Squamish
PHONE: 604-898-9336
WEB SITE: www.wcra.org/heritage
E-MAIL: park@wcra.org

John Godfrey

Opened in 1994, the West Coast Heritage Park provides a home to the West Coast Railway Association's large collection of locomotives and rolling stock. Located in a beautiful 12-acre mountain valley setting, the museum offers visitors a chance to learn about railway history in Canada's westernmost province.

CHOICES: The park exhibits a typical railway facility of the mid-20th century, complete with stations and other buildings. You are also able to see railway equipment in various stages of restoration. The collection of more than 50 vintage railway cars and locomotives includes cabooses, snowplows, a restored 1890 business car, and the only surviving Pacific Great Western steam engine. A mini train ride circles the park.

WHEN TO GO: The park is open year-round, except for Christmas and New Year's Day. Summer months provide the least likelihood for an encounter with the area's famous "wet sunshine."

GOOD TO KNOW: Many good restaurants and chain eateries can be found in Squamish. Shannon Falls Provincial Park contains the province's third-highest waterfall, which falls more than 1,000 feet.

WORTH DOING: Incorporate a visit to the museum with a scenic drive along the Sea to Sky Highway for a nice day-long family outing. The Sea to Sky Highway travels through five different biogeoclimatic zones, from coastal rain forest to mountain forest. This predominantly two-lane road goes from Vancouver to Whistler.

DON'T MISS: Royal Hudson no. 2860 now calls the park home. It was one of the last Royal Hudson locomotives built for the Canadian Pacific Railway by Montreal Locomotive Works in June 1940.

GETTING THERE: From Vancouver, it is about an hour's drive north on Highway 99 along spectacular Howe Sound, North America's southernmost fjord, to Squamish. Turn left on Industrial Way until Queens Way and then turn right and follow the signs.

MANITOBA

Winnipeg Railway Museum ❶

Located in the VIA rail station, this railroad museum is dedicated to preserving Manitoba's rail heritage. Various locomotives are on display including the *Countess of Dufferin* the first steam locomotive to operate in western Canada. It also displays baggage cars, freight cars, and a Canadian National caboose. The museum is open year-round.

SITE LOCATION: 123 Main Street, Winnipeg
PHONE: 204-942-4632
WEB SITE www.wpgrailwaymuseum.com
E-MAIL wpgrail@mts.net

Prairie Dog Central Railway ⊡

SITE LOCATION: Prairie Dog Trail, Winnipeg
PHONE: 204-832-5259
WEB SITE: www.pdcrailway.com
E-MAIL: info@pdcrailway.com

John Godfrey

This 36-mile round trip over the former CN Oak Point Subdivision from the north side of the Manitoba capital to the town of Warren offers a glimpse into prairie railroading of the past.

CHOICES: You can choose to travel in either open-vestibule or closed-vestibule coaches. All the wooden coaches, built between 1901 and 1913, are fully restored and air-conditioned – when the windows are open. Power is provided by diesel locomotive no. 4138, which was built in 1958 for the Grand Trunk Western Railroad. The train makes a stop in Grosse Isle on the way to Warren. Special excursions include Halloween, Santa, and family trains.

WHEN TO GO: Trains operate regularly on weekends from mid-May through September. Special runs also operate on Victoria Day, Canada Day, and Labour Day, and other select holidays.

GOOD TO KNOW: Ex-Winnipeg Hydro 4-4-0 no. 3, nearing completion of an extensive rebuild, is expected to return to service shortly. Built in 1882 by Dubs in Scotland, it would be among the oldest operable engines in North America. The railway's station, constructed in 1910 by the Canadian Northern Railway, is a Canadian Heritage Railway Station. It was moved from St. James Street to its present location in 2000 and renamed Inkster Junction Station.

WORTH DOING: Secure a ticket in either combine no. 104 (built in 1906) or coach no. 105 (built in 1901). These beautifully maintained relics are rolling time machines to another century.

DON'T MISS: When stopped in Grosse Isle and Warren, explore the towns' public markets. Grosse Isle is home to the 72-mile Prime Meridian Trail, a recreation and conservation trail built on an abandoned rail line.

GETTING THERE: The railway is located north of Winnipeg on Prairie Dog Trail. It is on the north side of Inkster Boulevard between Route 90 and Sturgeon Boulevard. Air, car coach, and rail service is available to Winnipeg.

NEW BRUNSWICK

New Brunswick Railway Museum ❶

The museum contains more than 20 pieces of rolling stock that includes locomotives, passenger cars, freight cars, maintenance-of-way equipment, and cabooses. Some of the cars are open for viewing. The museum also displays a speeder car, telegraph office, and smaller artifacts. It is open June through September. The museum has run excursion train in the past and may do so again at a future date.

SITE LOCATION: Route 114, Hillsborough
PHONE: 506-734-3195
WEB SITE: www.nbrm.ca
E-MAIL: info@nbrm.ca

NEWFOUNDLAND

Railway Coastal Museum ❶

The Railway Coastal Museum contains a large collection of items relating to Newfoundland's rail and coastal boat services. The museum is housed in the restored 1903 Riverhead station, and you can walk along the platform where passengers boarded the *Newfie Bullet*. The museum is constructing a train park for displaying rolling stock. It is open year-round.

SITE LOCATION: 495 Water Street W, St. John's
PHONE: 866-600-7245 or 709-724-5929
WEB SITE: www.railwaycoastalmuseum.ca
E-MAIL: info@railwaycoastalmuseum.ca

Railway Society of Newfoundland Train Site ❷

The society maintains a collection of narrow gauge rolling stock from the Newfoundland Railway. Several trains are displayed including the *Newfie Bullet*, once Newfoundland's fastest passenger train. Steam locomotive no. 593 is displayed with a representative selection of cars. A snowplow train is also featured. You can walk through all the railcars. The museum is open daily during the summer.

SITE LOCATION: Marine Drive and Station Road, Corner Brook
PHONE: 709-634-2720
WEB SITE: www.cornerbrook.com/tourism/ttrain.html

NOVA SCOTIA

Orangedale Railway Museum ❶
The museum was originally built in 1886 as a Queen Anne-style station. The ground floor includes a replica of the original office and waiting rooms. The second floor has been restored as the station agent's living quarters. The museum also displays a small diesel locomotive and several railcars. It is open June through October.

SITE LOCATION: 1428 Main Street, Orangedale
PHONE: 902-756-3384
WEB SITE: fortress.uccb.ns.ca/historic/oranstat.html

Sydney & Louisburg Railway Museum ❷
The museum features rolling stock, artifacts, and photographs relating to the Sydney & Louisburg Railway. Housed in an 1895 S&L station, the museum also contains historical exhibits about Louisburg. An original freight shed and roundhouse also hold displays. You can also view Nova Scotia's oldest passenger coach.

SITE LOCATION: 7330 Main Street, Louisburg
PHONE: 902-733-2720
WEB SITE: www.novascotiarailwayheritage.com/louisbourg.htm

ONTARIO

Chatham Railroad Museum ❶

Housed in a retired 1955 CN baggage car, the Chatham Railroad Museum includes interactive exhibits and photos on local as well as national and international railroad history. Open May to September, it is located across from the VIA rail station.

SITE LOCATION: Queen Street, Chatham
PHONE: 800-561-6125 or 519-352-3097
WEB SITE: www.chatham-kent.ca
E-MAIL: cktourism@chatham-kent.ca

CNR School Car ❷

Back in the good old days, you didn't have to walk miles through the snow to get to this school. Instead, it came to you. This car was one of seven railway schools that served children and adults along northern Ontario railways. Tour the car and see how teachers brought learning to isolated students. It is open Thursday through Sunday Victoria Day weekend through September.

SITE LOCATION: 76 Victoria Terrace, Clinton
PHONE: 519-482-3997
WEB SITE: www.schoolcar.ca

Cochrane Railway and Pioneer Museum ❸

Looking as if it could still ride the rails, Temiskaming and Northern Ontario Railway locomotive no. 137 provides the perfect introduction to the museum housed in the coaches and cabooses behind it. The preserved cars contain railway photographs and artifacts. Pioneer life in Cochrane is displayed by a replica of a trapper's cabin and various exhibits.

SITE LOCATION: 210 Railway Street, Cochrane
PHONE: 705-272-4361
WEB SITE: www.town.cochrane.on.ca

Fort Erie Railroad Museum ❹

This museum site features the restored Grand Trunk's Ridgeway station, which houses historic furnishings, telegraph equipment, tools, and other artifacts. Canadian National Railway steam engine no. 6218, a 4-8-4 Northern type, is the museum's centerpiece. Also on display are a fireless engine, a CN caboose, and other equipment. The CN's B-1 station that monitored traffic over the International Railway Bridge is also on site.

SITE LOCATION: 400 Central Avenue, Fort Erie
PHONE: 905-871-1412
WEB SITE: www.museum.forterie.ca/railroad.html
E-MAIL: museum@forterie.on.ca

Halton County Radial Railway ❺

The railway offers 20-minute rides on a variety of restored streetcars, dating back to the 1890s, through scenic woodlands. The museum displays more than 75 vehicles and features the largest collection of operable streetcars in the country. Its Rockwood station was built in 1912 for the Grand Trunk Railway. The museum is open on weekends May, June, September, and October and daily during July and August. Admission includes unlimited streetcar rides, and you can enjoy lunch in one of three picnic sites.

SITE LOCATION: 13629 Guelph Line, Milton
PHONE: 519-856-9802
WEB SITE: www.hcry.org
E-MAIL: streetcar@hcry.org

Komoka Railway Museum ❻

Kamoka's restored Canadian National station houses a collection of artifacts and photos dedicated to rail history in the area. It includes tools, lanterns, and a tiny flag stop station. Also on display are a 1913 Shay locomotive and a steel-sided baggage car. The museum is open Friday through Monday during summer and on Saturdays the rest of the year.

SITE LOCATION: 133 Queen Street, Komoka
PHONE: 519-657-1912
WEB SITE: www.komokarailmuseum.ca
E-MAIL: station-master@komokarailmuseum.ca

Memory Junction Museum ❼

Memory Junction features several structures including the original Grand Trunk station, a baggage shed, and an unloading depot. A rare N-4-a locomotive is on display along with a wooden, outside-braced 1913 boxcar and other railcars. The museum includes local historical and railway artifacts. It is open mid-May through mid-October.

SITE LOCATION: 60 Maplewood Street, Brighton
PHONE: 613-475-0379
WEB SITE: www.memoryjunction.netfirms.com
E-MAIL: re.bangay@sympatico.ca

Muskoka Heritage Place ❽

Muskoka Heritage Place contains Pioneer Village and the *Portage Flyer*, a restored 1902 steam train that takes you on a short trip to the past. After boarding at the station museum, you travel along the Muskoka River to Fairy Lake, where you can watch a turntable in action. At the museum, you can view exhibits on the Portage Railway and send a telegram. You can combine a Pioneer Village tour with a train ride or just ride the *Portage Flyer*.

SITE LOCATION: 88 Brunel Road, Huntsville
PHONE: 705-789-7576
WEB SITE: www.muskokaheritageplace.org
E-MAIL: village@muskokaheritageplace.org

Northern Ontario Railroad Museum & Heritage Centre ❾

This museum emphasizes railroading history in northern Ontario and includes additional exhibits on mining and lumbering. Artifacts are displayed in the Museum House, which was used by the Canadian National as a superindendent's residence. In nearby Prescott Park, it displays a U-1-f bullet-nosed steam locomotive, a wooden CNR caboose, and other equipment.

SITE LOCATION: 26 Bloor Street, Capreol
PHONE: 705-858-5050
WEB SITE: www.northernontariorailroadmuseum.ca
E-MAIL: normhc@vianet.ca

Port Stanley Terminal Rail ❿

Excursion trains depart from a historic station next to the King George lift bridge. Early diesel locomotives pull open and closed coaches that have been converted from cabooses. Regular one-hour excursions run to Whytes Park. A variety of special trains run during the season, and some travel the entire line into St. Thomas. You can view the PTSR's fleet of equipment in the yard just north of the station.

SITE LOCATION: 309 Bridge Street, Port Stanley
PHONE: 877-244-4478 or 519-782-3730
WEB SITE: www.pstr.on.ca
E-MAIL: info@pstr.on.ca

Smiths Falls Railway Museum of Eastern Ontario ⑪

This museum is housed in a restored 1914 Canadian Northern Railway station that contains thousands of artifacts relating to the Canadian Pacific, Grand Trunk, Canadian National, and other railways. The national historic site displays a 1912 steam locomotive, a CP diesel, a dental car, and passenger cars. It is open mid-May to September.

SITE LOCATION: 90 William Street, Smiths Falls
PHONE: 613-283-5696
WEB SITE: www.sfrmeo.ca
E-MAIL: sfrmchin@superaje.com

York-Durham Heritage Railway ⑫

The York-Durham Heritage Railway operates excursions and special trains between Stouffville and Uxbridge. Diesel locomotives pull passenger coaches built between the 1920s and the 1950s. The Uxbridge station, which was built in 1904, contains displays of rail artifacts. Caboose rides are available.

SITE LOCATION: 6176 Main Street, Stouffville
PHONE: 905-852-3696
WEB SITE: www.ydhr.on.ca
E-MAIL: ydhra@ydhr.on.ca

Waterloo Central Railway ⑬

The railway operates excursion trains through southern Ontario behind a 60-ton diesel locomotive. You can take the entire 12-mile round trip or detrain at St. Jacobs, where you can look around, and take a later train back. The railway also operates a 0-6-0 steam switcher and various special trains throughout the year.

SITE LOCATION: 10 Father David Bauer Drive, Waterloo
PHONE: 519-885-2297
WEB SITE: www.steam-train.org
E-MAIL: form on Web site
DISCOUNT: Receive $1 off each regular round-trip ticket.

Algoma Central Railway

SITE LOCATION: 129 Bay Street, Sault Ste. Marie

PHONE: 800-242-9287 or 705-946-7300

WEB SITE: www.algomacentralrailway.com

Jim Wrinn

The Algoma Central Railway offers the chance to ride into unspoiled Canadian wilderness from Sault Ste. Marie north into Ontario as far as the spectacular Agawa Canyon or to the end of the railroad at Hearst. Either way, you will not go away disappointed.

CHOICES: You can ride the tour train to Agawa Canyon and back, or you can ride the entire railroad – almost 300 miles one way – to the end of the line at Hearst. Or, best of all, you can do both: ride the canyon train out and then catch the regular train to Hearst and back. Going to the canyon, you'll see mixed forests, mountain lakes, and streams, and past the canyon, there are boreal forests, muskegs, and moose. The railway also offers winter snow trains and wilderness adventure trains.

WHEN TO GO: The railroad runs year-round. Fall bookings can be intense so plan ahead. The average daily temperature stays below freezing during December, January, and February.

GOOD TO KNOW: The tour train is usually packed, but the regular passenger train is more relaxed. You'll stop at only the canyon on the tour train, but the regular train pauses to let fishermen, hunters, and other outdoor types get off at just about any point. It's a lot of fun to see what people will load onto the baggage car.

WORTH DOING: There is much to do in Sault Ste. Marie, such as strolling along the boardwalk, visiting a casino, and touring the locks. Winter activities include skiing and snowboarding.

DON'T MISS: For scenery viewing, ride one of the railroad's two dome cars. Find a good vantage point at mile post 19, where the railroad crosses the Montreal River on a huge curving trestle perched atop a dam. For a wilderness experience, you can camp out overnight in a caboose at Agawa Canyon.

ETTING THERE: Sault Ste. Marie is located at I-75 and Highway 17. Signs show the way the depot, which is located downtown.

Canada Science and Technology Museum ⑮

SITE LOCATION: 1867 St. Laurent Boulevard, Ottawa
PHONE: 866-442-4416 or 613-991-3044
WEB SITE: www.sciencetech.technomuses.ca
E-MAIL: cts@technomuses.ca

John Godfrey

The Canada Science and Technology Museum's rail collection contains 1,000 artifacts that range from photos to locomotives and dates back to the early days of Canadian railway history. The museum also operates a demonstration train ride. Other exhibits focus on Canadian inventions, communications, and space.

CHOICES: Locomotive Hall showcases four locomotives, but other equipment is displayed throughout the museum and outdoors in Technology Park. Technology Park also includes a lighthouse, windmill, and Atlas rocket. With an assist from the Bytown Railway Society, the museum operates a two-truck Shay on Wednesdays and Sundays in July and August on a few hundred feet of track that borders the parking lot. A century-old business car and caboose form the usual consist.

WHEN TO GO: The museum is open year-round but is closed on some Mondays during winter. It also closes down for about four days for its annual cleaning. Look for the Festival of Technology in July, when you can watch demonstrations of some of the museum's artifacts.

GOOD TO KNOW: For a small fee, you can try museum's space simulator. Missions include trying to save a colony on Mars and flying toward a comet on a collision course with Earth.

WORTH DOING: In Ottawa, the country's capital, there are numerous attractions and activities. Sites to see include the Rideau Canal, Canadian War Museum, and National Gallery of Canada. You can even watch the changing of the guard at Parliament Hill.

DON'T MISS: In Locomotive Hall, you'll find four unique engines: CNR no. 40, built for the Grand Trunk Railway in 1872 and Canada's oldest mainline steam locomotive; Canadian Pacific no. 926, which spent 50 years hauling freight and passenger trains between Winnipeg and Calgary; CNR no. 6400 with its distinctive semi-streamlined design and painted olive green; and CP no. 2858, one of five preserved CP Hudsons.

GETTING THERE: Scheduled air, bus, and rail service operate to Ottawa. The museum is located approximately 10 minutes southeast of downtown Ottawa. Exit Highway 417 at St. Laurent south and turn left on Lancaster Road. You can also reach the museum by the no. 85 or no. 86 city bus.

Credit Valley Explorer 🔢

SITE LOCATION: Townline Road, Orangeville
PHONE: 888-346-0046
WEB SITE: www.creditvalleyexplorer.com
E-MAIL: info@creditvalleyexplorer.com

John Godfrey

The *Credit Valley Explorer* offers three excursion options on its round trip between Orangeville and Brampton over a route that was completed in 1879. The ride, aboard 1950s rail coaches, takes you through rolling hills and deep valleys, over the Credit River, and across a 1,146-foot-long trestle bridge.

CHOICES: The 43-mile, three-hour excursion departs Orangeville and travels through the Caledon Hills, Cataract, and the forks of the Credit River to Inglewood and Brampton before returning. Scenic excursions operate year-round, dinner trains run from June to September, and brunch trains operate Sundays September to May. In addition to meals, trips include informative commentary and, often, live music. Some special trains also operate from other departure points.

WHEN TO GO: Each time of year offers a different experience. Late spring and early summer give you a chance to see the countryside before the foliage becomes dense. Autumn is busy, and the trains are full, but the fall colors are spectacular. In winter, the train takes you on an excursion through the snow-covered landscape.

GOOD TO KNOW: For a refreshing pre- or post-trip stop, walk a few blocks to the Train Station, a restaurant housed in a former CPR station. You can also take a walking tour through Orangeville's historic downtown.

WORTH DOING: The Hills of the Headwaters is a great place to experience the great outdoors, no matter what the season. Hiking trails abound, and you can also fish, golf, and ski in a variety of locations.

DON'T MISS: Just relax in reclining first-class seats, look through the large windows, and enjoy the scenic views.

GETTING THERE: Orangeville is about an hour's drive from Toronto in southern Ontario. Trains depart from the railway yard on Town Line Road. From Highway 10, take Broadway to Town Line Road and turn left. Follow Town Line Road to the entrance.

Elgin County Railway Museum ⑰

SITE LOCATION: 225 Wellington Street, St. Thomas
PHONE: 519-637-6284
WEB SITE: www.ecrm5700.org
E-MAIL: thedispatcher@ecrm5700.org

John Godfrey

The railroad has been a part of life in St. Thomas since 1856. Over the years, a total of 26 railways have passed through town, helping it garner the moniker of the Railway Capital of Canada. Located in the former Michigan Central locomotive shops, the Elgin County Railway Museum helps preserve and display the railway heritage of St. Thomas and the surrounding area.

CHOICES: Equipment restoration is ongoing at the museum, and it displays a variety of equipment including a CNR Hudson, a Grand Trunk Western caboose, a Pullman sleeper, and an electric-powered car that transported children to school in the 1920s. In St. Thomas, the BX interlocking tower is available for touring by appointment.

WHEN TO GO: The museum operates daily between Victoria Day and Labour Day. Thomas the Tank Engine regularly stops by in July. It also hosts a Railway Nostalgia Weekend.

GOOD TO KNOW: A short drive from the regional center of London, St. Thomas is a small town with all services. Its Iron Horse Festival coincides with the museum's Railway Heritage Day.

WORTH DOING: Combining a visit to the museum along with a ride on the nearby Port Stanley Terminal Rail makes for an interesting day of exploring the preserved rails of southern Ontario.

DON'T MISS: The museum celebrates the Canadian railway on Railway Heritage Day, which is usually held in August. During the celebration, short train trips often operate within town.

GETTING THERE: VIA Rail Canada offers scheduled passenger service through London to the north. In addition, scheduled air service is available to that city's airport. If you're tied to the rubber tire, the museum is two hours from Toronto, two hours from the U.S. border at Detroit, Buffalo, or Niagara Falls, and one hour from Sarnia and Port Huron. Once in St. Thomas, you will find the museum on Wellington Street between Ross Street and First Avenue.

Ontario

Polar Bear Express 18

SITE LOCATION: 200 Railway Street, Cochrane
PHONE: 800-268-9281
WEB SITE: www.polarbearexpress.ca
E-MAIL: choochoo@polarbearexpress.ca

John Godfrey

Ontario Northland's *Polar Bear Express* transports you to the shores of James Bay and the edge of the Arctic. Its *Dream Catcher Express* takes you on a brilliant fall foliage trip out of North Bay. The *Northlander* travels between northern and southern Ontario.

CHOICES: The *Polar Bear Express* provides passenger excursions between Cochrane and Moosonee on James Bay. You can take a day trip, with several hours for exploring the area, or stay over and return on a different day. The train features a family car to keep young travelers busy. The *Northlander* passenger train operates between Toronto and Cochrane over the CN south of North Bay. In fall, you can relax aboard the *Dream Catcher Express* between North Bay and Temagami and view the brilliant colors.

WHEN TO GO: With trains operating year-round, the choice is yours. In summer, the *Polar Bear Express* runs every day but Saturday, and the *Dream Catcher Express* runs on a limited schedule.

GOOD TO KNOW: In Cochrane, the Station Inn provides handy overnight lodging on the upper floors of the train station.

WORTH DOING: On the *Polar Bear Express* layover, be sure to take one of the side trips to the island of Moose Factory, a former Hudson's Bay Company fur-trading settlement. If you want to see polar bears close up, you can visit the Polar Bear Conservation and Education Habitat, a polar bear rehabilitation facility, in Cochrane, where you can see the bears in natural habitat and even swim alongside them (with a window in between).

DON'T MISS: Aboard the *Polar Bear Express*, take in the scenic views from the dome car.

GETTING THERE: Cochrane, North Bay, and Toronto are connected by bus and train service. VIA and Amtrak service connects Toronto with southwest Ontario and New York. Scheduled air service is available to Toronto and to Moosonee.

284

South Simcoe Railway 🔟

SITE LOCATION: Mill Street W, Tottenham
PHONE: 905-936-5815
WEB SITE: www.southsimcoerailway.ca
E-MAIL: info@southsimcoerailway.ca

John Godfrey

The South Simcoe Railway operates over four miles of former CN trackage through rolling countryside approximately an hour north of Toronto. Most excursions are powered by a diesel locomotive, but the operating roster also includes two steam locomotives, a former CP 4-4-0 and a 4 6 0.

CHOICES: Regular excursions from Tottenham to Beeton and back take about an hour. As the train rolls through Beeton Creek Valley, the conductor provides an informative commentary. Passengers are carried in steel heavyweight coaches. The railway also operates a Santa Claus Express and other specials.

WHEN TO GO: The railway runs multiple trips on Sundays and on holiday Mondays, as well as some additional dates, between Victoria Day weekend and Canadian Thanksgiving.

GOOD TO KNOW: The town of Tottenham has a variety of quaint shops and eateries. Across the road from the railway is Tottenham Conservation Park, which offers camping, fishing, and hiking trails.

WORTH DOING: For a unique combination rail-water excursion, the RMS *Segwun*, the oldest operating steamship in North America, sails June through October on the Muskoka lakes, about a two-hour drive north to Gravenhurst.

DON'T MISS: Take one rail trip and then follow one of the others for some great photos. The engine faces south into the sun, and the relatively slow pace of the train makes it easy to follow.

GETTING THERE: No public transit is available to this neck of the woods. From Highway 400, take Highway 9 west nine miles to Tottenham Road and turn right. Continue into downtown Tottenham and turn left onto Mill Street.

PRINCE EDWARD ISLAND

Elmira Railway Museum ❶

The museum offers a look at railroading on the island in the early 1900s. It features re-created buildings representing the original wooden station house, platform, freight shed, and master's office. The station building contains two rooms of displays and artifacts. A miniature train operates around the museum, and a variety of special events take place on the outdoor stage, which was built from the base of a flatcar. The museum is open June through September.

SITE LOCATION: 457 Elmira Road, Elmira
PHONE: 902-357-7234
WEB SITE: www.elmirastation.com
E-MAIL: elmira@gov.pe.ca

QUEBEC

Railway Interpretation Center ❶

Housed in a 1917 station, this museum (Centre d'interpretation ferroviaire de Vallee-Jonction) relates the history of the Quebec Central Railway. On display are a CN 4-6-4T steam locomotive, a caboose, a tank car, and a boxcar. In August, the museum holds a railway festival.

SITE LOCATION: 397 Rousseau Boulevard, Vallee-Jonction
PHONE: 418-253-6449
WEB SITE: www.garevalleejonction.ca
E-MAIL: garevalleejonction@globetrotter.net

Canadian Railway Museum (Exporail) ❷

SITE LOCATION: 110 St. Pierre Street, St. Constant
PHONE: 450-632-2410
WEB SITE: www.exporail.org
E-MAIL: info@exporail.org

John Godfrey

The largest collection of railway equipment in the country is well worth a stop for anyone interested in Canadian railways and rail transit. Locomotives, rolling stock, and streetcars from many parts of the country tell of the evolution of both industries from a uniquely Canadian perspective.

CHOICES: The museum's collection boasts 160 railway vehicles, including locomotives, streetcars, and rolling stock. A number of special events and exhibits scheduled throughout the year are geared toward modelers, transit enthusiasts, and those with a love of railways. The museum has several train ride options. A streetcar runs daily during summer. On select summer days, you can ride on a demonstration passenger train pulled by a replica of an 1849 steam locomotive. The *Museum Express* runs occasionally between the museum and downtown Montreal.

WHEN TO GO: The Canadian Railway Museum is open daily between mid-May and the beginning of September. During September and October, it is open Wednesday through Sunday. The remainder of the year, the museum is open only on weekends and holidays.

GOOD TO KNOW: Wear good walking shoes and dress for the weather. The main building contains only a portion of the collection, and you can explore the rest of the site from stops along the streetcar loop. You'll be able to see Barrington Station, a restored, rural flag stop station from southwestern Quebec.

WORTH DOING: There is much to see and do in Montreal. You can discover centuries of history in Old Montreal and explore Olympic Park.

DON'T MISS: Unique pieces in the collection include former CPR 4-6-4 2 no. 850 that pulled the 1939 Royal Train; MTC 350, the first electric streetcar in Montreal; and former CNR 6711, which pulled the first conventional train through the Mount Royal tunnel in 1918 as well as the last in 1995.

GETTING THERE: The museum is located 12 miles from downtown Montreal. Montreal has extensive air, bus, and rail service. Amtrak's *Adirondack* connects the city with the rest of its network in Albany, N.Y. CIT Roussillon provides bus service near the museum. AMT operates rush-hour commuter trains between the Lucien L'Allier station and St. Constant that stop adjacent to the property.

SASKATCHEWAN

Rusty Relics Museum ❶

Rusty Relics Museum portrays pioneer life in Saskatchewan. Housed in Carlyle's 1910 station, its collection features several buildings, machinery, and artifacts. Railway items include a caboose, a jigger, a tool shed, and a working telegraph. It is open Monday through Saturday June to Labour Day.

SITE LOCATION: 306 Railway Avenue W, Carlyle
PHONE: 306-453-2266 or 306-453-2363
WEB SITE: www.sesaskmuseumsnetwork.ca

Saskatchewan Railway Museum ❷

This seven-acre museum contains more than 10 buildings, including a station, express shed, interlocking tower, and tool sheds, from the Canadian National, Canadian Pacific, Canadian Northern, and Grand Trunk Railways. On display are a variety of freight cars, passenger coaches, streetcars, cabooses, and a CPR S-3 diesel locomotive. You can take a guided tour or explore the museum on your own. The museum also offers short motor car rides.

SITE LOCATION: Highway 60, Saskatoon
PHONE: 306-382-9855
WEB SITE: www.saskrailmuseum.org
E-MAIL: srha@saskrailmuseum.org

Reference maps

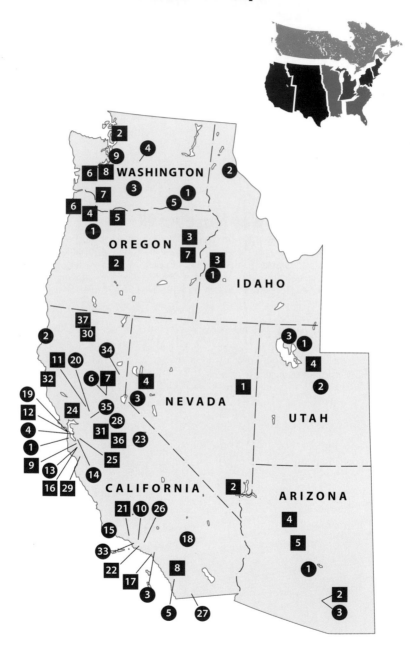

■ = train and trolley rides

● = museums and other sites

290

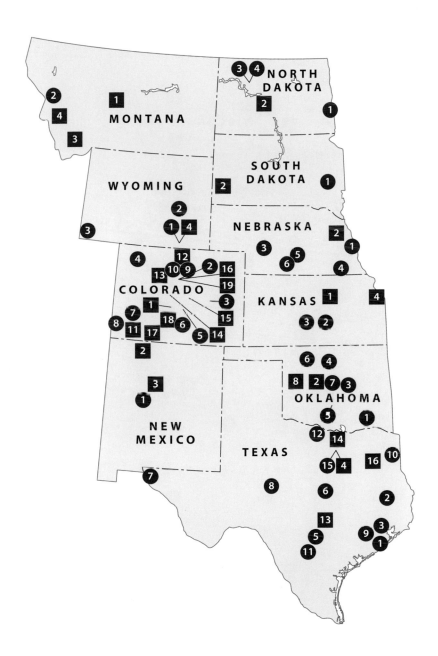

= train and trolley rides

= museums and other sites

MINNESOTA

WISCONSIN

IOWA

ILLINOIS

MISSOURI

ARKANSAS

MISSISSIPPI

LOUISIANA

00 = train and trolley rides

00 = museums and other sites

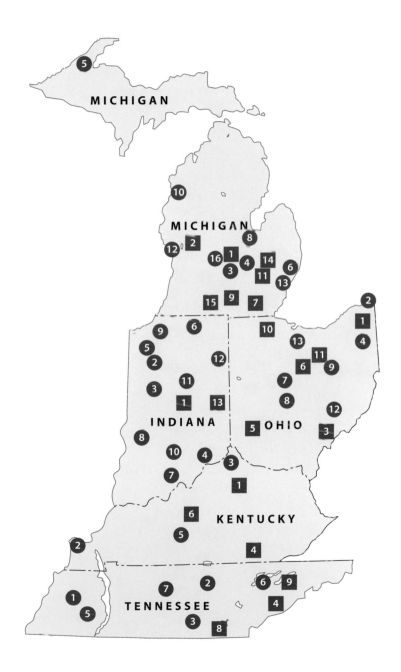

= train and trolley rides
= museums and other sites

= train and trolley rides

= museums and other sites

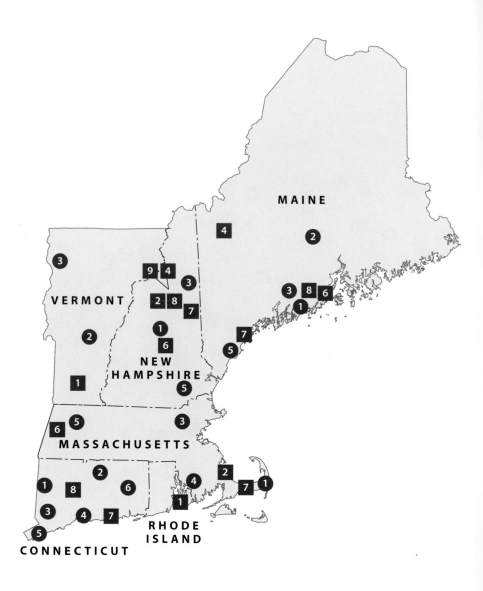

MAINE

VERMONT

NEW
HAMPSHIRE

MASSACHUSETTS

RHODE
ISLAND

CONNECTICUT

⬛ = train and trolley rides

⬤ = museums and other sites

Index

M

N

Printed in China